Asexual Perspectives:
47 Asexual Stories

Love, Life and Sex
ACElebration of Asexual Diversity

Sandra Bellamy

Published by Quirky Books. Registered address: Quirky Books, Miss Sandra Bellamy, Apt 3777, Chynoweth House, Trevissome Park, Truro, TR4 8UN.

Dedication

This book is dedicated to every Asexual around the globe who has ever felt they are alone, misunderstood, don't belong, and not accepted for who they are – even within the ace community. You most definitely exist and you most definitely belong!

Contents

Contents

"Why spend time trying to fit in?

... when you are beautiful just as you are!"

"Why are you trying to be ordinary?

... when you were born to be extraordinary!"

Preface

This book is based on 9 observations

Observation no 1

There are thousands of asexuals around the globe, some just like you, and some who are very different to you, and they too, feel alone in this world, and want to connect with other asexuals, just like you!

Observation no 2

There are asexuals who right now want love, companionship and relationships, without sex. And there are those who enjoy their own company and are happy to stay single forever.

Observation no 3

Whilst all asexuals have one thing in common – the lack of sexual attraction towards a specific person, they are all different in their likes, needs, wants and dislikes. This can make fitting into the asexual spectrum and finding a suitable relationship difficult.

Observation no 4

Right now, there seems to be a growing number of people within the asexual community who feel it is their right to tell others what type of asexual they can and can't be, and while suggestions and advice can be helpful to discover where they fit on the spectrum, blatantly denying that person the right to express their own asexual identity is wrong!

Observation no 5

There are a number of myths about asexuality and stereotypes – even within the asexual community, and these need to be addressed and broken through!

Observation no 6

The world has changed with the advancement of technology and social media, and now is it easier than ever to connect with other asexuals around the globe, for relationships, friendships, and to arrange meet-ups!

Observation no 7

The asexual community has expanded vastly since the early days of Aven and there are new terms coming out to describe the way in which asexuals identify that were not around years ago. This can invariably lead to some discrepancies in terms of identifications.

Observation no 8

You don't need to fit in to an exact specific asexual box to still be asexual. If you don't experience sexual attraction towards a specific person, you are asexual. If you cannot feel sexual attraction until you have formed a strong emotional bond with a specific person, you are still on the asexual spectrum. If you experience sexual attraction but only under specific circumstances or you experience it but not enough to act on it, you are still on the asexual spectrum. It's up to you to be honest with yourself and others in determining your own asexual identity!

Observation no 9

If you feel alone; are unsure of your identity or sometimes get confused; unsure what asexuals really think of Love, Life and Sex, and what experiences they have had or are having; and how they manage their relationships, look no further than this book. In this book I will reveal my own asexual perspective as well as perspectives from 46 asexuals from around the globe. Dispelling myths, breaking stereotypes, sharing their own personal journey to help you in yours and with a surprising over-riding message!

If any of these observations have resonated with you and if you haven't done so already, please invest in this book and I will reveal to you **Asexual Perspectives, 47 Asexual Stories, Love, Life and Sex, ACElebration of Asexual Diversity!**

But before we begin our journey together, I think there is something you should know...

Prologue

It's February 4th 2014, and even though I am rushing to get there I am apprehensive at the same time. I am not meant to be doing this, or going here. I was told I would never have to do this again, but that was before I got the unexpected phone call and here I am. Everything happens for a reason, right? Or so I keep telling myself.

It's not a big waiting room and other than the little window I pop my head through to tell them I've arrived, there is not much contact with staff. There are some pictures on the wall, a stay SAFE poster and a few magazines on the small brown coffee table in front of me, oh and a water cooler, which I just have to use before I sit down. Then I remember the toilet!

It's an anxious wait, she sounded nice on the phone, but you never can tell! All kinds of thoughts rush through my mind. How come the previous lady said I knew all of the answers myself? That I was answering my own questions and there was no longer a need for me to come? Why had I not been told I had been put on a waiting list? It seems so strange and out of the blue. Did this happen to others too?

As I scan the environment is seems so surreal that I am back here again, like déjà vu. I thought my problems were over and that I can look after myself and that I know what is best for me, better than anyone else. Why then, did I accept and now I am here? Because I do believe everything happens for a reason and that it is good to take any help offered in life! I keep holding onto this point in my mind, and think of it over and over again, repeating the same thing as a form of reassurance.

"Hi Sandra, come on through". Her voice is mild and comforting. It's too late to back out now and at least she seems nice!

Part I

"This Can't Be Right!"

1. Pain Into Gain

"I think there is something I should tell you, I was told I did not need to come again by the previous counsellor. And then I got a phone call from you and I did not know why I had been put on any waiting list, as the previous counsellor said I no longer needed counselling because I knew all of the answers to my own questions and I am still trying to work out exactly why I am here. The only thing I can possibly think it was, was that the previous lady, I forget her name, as it seemed liked over a year ago, in fact I think it was over a year ago, I told her I had a problem with not wanting sex in a relationship and she thought that was because a guy tried to take advantage of me when I was only fifteen. But it isn't the reason, as I had all my sexual relationships after that incident. It's really difficult for me to talk about it, because until I spoke to her, I did not even realise it was attempted rape, because I didn't actually say no and I liked kissing him. He showed me a condom and I was very naive back then and sweet and innocent. I was brought up in the countryside and did not even think about sex, it never crossed my mind that he was thinking about doing *that* with me and when he opened the drawer and showed me this condom, I just said nice, I had no idea he was thinking about me and him using it – well he didn't, I mean he did not even try to use it. He tried to… remove my underwear and forced my hand on his penis and it was disgusting and I closed my eyes, I really didn't want to see that. It was horrid. I managed to physically stop him

3

having sex with me, by crossing my arm over me and physically blocking him. I have hardly told anyone about this. I was invited to join a group that specialised in talking about rape, with other rape victims, but I do not consider what I went through to be that bad compared to what others who have actually been raped, have gone through, and to be honest, I don't think it is going to be any good to go there and listen to other people's horrific stories as I feel it will make my mind worse. I used to just call it a bad incident in my life, to myself. I was fifteen at the time and he was eighteen, so I would have been underage."

She listened patiently, not saying much, and that was the beginning of what I thought, would be a good way forward for me in my life, to chat this through and find out how I can have a loving relationship without sex, as I did not associate sex with love. Despite that being the best thing about my last long term ex of eight and a half years, he was good at, dare I say it, having sex with me, and in this respect I thought I would not get another better than him. Despite the fact that in the end, he was horrid to me and very abusive, he was the most gentlest and kindest person I had been with in this way and was very good at foreplay – although I had always preferred his finger to his penis, but he liked sex and I would rather have preferred just to have his finger forever. When I had sex with him, it was the only time I got to see the reason why I fell in love with him in the first place and looking back now, this is the reason I liked that time with him, not because of the sex itself. I was petrified of getting pregnant, even though I was on the pill. He preferred to do it the natural way and would prefer to wait a couple of months to do it this way, rather than to use a condom. I preferred the security of using the condom with the pill, as I knew I never wanted to have children in my life and to be pregnant for me, would be the worst thing in the world. This is not the type of thing you can discuss with your mum, "Hey mum, I don't want to leave my boyfriend (now ex), because he is the best I have ever had in terms of sex and catering to my needs in this way. Even if we do not have it for a couple of months, he will still be with me."

I did not like the movement of his penis at times, as it reminded me of that incident when I was fifteen and my hand had been forced. I also cried sometimes after sex, as it felt too emotional for me and too raw - like I had a physical open wound that had been opened up more.

"I would like to be in a relationship again but I just don't want sex. I don't associate sex with love and I really don't want to do that again in my life. Surely there must be people who have relationships without it? I just want a guy to love and like me for my personality and to stay with me because of that. Sure I would like a guy to like the way I look, but stay with me because he knows there is not another like me in terms of personality. But I seem to attract the wrong guys, the guys who want it all the time and I am worried I will never find a guy to love me without sex."

She looks down on me with a serious face and says in a concerned tone of voice, "I'm worried about you, because if you want a good guy, you will need to have sex to keep him".

I think to myself this can't be right! Why should I have to have sex to keep a good guy when I don't want to? On arriving home I Google 'I love kissing but not sex' and that is when I discover the term asexuality and Aven (asexuality.org), that is the biggest online community for asexuals, and I begin to research into it.

Week 4's session was cancelled. Week 5 is here and I am a bit nervous considering how our last session went, but relieved to think I have found the answer to my problem.

"I think I may be asexual. I Googled I love kissing but not sex, because I really don't like sex but love kissing, and it came up with asexuality and it sounds like me. Can you look it up for our next session? I think it will really help." She nods silently.

But when week 6 came, she had not done so.

"The NHS computers won't let me look up such a site."

"How come?"

"Because they won't let us access that type of material."

"So why didn't you look it up on your computer at home? You could have done that?"

Her silence says everything. She seems not bothered and disinterested, and our whole session goes badly because I feel she is not listening to me or interested in what I have to say. I feel bad about myself and start to get upset.

"I think it's best if we do not see each other again."

I needed time to think, although she was making me feel bad, I did not want to let go of counselling when I still needed help to understand myself in light of my new discovery that I may be asexual.

"I need time to think about it. To think about what's best for me. I don't want to say right now that I want to stop. I need time to think ".

"Take my number again and call me after you have made a decision."

"Okay."

I feel distraught, like I've been on an emotional roller-coaster ride these past few weeks and I wasn't meant to be here in the first place. After leaving, I keep churning things over in my mind. I can't go back as she is not supportive and is not going to help me to understand my asexuality. She was adamant that I needed to have sex to keep a good guy and that really upsets me. She is not going to listen to what I have to say in future sessions and is really no good for me. I had left counselling once and I could do it again. In fact it wasn't just once. I left it before, another time, when I went to see a counsellor for anxiety after I had freed myself from depression and she started to make me feel depressed again, so I had to leave and get myself back into a happy and healthy state of mind. She clearly had never had anxiety in her life, because if she had, she would not have been saying those things she did. But I digress.

The next day, March 12th 2014, I phoned her, "I won't be coming back, I want to cease counselling as it is not good for me and I am alright as I am."

It was a distinct turning point in my life and I have never looked back! I guess everything really does happen for a reason! But maybe not the reason we first thought!

But let me ask you this, have you ever struggled with something for so long, to finally feel relief that is it over, only to find out that a new problem has just begun?

1. Pain Into Gain

Well that is what happened to me.

Although nothing could seem worse than what had just happened I now faced the uncertainly of what asexuality actually was and how did I fit into it? But first of all, I had some people to tell.

I phoned my mum and explained about asexuality and that I feel I may be asexual and it must have just clicked with my parents because during the next phone conversation they seemed to have looked up the term and my mum said, "It sounds like you". This was such a relief to hear! If only everyone could be like my mum but they weren't.

Soon after telling my mum, I told a friend who walked part of the same way home as me that I think I am asexual and I explained what it meant.

She laughed, "But you are ALWAYS talking about guys, come on!"

"I agree I talk about guys a lot, particularly foreign guys as I am very aesthetically attracted to them but I don't want to have sex with them, because I am not sexually attracted to them."

She didn't believe me and kept persistently laughing and repeating what she previously said, then added, "You just haven't met the right person yet."

She went off to her home and I headed for mine. After this experience I was wearier of telling others until I had done some more research. But what followed was not the reaction I had hoped for!!

2. I Didn't Expect That!

In the months that followed, I joined a dating site for asexuals called Asexualitic.com. That was not long after I had a bad experience of dating a sexual guy in July. I enjoyed kissing him, he was 21, foreign, aesthetically very attractive and the best kisser I had in my life! But... at the end of the night he asked me to be his girlfriend and I told him I don't like sex, and then he said "No problem, I can have sex with other girls and you can be my girlfriend." I was disgusted. Just because I am asexual does not give a guy the right to be with other girls. If he loved me for who I am, why would he want to do that? But that was just it! He needed the sex and that was when the penny dropped – however much I liked him, I could not do that to myself and disrespect myself like that. There was no way I wanted to have sex with him, ever, and he had no right to treat me that way, but I finally understood why I could never date sexual guys again – because they would always need sex, and I didn't want that ever again in my life. It would be like self-abuse.

I remember being so nervous about creating a profile on Asexualitic because even though I had dated heterosexuals up until that penny dropped, I had also been happily single since 2011. It never occurred to me that I would have a chance of finding real love, for life, without sex, until I discovered I am asexual and there are asexual dating sites. I just put something like, 'Hi, I am

Sandra, I am a heteromantic asexual and I am happy being single'. I even spelt heteroromantic wrong. But I loved passionate kissing too, and then I spotted a guy who organised asexual meet-ups, not bad looking actually, but too old for me and not my type; more like an army type! And I messaged him to learn more about what type of asexual I am, because I noticed a lot of terms on this site but didn't know what exactly best fitted me, other than being a romantic asexual who is only attracted to guys. He said because I like the passionate kissing, I was definitely a Grey A. Because I understood he must have so much experience to hold regular meet-ups, I pondered it for a while; then agreed with it. At first I thought the Grey A concept was a bit weird, like you don't really fit in, and especially since I hate all other grey areas of life because I am a black and white girl, but as I noticed so many people on that site didn't seem to like passionate kissing, I began to feel comfortable that the term as I saw it – having Grey Areas, fitted me well. This was particularly noticeable when an asexual foreign guy private messaged me back saying he was worried in case the kissing went too far and without saying the exact words – it would seem he thought I am too sexual for him, even though I don't want sex ever again in my life. Since that time, I have had conversations with asexual guys, both on and off that site, which also fit into the Grey A category because they have Grey Areas, (even though some of them only classify themselves as a heteroromantic on their profile). Trying to get Grey Areas to match is another almost impossibility. Some guy's Grey Areas are too sexual for me. Especially as I don't like nudity and a lot of asexual guys seem to still like the physical closeness with clothes off, but not needing to go to the level of intercourse!!

It was a while before I became an official member of Aven (asexuality.org), the largest online community for asexuals. I had read some of their forum threads but had not taken the leap of becoming part of it. I guess I was a little nervous because I had never taken part in an online forum before, so I had no clue about what to expect or how to create posts and post them. When I finally decided to take the plunge, I introduced myself in the wrong way in the 'Welcome Lounge'; by saying I was looking for a relationship. I was told off by a Moderator who changed my comment and gave me a strict warning, "This is not a dating site! There are other sites for that." I explained that I had tried those, and had no luck as I was looking for a heteroromantic foreign guy, which is difficult with me living in the UK and not wanting to move. It didn't matter what I said – it wasn't the place for it. Even now I find this tough, because it is hard enough as it is to find another asexual without being restricted on Aven.

One day, when I was talking in the forums on Aven, and explaining how I defined my asexuality and the 'Grey A' part of it, I was told I could not define myself as a Grey A because I did not experience sexual attraction and not 'under limited or specific circumstances' and that was what a Grey A meant. At that time, Aven Wiki also defined Grey A as a 'catch all term' for those who did not quite fit the asexual box and as I was sometimes seen as too sexual for some asexual guys because of the passionate kissing and how close I like to get with my clothes on; but not sexual enough to be with a heterosexual guy, as I did not like, need, or want sex, I felt I fitted this definition well. (I tried to find this information again on the Aven Wiki page as I write this book, but it may have been edited out because now I cannot find it.) I reiterated my point of view, which someone else shared, but again I felt put down and belittled, as this one particular person was hell bent on forcing me not to define myself as that. This is a community that is in the minority of sexuality – yet in that moment I felt very singled out and that I did not quite belong. It was this moment that sparked the idea for this book, especially as others have since approached me and said they feel singled out in the asexual community too.

3. Discovery

I noticed that although asexuals share common ground with each other because of their asexuality and lack of sexual attraction; there are so many variations between us, in terms of experiences, in what we like and don't like. I think it's really important to recognise this; and that we all have something to contribute to the world and towards helping others to better understand their asexuality. Our diversity should be embraced and celebrated, not be treated with hostility and torn apart.

I am still very thankful and grateful for Aven and the rest of the asexual online community, who do a great job in connecting us with fellow asexuals and I have made some awesome asexual friends because of it, I just feel that we need to better understand and appreciate each other's identities, in order to be accepted for our own and this book will help you to do just that.

Besides there being some hostility even within the ace community there are also stereotypes and confusion over what asexuals do and do not do, have and have not done, in terms of love, life and sex – including what they really think about masturbation, porn and kinks. This invariably leads to lots of questions and advice being sought, especially by newbies of asexuality. With this in mind I wanted to interview a broad range of asexuals from around the globe, across the asexual spectrum, to bust through

the myths and stereotypes; to gain more insight; more understanding; and get valuable help, advice, wisdom and support. I
think all the asexuals I have interviewed, have done a tremendous job in this respect and in particular when they reveal what
advice they would give to a younger version of themselves or
those just starting to know about asexuality. So whether you are
just starting out on your asexual journey or you have known you
are asexual for years, I think we can learn from each other and
spread the word of asexuality to a larger audience by celebrating
our diversity.

4. Introduction

Who Is This Book For?

This book is for asexuals. It is not another book written as an introduction to asexuality or an overview of what asexuality is, but rather a book that assumes you already identify as asexual or have some understanding of what it means to be asexual.

However, if you are completely new to this concept and/or, you thought this book is about sexuals, then please think again and read on with a very open mind. Get ready to be educated about the sexual orientation that is in broad terms, the lack of sexual attraction, think of the 'A' in 'Asexual' standing for 'Absence' of sexual attraction and you can't go far wrong!

About This Book

Within this book you will discover 46 Asexual Perspectives of Love, Life and Sex. In order to give an overview of the diversity of asexuality, and to be fair and consistent, I interviewed each asexual and gave them all the exact same set of questions and asked that they answer as many as possible with no word limit. As we are talking about very personal and intimate details each of their perspective in answer to the questions is referred to as a 'story'. I gave them the option of not answering all questions if they felt uncomfortable. This is why you will see the exact same set of questions purposely repeated throughout this book, but with some omitted depending on if that question was answered or not. I have purposefully kept editing to a minimum so that each asexual can have their own voice shine through their words. This 'Quirky Book' is not about every answer being perfectly grammatically correct and it won't be, this book is about real asexuals, who exist, and who want to share their real life experiences to help you, in their own words; using their own dialect; colloquial language; grammar and spelling of words. So besides British English you will also see a lot of American English used throughout this book, even though I am British. You will also see 'text speak' such as 'Lol' – Laugh Out Loud! You will see the word '**ace**' used at times; that is slang for a person who is 'asexual' as well as the word asexual. You will see the word 'Aven', which stands for 'Asexuality Visibility Education Network'. This book is written in an informal conversational style, similar to what you would find on a blog or how you would speak to, or text message a friend. At the end of each story, I have given each interviewee the opportunity to share any extra information with you about themselves, such as which country they are from, to show that I got a diverse range of backgrounds and ethnicities into the book. All asexuals were given the choice to use their real name, be anonymous, or give an alias name. So the names you see may or may not be real, but all other details are true, as they have been presented to me from their own asexual perspective. It's up to you to read on and discover if you share that perspective or not!

I feel truly blessed that all interviewees have been willing to open up and share their most intimate moments, thoughts, feelings and emotions with you. What you are about to read is unique, amazing, interesting, sometimes candidly humorous, fascinating and insightful. This is their story, now it's their time to tell it.

Part II

Asexuals Sharing Their Perspectives on Love, Life and Sex

5. Phillipa Duke's Story

When did you first discover you are asexual?

I first figured out I was Asexual about 9 months ago.

How did you discover you are asexual?

I was about to hit the 1 year milestone of my first relationship and the pressure to have sex with him was building. He was a virgin and so was I, so I thought that the desire to want to have sex with him would just happen like the flip of a switch one day, but it didn't. 6 months in to the relationship he told me he was in love with me and I told him that I cared about him, but that my "train isn't at the station yet". As we hit about 7 months the gentle pressure started for sex and by month 9 questions were being asked like "Don't you find me attractive?" I knew about asexuals due to a friend being one, but I never considered myself being one because I had a boyfriend. I tried to convey how I felt to him but I couldn't find the right words. I was just waiting and waiting for that moment where I would just feel "ready", and I built it up so much in my head that I had to force myself to do something to appease him and make him back off a bit, like to give me a grace period where he was satisfied and wouldn't pressure me again for a while. One night, like the many before, he would reach over in the single bed we shared when he came to visit and he would try to start something, try to get a response out of me, even though his many attempts had never worked before. I felt nothing, he only ever got as far as my breasts, which is when I would notice what he was trying to do and jokingly brush him off and moan about wanting to sleep. One night I was resituating myself in bed and I guess I must have moved the wrong way because he said, "If you're going to do that, you're going to have to deal with the consequences." It was painfully obvious that he was sexually charged and this had been going on so much that I just thought I should get it over with, so I touched him through his boxers.

My motives for doing this gives me goosebumps when I think about it and I just want to erase that night from existence. I had been talking to my mum and her boyfriend about his wants growing faster than mine, even though my wants weren't growing at all. The advice I was given was to just do something to ease his tension, such as to give him a hand-job. You trust your parents and you value their advice, but I wish I saw that for the terrible damaging advice that it was.

When it came to the act itself everything about it was emotionally detached and if he were at all a respectable man he would have noticed this from the first second and would have stopped me, but he didn't. I told him I would do it, that he wasn't allowed to look at me, or touch me during or after. I said not to kiss me and to keep his boxers on because I didn't want to see it. If those aren't warning signs that this isn't done out of love or mutual want, then I don't know what are. When I was done, everything I did for the rest of his visit was on autopilot and as mechanical as a robot. I cleaned the sheets of the evidence whilst he had a shower; I just walked around with a bad feeling, like waiting for a shoe to drop, up until he got in the taxi and went home. I felt relieved to see him go, and I refused to think about what I had forced myself to do like it was a bad dream or it wasn't me that did it. Thinking back on it now, it makes my hands clench and I shake them like trying to remove something, to get rid of the feeling. I feel like physically removing my hand from my body because when I am reminded of this, it's not my hand anymore. I get shivers and I have to force myself to think of other things because of that feeling of violation and shame because I did this willingly to myself.

It's quite frightening how pressure for sex from someone that you think you love can get under your radar. I am a very confident and headstrong woman and it took hindsight to realize just how much pressure I was under to not just have sex with him, but to really WANT to have sex with him, to feel that desire. I never looked at him and felt physical attraction. I never actually felt love for him, just my idea of what love might be by rationalizing what others described as love and comparing it to my situation.

He told me he wanted to treat me to a holiday and he suggested a number of places until we settled on Thailand. I am a student and even with saving I only managed to contribute something like £400 for a trip costing around £2000, so he willingly paid the rest. The destination looked heavenly and we were both very excited and planned everything we would do on the main island and the romantic getaway island meticulously. There was this unspoken expectation that this island would suddenly inspire me to flip that sexual switch and that we would finally have sex together on that holiday. I think he got so excited for the trip that this expectation became less of a hope and more of a concrete rule; that I had to have sex with him because he has paid for it, it's a romantic place and it became something like a contract. I got very bad sunburn on this trip because he didn't put the sun cream on my back properly on the boat over, so I couldn't even

23

lay on my back. The extreme humidity, heat and altitude of the island gave me nosebleeds and a bit of psychedelic sight. Our hotel room was around 300-400 steep steps up a hill, so by the time I got up there I would just strip and sit in the shower under freezing cold water to cool down, get rid of the sweat, soothe the sunburn, and just gather myself because those combinations of things absolutely knackered me out for the first few days.

Half way through the holiday he tried to start something and I very plainly said, "You do know we aren't having sex right? I mean, I have seriously painful sunburn and I am barely able to stand by the time we get back up here (to the hotel room)." I was watching some Wimbledon on the hotel TV at the time so I didn't see his face, but after a while he said that's ok and we carried on as previous on our holiday. Suddenly he got awful. The rest of the holiday was spent with him refusing to hold my hand at all, him walking ahead of me instead of holding my hand and walking beside me, him doing things he found fun or going places he wanted to go, even though one of the days I really hurt myself and told him it's too painful to walk, he carried on with me trailing painfully behind him. At the airport I was just talking about normal things and he randomly said, "Just fuck off", which is the first time he had ever said anything like that to me. I thought all of this behavior was because he was a bit feverish from an infected burn at the time and a small monkey bite he'd gotten.

On the plane he had registered me for a lactose-free meal despite my not being allergic to anything anymore. I took the tray and everything was horrid and more than just lactose-free, but gluten-free and barely edible. Despite him knowing that I hadn't eaten for quite a long time, when they came around with his meal a little later because he had a different one, he didn't want it. I asked if I could have it instead and he said no and the lady took it away.

When we got back to England the stress was so high I couldn't wait to get away from him. I jokingly refused to kiss him partly because I was a bit silly and worried he had rabies from the monkey bite and partly because I didn't think he deserved one from the way he had been acting. He said, "Are you seriously not going to kiss me?" And then he walked away with his bags and a hug. Three days later after no word he sends me an email on Skype breaking up with me, telling me how I have become an awful, selfish person. His own granny contacted me to tell me how disappointed she was that her grandson couldn't "Enjoy his holiday to the full". She was literally disappointed that I ruined her grandson's holiday by not having sex with him. I called him out on his real reason being my not having sex with him and he admitted that he'd been planning to leave me for just over a month but that he had hoped to take my virginity on holiday first and dump me when we got home. I am so very, very, glad I had that painful sunburn now, because I may have actually gone through with it if I didn't have those excuses to protect me. Two months after this breakup I was in a state of flux trying to make sense of it all and what it was I really wanted, when one day I just sat there and said to myself, "I'm asexual" and everything fell into place like the last puzzle piece.

I have always looked at people and seen physical attributes that I would label as attractive, but not in a sexual way, so in a world where I didn't feel gay, bi, straight, or anything widely known about, I just adapted my perception to fit a way of thinking. Looking back now I know I have always been Ace and have been applying different coping mechanisms to try and be a sexual being like everyone else, at least in my mind.

How do you identify yourself asexually?

Since then, I now know that I am specifically a sex-repulsed Aromantic Asexual with the tendency to Squish, in the friendly way. I am uncomfortable with receiving flirty touches and attentions and I don't like it when people mention the way I look when I dress nicely. I don't want it acknowledged I just want to get on. I have also discovered whilst playing drunken spin the bottle that I am completely comfortable sharing a kiss with someone when I know there are no sexual motives behind it, which surprised me.

Are you 'out' about being asexual? If not, why not? If you are out, whom to, and how did they react?

I am out to everyone that matters, including all of my flatmates and any coursemates that happened to be around when it has been mentioned. My mum thinks that I am still finding myself and that one day a man will walk in and I'll suddenly be straight again, but I think that is rooted in her want for grandchildren because I was the child most likely to have kids. I've said adoption exists for a reason and her answer is to "get a turkey baster" if you know what that means. She would prefer grandchildren by blood, but beyond that she takes no issue. It's not a big deal in my life because I cut out the cancerous people in it long ago, and they are the ones that would have had a problem with it so that pre-weeding made it very easy to just be myself. My granny's response was, "What is that?" And then shocking me because she hasn't got the most accepting opinions on certain LGBTQIA communities; said that she doesn't doubt it for a second because her own mother was just like that, and the only reason she ever did the deed with my now deceased grandad, was to have children only, and they stopped at two. She suspects that these generations of built up lack of sexual desire have just burst like a balloon into my mum and that she liked sex so much she refused to pass the gene or desire on to me. It's quite funny because I am from a very sexually open household and I therefore can have a filthy mind, yet I am the exact opposite of my mother in sexuality.

The only major problem I have had is with my flatmates from September 2015 to November 2015, and that situation was so short because I couldn't live with the shocking acephobia they subjected me to. One of the first things one of the girls said upon meeting everyone was "How does everyone feel about gays?" And I assumed she brought it up to maybe say that she was gay herself, so I said I was fine with it because I am Asexual and everyone else said that they were OK with it, despite them all clearly not having a clue what that means. This proved to be the start of a clash of epic proportions between my laid back, natural, hangout in pyjamas on my laptop ways, and their collective flock-like fresh out of school, lives out of daddy's back pocket, obsessed with beauty, makeup, partying, and most of all SEX filled lifestyles. I study the therapies and from what I have learned I would genuinely diagnose one of them as psychopathic with another displaying borderline psychopathic behaviours from the way they went about themselves. Their abuse became shockingly intrusive to the point where they would invite strangers into the flat to scream at me through the door all manner of vile things, along with homophobic slurs, so I think they thought being asexual was the same as being lesbian. My accommodation did nothing to help me, despite my recording everything they were saying. When I cried, they laughed. I had about two breakdowns in those two months, one of which ended with me on the phone to the Samaritans because nobody would help me. As soon as a transfer was available I was out of there, in four hours all packed and free of them. They had actually been to my new flat before me and warned my new flatmates about me, and how I might try to paint them as horrible people but actually I was just playing the victim. Luckily my new flatmates decided to get to know me on their own and realized exactly how wrong my previous flatmates were about me. I was a lot more tentative in telling them about my sexuality this time, but when I did they were respectfully inquisitive and absolutely respectful and understanding. One of them even Googles things randomly about asexuals and we sit and have lengthy discussions about what he's found, he's that interested in how I see the world differently.

I had a taxi driver overhear me talk about my breakup on the phone and he told me I needed to go see a doctor and looked at me like I was an alien and he clearly agreed that I owed my ex sex, but I was out of that cab within five minutes so I won't let that bother me. I sometimes get a bit annoyed when people ask highly intrusive questions about masturbation or if something happened to me and that I should see a doctor and I'm too young to know this so definitely about myself, but just like with my mum, the proof is in the pudding. All I can do is just carry on as I am and when I am still asexual ten years down the line my mum will concede that it's not a phase.

What's your deepest fear, concern or worry, about being asexual?

At first I was very concerned about being alone, as even when I found the LGBTQIA community where I live, they were still all based on a sexual orientation that involved sex, so there was no Asexual point of relation. The three asexuals in the group were so cliquey that I think they were so used to being the only super special asexuals in the world; that they were unable to accept there are others such as myself and my friend. My friend has been an absolute pillar in this as without her I wouldn't even know what an asexual was and where would I be today without that knowledge? I can really relate to her and talk with her about this, which is something I value greatly along with our friendship in general.

I have reached the healthiest mental place in my life so far and I am very happy with my life now I have resolved my fear of loneliness. I can easily say that I am lonely, but I mean it as in yes I would like more friends but I am so content in my own company that I don't need friends to find my own value and to be happy. I really want to get a pet hamster for companionship and then move on to getting a dog and way down the line adopt. Being alone isn't a curse; sometimes it's exactly what you need.

Why do you feel, in general, that society doesn't accept asexuality as a form of sexual orientation in its own right? And what can be done about this?

I take huge issue with the lack of representation of asexuals in the media, which is what shapes everyone's thoughts and understanding of how the world works. I feel like now is the time for the Gays and Lesbians where more films and characters are being made with those orientations and one day it may be the asexual's turn, but not yet; one day friends, one day.

A lot of people just cannot comprehend a life without sex and even if they try these things it's abstinence for God. This world is sickeningly saturated with sex and all things love and relationships, so when you are essentially indoctrinated to find such vital value in it, it is incredibly difficult to try and see that others don't live the same way. Some people just think that asexuals are young fools, pretending to try and seem different and interesting, which really doesn't help because I knew plenty of people when I was at school that caught the "Bi-bug". Left right and centre, everyone was saying they were Bi, because a really popular group started claiming they were, but by the time we left school I could count the people that still identified that way on one hand. I think people just suspect that we aren't being honest because like sex, this world is filled with dishonesty too.

What's your view on love? Have you been in love before?

I have never been in love; I genuinely don't think I am capable of that kind of attachment to anyone other than family. I really find love cute sometimes and I love reading fanfictions and watching Anime and whatnot that just tears out my still beating heart and stomps it on the floor with disastrous, painful love tragedies as the plot, along with heart-warming love stories where they overcome things. I have absolute respect for it and its value to most, I just don't experience it.

Are you currently in a relationship, and if so, is it with another asexual? If yes, do they identify the same as you or how do they identify? Or is it a sexual person? And how is either working out?

No relationship. Never again, thank you. I will have a house full of dogs, adopted children and maybe a rabbit and hamster. That is all I want and need.

If you are not in a relationship, would you like to be in one and if so, why, and what type of relationship – romantic? Platonic? What would your ideal relationship look like? And would you be in a relationship with a sexual person or not, and reason why?

Similar as above, absolutely no thank you. The most I would want is a super close best friend that I maybe develop a want to cuddle with, but nothing more. I don't need it at all.

What is your view about sex? Have you had sex before and if so, how did it make you feel? If you haven't, would you?

I think sex is a functional thing kind of like cogs and grease and motion. I can't see how there can be emotion attached to the rubbing together of bodies because I find it so disjointed an act from an emotion. I kind of die inside when I hear flatmates panting and squeaking beds because it makes me uncomfortable and they know that and apologize, but I tell them I have absolutely no problem with them doing what they do, they can go at it like rabbits, just please don't talk to me about it because I don't understand it. I respect it absolutely; I'd just rather not be around when it goes on or gets talked about.

Do you believe if a sexual person had a relationship with an asexual, it can work? And what do you think about it being fair or not?

I know that I would be highly suspicious if someone told me they could deal with not having sex after a life of it being part of the relationship process. I would be questioning them at every corner waiting for them to try it on or something. I really don't think I could trust that they are telling the truth or truly understand just how big of a NO it is, as to me ever having sex with them. I'd suspect they would want to change me like they think they have the cure. No. NO, NO, NO, I don't have enough trust in me to do that. Just like I can't turn my sexual on, how could they turn their sexual off?

Asexuality is the lack of sexual attraction, as an asexual, what does this mean to you?

This is like the lack of sexuality, because by not feeling it, you are kind of not a sexuality at all. I mean I identify as asexual but I feel like it's safe, kind of like if a whole kitchen symbolized all of the sexualities, we are the innocent piece of cake in the corner. Like we are just gunna be cake, you carry on cooking at your leisure.

Do you believe sexual attraction and sexual desire are the same thing or different, please explain?

I don't understand either, as in I can't relate to them, so I can't really differentiate them. If you put two spiders in front of me I know they are spiders but I couldn't tell you about them or their differences.

Do you think sexual arousal and sexual attraction are the same or different, please explain?

VASTLY different in my opinion. Masturbation is a thing, just like how the cogs turn in a machine; the body can experience it in my opinion. Sexual attraction is wanting someone else's… cogs… to mingle with yours in a greasy transaction. Arousal is a bodily function; sexual attraction is a different ball game.

What's your view on living with someone?

It would be really sweet to live with someone but in my experience people can be nightmares in terms of sharing responsibilities within the home. I'm going to live on my own very soon because I feel like I'm the only one I can rely on to take care of the place. Plus, it will be a safe haven just for me and I don't want to tamper with that at this point in my life.

Would you like kids and if so, how many? And how do you hope to conceive these? If you already have kids, did you know before you had them that you are asexual and how did that impact your life?

Adoption would be lovely, 3 would be my maximum but I know I want at least 1. There are plenty of children around in this world without a family, why would I go for artificial insemination, which makes me shudder at the thought, just to have a child by blood? Blood relations are overrated in my opinion.

What's your view on marriage? And if you were to get married, would it need to be with another asexual?

In an alternate universe I like to imagine the best wedding ever, but that might just be because I really like weddings and I feel like I could do it better than the ones I have been to. I just want a great big shindig. I don't have a clue what I would do if another asexual liked me, let alone wanted to marry me. They would be the only ones I would even begin to entertain.

What's your view on nudity? On porn? On masturbation? On BDSM and kinks?

Being raised in a highly open and honest sexual environment where nothing is taboo to talk about, I don't kink shame. Some I really don't understand and some are actually illegal, so if it is a really dark kink like killing kittens or something, I will obviously not approve. As long as nobody dies or ends up with mental scars or is subjected to abuse they don't want, I'm fine with it.

How difficult is it for you to be asexual, in a sexualized world?

It's easy as pie to be myself in general because I don't let cancerous people near me. I think it's easier for asexuals because we easily pass as straight, I mean we are the closest sexuality to straight and by not being with someone people just assume you are a straight singleton. It is a bit like walking through a minefield sometimes with all of the sexual madness I'm surrounded with, and that is when I take a step back from it all and get on with my own stuff.

Can you tell me about a time when you have had to deal with intrusive questions or a difficult situation due to your asexuality, and what happened?

Now I just tell people when I suspect they are about to get intrusive, how inappropriate it is to ask certain questions of anyone, so why do people get a special pass with me? In the past I've just not answered; they get the gist of why I'm not responding and soon stop.

What are the positives about being asexual?

Life feels so much easier. I know what I want, I know what I am, and I luckily know I won't have to deal with some crazy love triangle in the future. I'm safe as houses from all of that emotional mess, and STIs.

If you could have one wish about being asexual, what would it be and why?

I would wish that this world wasn't so vapid, vain and obsessed with all things sexual and the existence of correctional rape or rape in general. I can literally feel my brain melting when I look at the things kids these days find gospel. Kim Kardashian. Honestly? This generation is doomed, I'll pass on my wishes to them; they need it.

If you were to look back at your life, what advice would you have given a younger version of yourself in regard to asexuality?

Stop embarrassing yourself trying to make the boys fancy you! You don't want them to fancy you! You just don't have a clue what you are even doing! You don't even realize you are responding to what society has taught you and not what you are. Be calm young one, pay more attention in Design and Technology instead of someone you think you like.

What advice would you give to others who are just discovering about asexuality and considering whether they are or not?

I have answered this question before when interviewed about my art work on an asexual artist's blog (see link):

"I have a phrase that I tell people when I am asked how I am so confident (not full of myself, just happy with who I am in my own skin and how it shows).

'You have to live your life for you.'

Now on the face of it that seems really selfish, like 'oh but what about kids, what about family, what about a career in helping others oh you are so selfish' but if you think about it, it makes a lot of sense. You have one life. That life is yours. It's not your parents', it's not your best friend's, it's not your bullies', it's not society's, and it's yours. If you live your life trying to match up even in the slightest way to what others want for you and from you by going against what you feel, you are giving others power over your life. That life is yours, a lot of these people may not be around forever, especially the friends and bullies. Life goes on and things change, but you have to be your own anchor. You need to take courage and be what some would call 'selfish' and live your life for you, even if that means breaking the strongest of ties to those you love to do it. Loneliness is not a curse. I can happily say that I am lonely, or more accurately alone, because I am content. I am in the best place I have ever been in my entire life and I am alone/lonely at the same time. It doesn't have to be a curse. I am secure in who I am and yes you miss people and crave acceptance from others at first, but once you realize that all the approval and love that you need is within you, the easier it will be to live life the way that feels right.

Regardless of where I face hate, erasure or misunderstandings, the way I deal with it is simple. Their opinions aren't valid. It's like if you asked a baby to write a paper on time travel. They may go absolutely ham and chips on that paper with crayons colouring in the page however they want, but at the end of the day it's all just nonsense and scribbles. (I love odd metaphors.) Babies aren't qualified to write papers on time travel, and neither are people that put down others because they consider asexuality to be a weak spot, or just too damn weird and unrelatable to even try to respect it. They are invalid, have absolutely no stock, and therefore do not have the right/power to upset you. You control whose comments get to you and you get to draw the line between what is valid and what is nonsense scribbled in crayon by a baby about your life. It's yours. You've got to live your life for you, in five years time it's highly likely you will never see these people again so don't give their words value. Strive to love yourself and be the best person you can be for you."

Do you have a story you would like to share or anything else you would like to say?

Keep calm and prepare for the zombie apocalypse. It's coming. Maybe.

Extra Info

What name would you like to go under for this book? Full name, first name, or alias?

Phillipa Duke.

What country do you live in?

UK.

What nationality and ethnicity are you?

White, British.

Links to your website/social media

https://phillipaduke.wordpress.com/

https://asexualartists.wordpress.com/2016/04/22/interview-phillipa-duke/

6. Robin's Story

When did you first discover you are asexual?

When I was 18 years old.

How did you discover you are asexual?

One of the people I knew continued to make me uncomfortable by making sex jokes, and eventually when she talked about having sex publicly, I felt uncomfortable to the point I tried to figure out why. In trying to figure out why, I talked to those who were the two closest people to me at the time, and as I came up with possible reasons for it, my feelings were invalidated with 'you should just expect two loving people to have sex.' It was the first time I was acutely aware people had a sexuality, and it made me feel scared. I was scared of thinking about, or seeing any couples after that, because it kept on reminding me that they might have sex behind the scenes, and to think that people who appeared to be so innocent on the surface had a sexuality felt so out of place and scary to me. After finding out about asexuality (I chanced across the term when someone said something acephobic. The person described someone who sounded like me, so I looked asexuality up), I joined ace (short for asexual) forums, and talked to ace people, and ended up feeling so much better about myself. I finally felt as if I was allowed to just be.

Looking back, ever since I first learnt about sex in my primary school in sex education, I've always been uncomfortable with the concept of me having sex with anyone. Maybe I've just always had asexual characteristics that I didn't notice were thought by others to be unnatural until I was 18.

How do you identify yourself asexually?

Panromantic ace/demisexual

Are you 'out' about being asexual? If not, why not? If you are out, whom to, and how did they react?

I am out to queer people only. I usually come out to people who I think will be a bit more understanding than the usual crowd. People who I've come out to don't really react much to me coming out as ace, and don't ask me questions about being ace or anything like that, but maybe because these people already have at least a vague idea of what asexuality is.

What's your deepest fear, concern or worry, about being asexual?

Obviously being sex-repulsed isn't a compulsory part of being asexual, but some asexuals, such as myself are, and so I find it hard to tell people who say sexual things that they are making me feel uncomfortable by doing that. I am worried about being thought of as strange for feeling uncomfortable about sex... sex which is normalized in society to a point that it's expected that everyone has sex at some point in a relationship.

Why do you feel, in general, that society doesn't accept asexuality as a form of sexual orientation in its own right? And what can be done about this?

I think the argument that crops up often is about how exactly we are oppressed. For example, gay people have been killed or their lives ruined by homophobia. It is thought that asexuals aren't oppressed in the same way, so asexuality shouldn't really be a minority sexual orientation in its own right.

A lot of people also think it's impossible not to feel sexual attraction to others. They think that the lack of interest in having sex stems from being a 'late bloomer.' However, this is invalidation, erasure and oppression, in its own right.

I think promoting ace awareness is the best way to stand up to this erasure, whether people believe us or not.

What's your view on love? Have you been in love before?

I think love takes on a variety of forms. However, what usually crops up amongst asexuals in terms of love would be platonic and romantic love. I can feel the clear distinction between both feelings, but the difference is hard to explain... most of the time, you just have to expect people listening to get you. I say that because some people can't feel the difference between romantic or platonic love, or can't feel romantic love at all. It's important to respect this fact, and to not normalise romantic love as something everyone feels.

I would say that I am able to feel romantic attraction, so I am not aromantic per se. However, I am on the aromantic spectrum, and here's why. I am grey-romantic (I rarely feel romantic attraction). I am demiromantic, so I like people who I have gotten to know well... I don't feel 'love at first sight,' and I can't understand that. Grey-romantic and demiromantic are both in the aromantic spectrum. I don't really have a preference or criteria for what kinds of people I love. I don't care about their gender. Ultimately, I think it's important to be loved as well as loving someone. As long as you're special to your partner and vice versa, that's enough. And that's even if you and your partner may not feel the same kind of love (e.g. they feel more of a platonic love for you, whereas you feel romantic love for them). But it depends on how both people feel about the love they receive. In that sense, aromantic-romantic relationships work in a similar way to asexual-sexual relationships, and I'll talk about that later.

Are you currently in a relationship, and if so, is it with another asexual (if yes, do they identify the same as you or how do they identify), or is it a sexual person? And how is either working out?

I am with another asexual. It's working out great.

What is your view about sex? Have you had sex before and if so, how did it make you feel? If you haven't, would you?

I'd say that one's sex life should be private, not just out of respect for your partner, but also because there ARE sex-repulsed people out there who do not want to hear about sex.

I have had sex, but only with my partner. And that's because I can only tolerate sex with people I love.

Do you believe if a sexual person had a relationship with an asexual, it can work? And what do you think about it being fair or not?

I think it really depends on the people involved. I know a few sexual-asexual relationships in which the sexual person, out of respect for the asexual partner, does not ever have sex with their asexual partner. However, I don't think the majority of sexual people are like that. Even those who respect the asexual partner's wish to not have sex, would still want to have sex, and so form a compromise with their asexual partner about it. For example, agreeing on the amount of sex to have within a certain time period, so that the amount of sex does not overwhelm the asexual partner. In other words, an asexual who wishes to have a relationship with a sexual partner should expect to have sex in the majority of cases.

As much as it depends on what the sexual partner wants, it also depends on what the asexual person is willing and able to tolerate in terms of sex. I also know that some asexual people do enjoy sex, so in that case, having sex with their sexual partner at their request, may not be a problem at all.

Asexuality is the lack of sexual attraction, as an asexual, what does this mean to you?

For me, lack of sexual attraction is not feeling the desire to have sex with someone when you interact with them directly or indirectly. I'd like to also state I am a demisexual and so feel exclusive sexual attraction to someone I form a close emotional bond with and otherwise I just don't feel sexual attraction.

Do you believe sexual attraction and sexual desire are the same thing or different?

I think sexual attraction is the desire to have sex with a particular someone and sexual desire is the desire to have sex itself.

Do you think sexual arousal and sexual attraction are the same or different, please explain?

Yes they are different things. I accept that you can feel both simultaneously, which is probably why a lot of people conflate the two but they are definitely different. I think sexual attraction is the desire to have sex with someone, whereas sexual arousal is the desire to relieve arousal of your genitalia.

What's your view on living with someone?

I think opinions differ on this, but personally I would want to live with someone I can tolerate, and feel comfortable with.

Would you like kids and if so how many? And how do you hope to conceive these? If you already have kids, did you know before you had them that you are asexual and how did that impact your life?

I think I would be most comfortable having kids by adoption or scientific methods.

What's your view on marriage? And if you were to get married, would it need to be with another asexual?

I am in no rush to get married myself, and I would like to leave it to my partner to decide whether she wants to or if she is ready to marry. I don't think marriage should be thought of as a compulsory element of a stable relationship. There are many stable relationships that don't involve marriage.

If I do get married, I would want it to be with someone I love... and hopefully with someone who won't just divorce me straightaway.

I think it would be great to marry someone who would respect my limited tolerance for sex and I think asexual people would tend to understand me more in this respect.

What's your view on nudity? On porn? On masturbation? On BDSM and kinks?

I think with being shown nudity, it really depends on whether the level of it is just right for the context. For example, life drawings should be able to have nudity. I don't really like to talk too much about porn, except that one should bear in mind they are fantasies that are not to be taken seriously, nor practiced (unless it's consensual and between adults). You can use porn as sources of sexual relief whether you are seeing it on your own or with your sexual partner, but you should leave it at that and not bring them into real life by practising non-consensual things like rape. You should also not go and talk to irrelevant people about the porn you enjoy. I mean you never know if there is a sex-repulsed asexual near you, and you don't want to make them feel uncomfortable. Personally, I only feel comfortable talking about sex or sharing my sexuality with my partner. Otherwise I feel really uncomfortable when people bring porn and sex up randomly. I don't know if people are familiar with Yaoi, but it's gay porn – often it's not a real representation of gay people, and the way it's talked about (and this is usually by straight girls too), just shows how fetishising they are of gay people. I'd appreciate it if people kept that sort of fetishising porn talk away from me.

As much as there being forms of fetish I see as unacceptable – for example, trans fetish or Asian fetish, (I just feel that these things contribute to harming oppressed groups of people), I think a lot of fetishes can be acceptable. For example, if BDSM is being practiced between two consensual adults, that is okay.

How difficult is it for you to be asexual, in a sexualized world?

It is very difficult for me, because there's basically sex everywhere: Books, media, and in the form of sex jokes in real life. Even in children's shows you get sexual innuendos that older audiences are supposed to appreciate, but it just makes me feel so betrayed by the show. It's because when you are searching for the rare forms of entertainment that have no mentions of sex at all, but all you end up getting is about sex, you end up hoping for the rare gem that you just happened to find to stay a rare gem...and that hope is what ultimately destroys you when the rare gem turns out not to be the rare gem.

Can you tell me about a time when you have had to deal with intrusive questions or a difficult situation due to your asexuality, and what happened?

I haven't had any situations like that, no.

What are the positives about being asexual?

I think asexuality is just a part of me, and it's not something to be considered good or bad.

If you could have one wish about being asexual, what would it be and why?

I wish people in the grey-ace spectrum weren't made to feel so isolated in the ace community when they are already made to feel alienated in the non-ace community. As a demisexual, I have more than often used 'asexual' rather than 'demisexual' to describe myself, because I am so worried about aces who aren't in the grey-ace spectrum judging me or being scared of me.

If you were to look back at your life, what advice would you have given a younger version of yourself in regard to asexuality?

I would have told myself it's okay not to be comfortable with sexual topics. It's okay not to understand why people have sex. And even if people around me don't understand why I act that way (and even I myself didn't know that asexuality was the cause of that), it's more important to be who I am instead of forcing myself to fit in, or pretending that I understand what others are saying about sex.

What advice would you give to others who are just discovering about asexuality and considering whether they are or not?

Finding yourself takes time. So don't rush it. Never rush it.

Extra Info

What name would you like to go under for this book? Full name, first name, or alias?

Alias: Robin.

What country do you live in?

United Kingdom.

What age are you specifically? Or what decade age range are you – 20, 30. 40s?

In my 20s.

What nationality and ethnicity are you?

British/South Korean.

7. Silje Vindklokker's Story

When did you first discover you are asexual?

I first started identifying as Ace a few weeks into my first year of college.

How did you discover you are asexual?

I think I always knew I was different but I wasn't sure in what way, so I picked a label (it was bisexual if you're curious) and rolled with it even though it didn't quite fit. A few weeks into my first year, a now very good friend of mine, questioned me about my feelings toward sex and relationships. She pushed me to think about things I've never been asked to think about before and it helped me figure myself out.

How do you identify yourself asexually?

I identify as a Sex-repulsed Asexual, who isn't sure about her romantic orientation.

Are you 'out' about being asexual? If not, why not? If you are out, whom to, and how did they react?

Can I say sort of? If someone asks nicely, I'll answer and not run away. I don't mind if people know, I'm just not going to shout it to every passerby. My family doesn't know because they can barely keep their heads on about me being vegan, I can't even comprehend how they'll deal with me not only dropping Judaism in favor of Wicca, but this too? Ha! I don't give 'em credit because they don't deserve it. Most of my friends know and they took it well. The others live in fantasyland so my words have no effect, I just leave 'em be.

What's your deepest fear, concern or worry, about being asexual?

Corrective rape; the 'cure' to all things different. Sorry, not the time for jokes. Oh, and I am concerned about not being taken seriously to the point where "No" and "I don't want to" sound like "ehhh maybe" and "Yes, Please" to certain people.

Why do you feel, in general, that society doesn't accept asexuality as a form of sexual orientation in its own right? And what can be done about this?

I feel that society does not accept asexuality as a form of sexual orientation because it loves to cling to the ever shifting idea of 'normal' and conforming to it, as well as the phrase "it has always been done this/that way", to the point where it becomes justification for behaviors and actions. I'm not sure what can be done about this but if society learned how to see people as people first, instead of everything else; religion, race, gender, sexuality etc., it would be easier to validate asexuality as a sexual orientation.

What's your view on love? Have you been in love before?

Oh boy, I've been pondering this question for a while and I still do not know. I personally feel I've never been in love. Does a fierce devotion and sense of loyalty count? Probably not. Wait, I love trees! They call to me and sooth my rage and anger toward this destructive world. I don't think that counts either. Eh, it's okay ill figure it out; can't miss what I never knew.

Are you currently in a relationship, and if so, is it with another asexual (if yes, do they identify the same as you or how do they identify), or is it a sexual person? And how is either working out?

I am not in a relationship currently.

If you are not in a relationship, would you like to be in one and if so, why, and what type of relationship – romantic? Platonic? What would your ideal relationship look like? And would you be in a relationship with a sexual person or not, and reason why?

I want to say yes, but people confuse me and they are so needy and complicated and I'd have to share with them. If I was ever contemplating a relationship, I might try romantic but I'm not sure. They'd have to be vegan, spiritual not religious, and I'd feel bad being in a relationship with a sexual person because in my mind they have these expectations even though they know I'm Ace, and they're only sticking around because of obligation. I see now that I'm a very particular person.

What is your view about sex? Have you had sex before and if so, how did it make you feel? If you haven't, would you?

I don't care if others have sex. I personally have no desire for, or interest in it. Just keep it far away from me.

No, I have not, but some have tried and let me tell you the sound of someone opening a condom is scary but the absence of that sound is terrifying.

Do you believe if a sexual person had a relationship with an asexual, it can work? And what do you think about it being fair or not?

Possibly, I'm not sure, I have had no experiences with this topic but I'd like to say yes it's possible.

Asexuality is the lack of sexual attraction, as an asexual, what does this mean to you?

When I look at someone I notice little things; eye color, the shape of their nose, jaw line, earring or absence of, teeth, other facial piercings, hair color and style. I cannot tell you what they're wearing, I can never remember because there is nothing of interest that low, except shoes. Besides that, I mostly think 'whoa what a rad friend you'd make', or 'whoa you're very attractive stay that way.'

Do you believe sexual attraction and sexual desire are the same thing or different?

I'm going to go with similar but different, one can desire sex but not be sexually attracted to a person but they can also go hand in hand.

Do you think sexual arousal and sexual attraction are the same or different?

Hum, yes I believe they're different but I only have blurry textbook terms and definitions. Arousal is physical and doesn't necessarily have to be triggered by sexual attraction. Sexual attraction is mental.

What's your view on living with someone?

Uh, I don't share well and there are complications with living with another but as long as I have my own room I guess it would be okay.

Would you like kids and if so how many? And how do you hope to conceive these? If you already have kids, did you know before you had them that you are asexual and how did that impact your life?

Oh, no. I knew when I was four and that notion still stands strong to this day. Change my mind my ass. Excuse my language.

What's your view on marriage? And if you were to get married, would it need to be with another asexual?

I believe it's a very outdated ritual where women are given away to another man because she's past her use at home and only usefulness left is as a child bearer/rearer and housekeeper. Oh and those rings are little finger shackles claiming that you are nothing but property. However, I don't have a problem with other people getting married.

What's your view on nudity? On porn? On masturbation? On BDSM and kinks?

I don't care if it happens, I just prefer if it's done, discussed, and kept very far away from me.

How difficult is it for you to be asexual, in a sexualized world?

It is not difficult per se but it can be annoying at times especially in the media. I would like to read a story or watch a horror movie without the sex and unnecessary romantic subplot. Unnecessary being the key word, I don't mind romance if the plot is beautifully executed. Oh, I do not like the assumptions and "uh huhs" to everything I say.

Can you tell me about a time when you have had to deal with intrusive questions or a difficult situation due to your asexuality, and what happened?

I haven't gotten any intrusive questions yet but Netflix and chill means something else! I found out the hard way. Oh and "hangout" doesn't mean hangout. Why aren't these things explained? Holy hell, I had to be saved by my friend, all's good nothing too bad happened, I got out of there before his drunk ass could do anything.

What are the positives about being asexual?

There are so many positive things about being asexual, the puns, inside jokes, and the community. Finding out everything is normal, oh and the promise of world domination. I especially like the sandbox. (The sandbox is part of a set of pictures designed to explain the different sexualities relating to different things found in the park or playground. So it goes: The Asexual Sandbox, Bisexual Swing, Pansexual Merry Go Round, Heterosexual Slide and Homosexual Horsie. I thought it was cute and they were done in the different pride colors.)

If you could have one wish about being asexual, what would it be and why?

I figure the equality for all should be my wish since it caters to the greater good, but I'm going to be selfish and say I really wish people would stop calling me innocent, prude, and celibate, good goddess it infuriates me to the point I contemplate violence. Violence is not the answer even if they don't believe me when I try to say otherwise.

If you were to look back at your life, what advice would you have given a younger version of yourself in regard to asexuality?

Younger self, it is okay to be different, embrace it. Oh and whatever you do, do not make friends with shallow, two-faced, conformists. They only care about themselves and will only bring you misery by trying to change you to fit their ideals by any means necessary. They are poison and not worth the confusion, self-hate and abuse. If somehow they ensnare you, stay strong eventually the storm will pass.

What advice would you give to others who are just discovering about asexuality and considering whether they are or not?

Don't feel like you have to be labeled, humans are too complex to shove into neat little boxes. Just take it one step at a time and if you decide that asexuality is you, there is a whole community comprised of the one percent ready to welcome you. If you decide you are not, don't fret there is always someone willing to listen and offer advice.

Do you have a story you would like to share or anything else you would like to say?

I think I covered everything; I have only been Ace officially for a little over a year and a half. Oh, wait! This is the most I have talked about sex. Ever. However, if it helps to ease the struggle of others; yay.

Extra Info

What name would you like to go under for this book? Full name, first name, or alias?

Alias: Silje Vindklokker.

What country do you live in?

North America but I want to live in Norway.

What age are you specifically? Or what decade age range are you – 20, 30. 40s?

20.

What nationality and ethnicity are you?

Half white, half Columbian and from North America.

8. Cassidy's Story

When did you first discover you are asexual?

Around November 2015. I was 28.

How did you discover you are asexual?

My husband and I had agreed to see other people and I was on OkCupid and found a girl whose profile I liked and she identified as a "grey ace" and I did some Googling and thought "holy shit that's me".

How do you identify yourself asexually?

I identify as a poly biromantic grey ace. I'm a cis woman. I'm sex positive and love physical affection. I think genitals are somewhere between silly and gross. I don't really enjoy touching them but will (willingly) to please my partner.

Are you 'out' about being asexual? If not, why not? If you are out, whom to, and how did they react?

I am out to some friends, my husband, a cousin, and anyone I'm trying to date. I'm not hiding it but it also doesn't seem pertinent to a lot of my relationships. It seems similar to a friend I have who doesn't like pizza. MOST people like pizza. People kind of assume that EVERYONE likes pizza. She doesn't. No amount of changing the toppings makes her like pizza. She doesn't go around proclaiming she doesn't like pizza and it really only comes up when a group is thinking about having pizza. She does, on occasion, eat pizza anyway. That's kind of how I feel about sex.

What's your deepest fear, concern or worry, about being asexual?

That eventually my sexual, (very sexual) husband, will leave me for a sexual partner. I don't really worry about this much though, our relationship is super secure.

Why do you feel, in general, that society doesn't accept asexuality as a form of sexual orientation in its own right? And what can be done about this?

It's kind of like music I think. When you meet a person you don't ask "Do you like music?" you ask, "What kind of music do you like?" If someone said, "I don't like music" my initial response would be something like, "But there are so many different kinds! You don't like ANY of it? Seriously?! Have you listened to...?" It's a seemingly universal human interest. Sex takes it one step further in that even other warm-blooded animals like sex. I totally get why people are confused. It's easier to wrap your head around, "they just like different sex than I do" than "they just don't want sex". I think it's kind of weird that everyone NEEDS to have a sexual orientation. I think it puts way too much importance on sex. I feel like sex is just something people do together. Like puzzles or jogging. My puzzle orientation is jigsaw and my jogging orientation is No. I think sex just needs to be taken off its pedestal.

What's your view on love? Have you been in love before?

I love love. I've been in love like 10 times. I live for love. I really don't know what else to say about it.

Are you currently in a relationship, and if so, is it with another asexual (if yes, do they identify the same as you or how do they identify), or is it a sexual person? And how is either working out?

I'm married to a very sexual, bisexual, gender queer, man type person. (That's how he describes himself.) It works because we are completely honest with each other. My coming out as asexual actually helped because he thought that I just didn't want to have sex with him but now he understands that I don't want to have sex with anyone. We do have sex fairly regularly (once a week-ish) but it's kind of like I know he does things for me that he doesn't enjoy (i.e. watching bad TV, clothes shopping), because I like it and he wants to spend time with me and so I have sex with him because he likes it and I want to spend time with him--but I get to pick the music. If he asks if we can have sex and I don't want to I say "no" and he respects that.

What is your view about sex? Have you had sex before and if so, how did it make you feel? If you haven't, would you?

I have had a lot of sex with a lot of people actually (which is why my friends are so confused by my recent discovery of asexuality), because since I didn't desire it the way other people did, it couldn't control me. I kind of used it as a weapon. (I'm in no way advocating this but it's what happened.) I could get people to do all sorts of things by having sex with them. Stay with me. Leave her. Drive a couple hours then spend the night. Feed me. Take care of me. Love me. It made me feel in control in a time in my life when I had very little.

Do you believe if a sexual person had a relationship with an asexual, it can work? And what do you think about it being fair or not?

I'm in one and it's working. As far as fair goes...life isn't fair. This is what I mean when I said sex is put up on this pedestal. Ok, so there's one thing that we don't both like. Big deal. He doesn't like drawing. I don't like Magic The Gathering (a trading card game). He doesn't like musicals. I don't like first person shooters. Big deal. There are a million and one things that we do both like and we love each other and we have an amazing life with great friends, a beautiful daughter, dogs, and more love than we know what to do with. So I don't want sex. Big deal.

Asexuality is the lack of sexual attraction, as an asexual, what does this mean to you?

I identify as a grey ace and to me that means I'm never going to look at a person and think "man, I would love to have sex with that person", although through the right combination of music and touching I can become physically aroused and orgasm, but it's so tedious and I can think of (and sometimes do think of), a dozen other things I could be doing.

Do you believe sexual attraction and sexual desire are the same thing or different?

I imagine they're different to sexual people. Like finding someone sexy and wanting to have sex with them are two different things. I don't particularly have either. Sometimes I do want to touch people though. Nothing sexual. I just want to pet them.

Do you think sexual arousal and sexual attraction are the same or different?

Yes. Arousal is a physical phenomenon (i.e. an erection or lubricated vagina), and attraction is a more abstract concept.

What's your view on living with someone?

I HATE living alone. I live with my husband, our daughter, two dogs and two ferrets. Honestly, I wouldn't mind getting some roommates. I like living with lots of people.

Would you like kids and if so how many? And how do you hope to conceive these? If you already have kids, did you know before you had them that you are asexual and how did that impact your life?

We have a daughter. She's two. I figured out I was asexual after I had her. I don't want any more children. Being pregnant was horrific. Birth was horrific. My asexuality hasn't impacted that part of my life. She was conceived because I got lax with my birth control because I wanted a baby even though we weren't ready. I told my husband he should wear a condom because I hadn't been taking my pill unless he wanted a baby. Now we have a baby. She's awesome.

What's your view on marriage? And if you were to get married, would it need to be with another asexual?

I like marriage. I like the security and the commitment. He's sexual and he's allowed to have sex with other people provided he is safe and doesn't produce any children. I'm allowed to have emotionally intimate connections with the same limitations (although I'm not sure how I could produce children in this manner), (that was a joke). The marriage is a safe and stable place from which to explore the world and come back to.

What's your view on nudity? On porn? On masturbation? On BDSM and kinks?

I personally enjoy being naked. I don't mind at all if other people are naked. My husband watches porn. I don't care at all. Sometimes I watch porn to make fun of the bad acting. I think it's funny and don't see how anyone could possibly find it sexy but I feel that way about most things. I've been known to participate in BDSM because I like to feel in control. I would probably make a great dominatrix. Most kinks I find comical but that's rude so I try not to laugh out loud.

How difficult is it for you to be asexual, in a sexualized world?

Not at all. I feel like I have the upper hand most of the time.

I've been sexually assaulted more than once and failed to report it because I figured it was probably my fault for playing with the proverbial fire and because I never *want* it so what's the difference? I know now that the difference is I said "No" and that is enough of a difference to matter.

What are the positives about being asexual?

Apparently sexual people have this inner dialogue, "I shouldn't have sex with her...but I really reeeally want to.... ok fine!" and it causes them turmoil. I only have these feelings about whether or not I should eat chocolate. Also I have enough body/mind fights going on without whether or not I should be playing pelvic peaknuckle with people. (I have anxiety, which causes my body to randomly think I'm in mortal peril at inappropriate times.)

If you could have one wish about being asexual, what would it be and why?

Um.... probably that I could turn it on and off at will. It would make my sex life with my husband easier.

If you were to look back at your life, what advice would you have given a younger version of yourself in regard to asexuality?

I would probably just tell myself it was a thing. I was a pretty smart teenager, I probably could have figured it out from there.

What advice would you give to others who are just discovering about asexuality and considering whether they are or not?

If you think you are then you are. There's not a litmus test. Identity is about how you feel about who you are. Some people think it's weird that I have had so much sex and still identify as being asexual and I don't really care because it feels right to me.

Do you have a story you would like to share or anything else you would like to say?

Pizza, music, and sex, are all great things but not everyone likes them.

Extra Info

What name would you like to go under for this book? Full name, first name, or alias?

Cassidy.

What country do you live in?

USA.

What age are you specifically? Or what decade age range are you – 20, 30. 40s?

29.

What nationality and ethnicity are you?

German Jew and Native American mostly, but I usually just go with white.

Links to your website/social media.

www.annebivalent.wordpress.com

9. Kenneth William's Story

When did you first discover you are asexual?

I began identifying as asexual a few months after turning eighteen, however, I would have earlier if I had known there was a word for how I was feeling. When I was in high school I understood sex as a concept, however, I didn't know it was okay not to crave it. I didn't understand my friends' need for it, or why it was such a big deal when I said I would never want to have sex with anyone I dated. It's clear to me now that if I had known the word, I would have begun using it around fourteen.

How did you discover you are asexual?

I had an upsetting conversation with the guy I was dating at the time over my lack of sexual desire and began Googling to try to figure out if there was a word for how I felt. I found AVEN, and after looking through the threads felt a surge of relief as I learned there were people who felt the same as me. What's kind of funny was that I was searching the word "asexual" because I had finished watching the show Sirens, which has an asexual character, Voodoo. I remember liking her because I could relate to her.

How do you identify yourself asexually?

Panromantic asexual with a bit of a preference for males.

Are you 'out' about being asexual? If not, why not? If you are out, whom to, and how did they react?

I am out to my cousin who I am close to and grew up with, and a few friends. My cousin was understanding, likely due to our closeness and experience with those who aren't the norm. I came out to the others while we were talking about their sexual exploits or making jokes, and they took it okay. There are some problems that arise, like assuming I haven't had good sex or met the right person yet, or that I am also aromantic. I am not out to most of my family because I don't feel the need to bring up sex, especially since they're religious, just to tell them I don't desire it. I also feel they would mistake it for celibacy, or that I want to wait for marriage. I come out to friends when it becomes relevant or easy to do. I do not mind talking about sex or sexual topics, so I don't always feel like I need to tell someone I'm ace.

What's your deepest fear, concern or worry, about being asexual?

Being alone forever. I crave a romantic partner, or at least the aspects of it, such as cuddling and kissing. I have no problem with immediately being written off as a potential partner due to my asexuality. I know sex is important to the majority of people and that most people wouldn't be okay in a relationship without it. I have never met another ace though, and I fear I will never meet one, and that if I do, we will still be too different in personality and our interests.

Why do you feel, in general, that society doesn't accept asexuality as a form of sexual orientation in its own right? And what can be done about this?

It would help if not having sex wasn't seen as a bad thing, or as an insult, you know, the "asexual nerd who can't get laid" stereotype. Having it mentioned in sex ed classes would also be a good start. If it becomes more well known then I think more people will come to accept it, as well as younger asexuals not feeling confused or broken. It also may be hard for sexuals to wrap their head around the idea that someone might not want, or even hate, something they love and crave. Sex is everywhere, and while I'm okay with that, it does make it more difficult to realize not everyone wants it.

What's your view on love? Have you been in love before?

Love is different for everyone. If I like you, I'm probably constantly insulting you and simultaneously trying to help you out. Love can exist with or without sex, but I don't believe in love at first sight. Crushes can form on sight, but crushes aren't love. They can possibly be a prelude, but I don't think you can really love someone until you actually know and spend time with them. I was actually a bit slow to crushes, one not developing until I was nineteen. I had relationships, but liking someone I wasn't currently seeing was new. I believe real love is long lasting, and is still present even when the "flame" is gone and everything settles. Love doesn't need to be in your face, love is love. It can also, obviously, be platonic, love for friends and family. I believe I did fall in love with my last boyfriend. We dated for three years before breaking up over the lack of sex. It was difficult for both of us, it was him who ended it, I cried, but got why he needed to end it. My gender was also a bit of a problem, but it was really a lack of sex that did us in. We remained friends, but splitting was difficult, and we continued telling each other "I love you" for quite a while, and every so often still do. At this time we've been broken up for over a year, but still cuddle and share a few kisses. I still feel I love him, but not that I'm in love with him. It feels like a stronger platonic love.

Are you currently in a relationship, and if so, is it with another asexual (if yes, do they identify the same as you or how do they identify), or is it a sexual person? And how is either working out?

I am not.

If you are not in a relationship, would you like to be in one and if so, why, and what type of relationship – romantic? Platonic? What would your ideal relationship look like? And would you be in a relationship with a sexual person or not, and reason why?

Yes, I would like a romantic relationship. I would prefer to date an asexual, however since I don't connect love with sex, I would be okay with a sexual who would have an open relationship with a set of rules we would both agree too. There would be no cuddling, kissing, or other romantic gestures for the other person; it would have to purely just be sex. They could also not bother me to have sex with them. We could talk about sex, joke about it, but I do not want to be in a relationship where I feel I have to have sex. I would want to know if they're taking advantage of being able to have sex with others, but it is hard to say now how much detail I would want. It didn't bother me when the guy I liked talked about sex with his past girlfriend, but I did get jealous thinking of things like kisses or cuddling.

My ideal relationship would involve a lot of physical elements, but no sex. Cuddling, kissing, wrestling and fighting would be enough. Someone who shares my interests and my rather rough and often mean personality; a partner in crime.

What is your view about sex? Have you had sex before and if so, how did it make you feel? If you haven't, would you?

I view sex as healthy and normal, but not something I will ever want in my life. I've given and received oral sex, giving it was boring, gross, and all I did was wonder how long I needed to try before it was okay to stop. Receiving it was also boring to me, with the added issue of trying to avoid eye contact. It was also awkward seeing a face I saw as adorable and cute, doing something I saw as pointless and unsanitary. I have no idea what to do with my hands either. I'm not interested in sex, it makes me feel bored, awkward, dirty, and it is upsetting. I don't mind light sexual things, a hand on my butt or thigh while cuddling, but I need to be very comfortable with the person. I don't like it if it gets too handsy. Everything sexual I did was to try to make my partner happy, and not something I would have ever done for myself. In the end it still didn't work out. I wasn't willing often enough, and it was often obvious I was bored or unhappy with what was going on. I actually got caught watching Futurama on the TV over my partner's shoulder. He realized it when I laughed, forgetting I was supposed to be moaning or something. He was pretty unhappy with me.

I also don't think leaving someone for lack of sex is wrong. I see it as just another need. If my relationship lacked something I saw as vital, and it couldn't be worked out, it would be okay for me to leave as well.

Do you believe if a sexual person had a relationship with an asexual, it can work? And what do you think about it being fair or not?

Yes, I do think it can work. Asexuals don't crave sex, but not all of them are repulsed by it and may choose to have sex to make their partner happy. They may also be okay with an open relationship, or the sexual may choose celibacy if sex isn't as important to them. I think it becomes unfair when either partner tries to guilt the other. It is unfair of the sexual to try to guilt the asexual into having sex, and equally unfair when the asexual partner tries to guilt the sexual into denying their own needs.

Asexuality is the lack of sexual attraction, as an asexual, what does this mean to you?

It means I don't look at someone and go how they look makes me desire sex with them. I experience aesthetic attraction, and I feel like a lot of the time sexuals don't understand the different between the two, or at least it can be difficult to explain to my sexual friends that I don't want sex with someone but I still think they're good looking. I look at someone and I like their long hair, or their brown eyes, and it ends there. I might want to cuddle them, hold them, have them near to me, but I don't think about sex or how they'd look naked.

Do you believe sexual attraction and sexual desire are the same thing or different, please explain?

I think they're very connected, but I wouldn't say that they are the same thing. I would describe sexual attraction as seeing a person or object and having sexual thoughts and feelings, and sexual desire as, well, desiring sex.

Do you think sexual arousal and sexual attraction are the same or different, please explain?

Yes, I do believe the two are the same. Without the physical sexual arousal, the two are the same to me.

What's your view on living with someone?

Live with whoever. I'd move in with a partner, but only if I truly felt we were compatible, for no other reason than I don't want to suddenly have bills I cannot afford myself. I don't care if people who are dating move in together. I think it's a good idea for people to live together before marriage, what if you learn you cannot live with them? They drive you crazy or it just causes too many issues?

Would you like kids and if so how many? And how do you hope to conceive these? If you already have kids, did you know before you had them that you are asexual and how did that impact your life?

Currently, I view myself as too young and not financially fit to have a child and I'm not sure if I do. I go back and forth on the issue, but overall, I think I would like a single child. It would have to be adopted or come into my life in a similar way, as I will never want to actually "have" a child.

What's your view on marriage? And if you were to get married, would it need to be with another asexual?

I don't think marriage is important, but I have nothing against people who choose to marry, nor do I hate the concept. I know very few people who are happily married and grew up knowing my married parents hated each other. While I do want a romantic partner to spend my life with, I'm okay if the two of us never get married. That wouldn't bother me. It would also make things much easier if we broke up. If I were to be married I would prefer it to be with an asexual. A sexual would be okay if we were in a good, healthy relationship, where I was not pressured to have sex and they were not forced to give it up.

What's your view on nudity? On porn? On masturbation? On BDSM and kinks?

I find porn repulsive to look at, but I don't care that it exists. It's there, people like it, and I see why. However, I find it very disturbing and upsetting to watch sexual acts between strangers. The first time I watched porn I was around sixteen, and my boyfriend had wanted me to watch it with him. At first I just didn't care or understand the appeal of watching a woman touch herself, but it quickly became disturbing to me to watch, and I didn't make it very far at all before getting too upset. My boyfriend realized I was upset and hiding my face, and turned it off. He was pretty upset by my reaction, and I was upset because I didn't know why it was so wrong for me to dislike it. It is also pointless in my life. I have no desire to be in the place of any of the participants, nor do I have any desire to masturbate to it. I don't often masturbate since I don't get any pleasure from it. I got some when my boyfriend did it for me, but I quickly got bored and it didn't carry on. Soon as he stopped the feelings were over and I'd want to eat or watch TV; something unrelated. I see nothing wrong with it as a thing other people do.

I'm okay with BDSM and kinks. I don't mind pictures or images pertaining to BDSM, unless there is nudity. I do not like most nudity in sexual scenarios. I don't mind it when it's really art, and I don't freak out seeing a woman's breast by mistake when she's breastfeeding. I got scared the first time I saw my ex-boyfriend naked, but I no longer mind it. That might be because of how close and comfy around each other we are. I don't mind being naked around him either, but he's the only one. I wear layers and avoid showing as much skin as possible around anyone else. I'm very uncomfortable with my body. I also don't like seeing people in skimpy clothes. I understand why they would want to, especially if it's hot, but I avoid looking at anyone scantily dressed.

How difficult is it for you to be asexual, in a sexualized world?

It really only becomes a problem when the assumption that I also love sex becomes too much. I don't like watching sex scenes in movies, but I make sex jokes, talk about sexual things, and don't care if my friends tell me what sexual things they do with their partners. It would be much, much more difficult if I couldn't deal with those things. It makes it much harder for me to find a date, and sometimes to relate to people. I also get bored of certain movies or shows when it becomes too clear that the plot is the characters have sex. Since I don't feel sexual attraction, I can't relate when my friends point out someone they think is sexy. I also have problems explaining that when I had a crush on a guy, I did not want to have sex, even though I found him attractive.

Being asexual often makes me feel like an outsider, like everyone else speaks this language that I do not. I also had trouble telling my ex that he had done nothing to turn me off to the idea of sex, since we were each other's first for many things.

It became an issue when I had a crush on a guy. I told our mutual friend who, while a great guy, quickly assumed it meant I desired sex. His advice for me was also often to do something sexual. I feel it was probably also confusing for my crush when he came on to me, and I turned him down. He stopped what he was doing and was very decent, which was great. He apologized for assuming he was going to get laid (his words), and that he thought that it went with me admitting to liking him. I don't have too much trouble knowing there's a connection between the two, but I do wish they weren't assumed to be the same thing.

Advertising that plays on sex is also kind of funny to me. I know they're trying to use someone "sexy" to boost their product, as well as language or music, but it doesn't get me. I either lose interest because I don't care about the people, or try to figure out what is actually being sold and what it does.

Can you tell me about a time when you have had to deal with intrusive questions or a difficult situation due to your asexuality, and what happened?

If I tell someone I'm ace, they will typically assume that it is okay to ask me if I masturbate. They will also often ask about my sexual history, or tell me my boyfriends were probably just ugly. I don't mind talking about my sexual history with friends, with people I'm comfortable around, I do not like getting these questions from strangers or acquaintances. They're weird and make me feel awkward. I also used to get protective of my ex when someone would blame him for my asexuality, because no one is to blame for it, and insulting helps no one.

I feel like flirting is also a difficult situation for me. Most of the time flirting expresses sexual attraction, and that's not something I want from strangers. It makes me sort of panic because I want to flirt back because it's fun, but I don't because I know that they're actually serious. I flirt and mess around with friends, and they do the same, because we both know that neither of us are serious. When it's with a stranger or acquaintance, I can't tell if they're playing or not. To me it's just a game, just playful conversation. It doesn't always dawn on me that people do it because they want something, whether it's sex or just a relationship.

I've been asked if I was sexually abused as a child, and if that was why I'm asexual. This is absolutely not an okay thing to ask someone. It's rude, inconsiderate, and dismisses the idea that someone can be asexual without trauma. My past isn't the cleanest, and while I'll talk about it with people I'm close to, no one else is entitled to this information simply because they feel asexuality can only be a result of an issue. When asked this, I am either forced to say I was, and have them dismiss my asexuality and ask more questions, or say no, and just deal with more questions, knowing I lied. There's never an appropriate time to ask someone this when they say they're asexual. What if they ask this of someone who is still getting over their trauma?

What are the positives about being asexual?

I'm not quite sure there are any. I feel pretty left out and like I'm missing a big part of life and love. I would never choose to be asexual; I dislike it. I would prefer to be a sexual person.

If you could have one wish about being asexual, what would it be and why?

That more people understood and accepted it as a real thing, more than just as someone who hasn't had good sex, or as a sexual who can't get laid.

If you were to look back at your life, what advice would you have given a younger version of yourself in regard to asexuality?

I would have told younger me I was asexual, that I'm not broken, and not to think I am. That knowledge would have stopped a lot of pain and confusion. Trying to force myself to be sexual and not knowing I wasn't broken or stupid, was a lot of unnecessary strife. I would have told past me that everyone in high school who obsessed over sex weren't wrong, but neither was I for not caring. I also would have warned past me that I wouldn't ever be ready for sex with my boyfriend. I don't regret dating him, and I would date another sexual, but I didn't know I was ace and it was unfair of me to keep putting off having sex, thinking I would eventually want to. It hurt me and it hurt him.

What advice would you give to others who are just discovering about asexuality and considering whether they are or not?

Don't listen to what sexuals tell you about who you are, because they don't know how you feel anymore than an ace understands how they feel. We have different orientations and have no business trying to force them on each other. Know that while it makes it harder to find someone it doesn't mean you'll be alone. Also, just because you're rare, it doesn't mean that you are also broken or have to be alone.

Do you have a story you would like to share or anything else you would like to say?

One of the things that really frustrates me as an asexual is the assumption that I must be pure and innocent, and cannot like certain things. It's very annoying to be told I cannot like a certain song or band because I don't like sex. I don't like to be told in a condescending manner that a certain song references sex or that the band I'm listening to has explicit lyrics. I know it does, I just don't care. It is equally annoying to talk about TV shows and be asked why, as an asexual, I would be watching a show that has sex scenes. I don't watch sex scenes, I fast-forward or get up for a moment, and feel I don't miss out on anything actually important.

It is also frustrating to come out to someone and have them say something along the lines of, "Aw, I'm sorry!" Why are you sorry? If I told you I was gay would you apologize? Why would you need to apologize for my orientation?

Extra Info

What name would you like to go under for this book? Full name, first name, or alias?

Kenneth William.

What country do you live in?

USA.

10. Niki's Story

When did you first discover you are asexual?

I had suspected that I was for several years but didn't really learn about the term and apply it to myself until a few months ago.

How did you discover you are asexual?

Looking around at other people my age and the media in general, it was easy for me to judge myself for not having the same interest in sex as my peers. The media (movies, books, anything really), put so much emphasis on how important sex was to growing up and finding out who you were, and I just never felt the need for that. For a long time I thought something was wrong with me because of that, like I was defective or immature for not wanting to have sex. It wasn't until I started coming across the term asexual in blogs online that I realized there were other people like me and that it wasn't something I should feel bad about. I started reading up on asexuality and realized the term applied to me.

How do you identify yourself asexually?

I'm still learning the terms but I'd say Grey-ace or sex-positive ace.

Are you 'out' about being asexual? If not, why not? If you are out, whom to, and how did they react?

I only really started fully identifying as asexual a few months ago, so I'm only out to a few people. My old roommates became the first to know, we were taking about sex (a very common topic for people my age) and expectations in a relationship. My expectations as an asexual just kind of came out. I was freaked out when I realized I'd just admitted that to them, but they were all very supportive if a bit curious; they really wanted to know what that meant from someone who actually identified that way. My sister also knows and is very supportive of me. That has meant a lot since she is a very sexual person. I haven't told my parents yet. It's not so much that I don't think they would understand; it's more that asexuality is often poorly understood and I need to wait till I have enough time to explain it all. I live really far away for school right now and it's not exactly the kind of conversation I want to have over FaceTime!

What's your deepest fear, concern or worry, about being asexual?

Being misunderstood and wrongly judged. It is so strangely vital in our society to want sex and be interested in sexual activities. People look at you very differently sometimes once they figure out that you don't like the idea of having sex, and they tend to make a lot of snap judgments. You have low self-esteem. You have no body confidence. You are sheltered or a prude. You are just a virgin and have to get over it. You just haven't met the right person. I've had people completely dismiss the idea of my being asexual because they just can't wrap their head around not wanting sex. Having people completely disregard or ridicule you and your identity is a big concern for me.

Why do you feel, in general, that society doesn't accept asexuality as a form of sexual orientation in its own right? And what can be done about this?

Our society is often so sexual and sex is viewed as such a critical part of love and relationships that I think a lot of social norms just don't leave room for asexuality. Culturally, we reject the idea that people can be disinterested in sex. Therefore, when most people are introduced to the idea of asexuality, it seems wrong to them. Lots of people associate it with odd or different people who just don't fit in and aren't all there, or who "couldn't get some anyway". They can't imagine asexuality, therefore they have to supply some kind of defect as to why certain people don't engage in sex. I think it is important to have a dialogue so people realize that being asexual is a normal and healthy way to be and isn't just some cover up for prudish people. The portrayal (accurately!) of asexuality in the media would really help with that.

What's your view on love? Have you been in love before? Please explain.

I haven't been in love before. I think it is separate from sex and valid for asexuals as well. I see it as more of a mental and psychological commitment than a physical one. You commit your emotional investment, your time. Having never been in a relationship I think it is hard to define without experience.

Are you currently in a relationship, and if so, is it with another asexual (if yes, do they identify the same as you or how do they identify), or is it a sexual person? And how is either working out?

I have never been in any kind of relationship before.

If you are not in a relationship, would you like to be in one and if so, why, and what type of relationship – romantic? Platonic? What would your ideal relationship look like? And would you be in a relationship with a sexual person or not, and reason why?

I would say that while I'm open to the idea, I do not want to be in a relationship right now. It's not necessarily about sexual identity, just too much going on in grad school! I'm honestly not sure what my ideal relationship would look like; I would want to be very comfortable. I really love the idea of being with someone who makes me feel more powerful and confident in myself, and whom I could support the same way.

People in really long-term relationships who really know their partner and are past the fancy dates and into hanging out playing video games with beer; those are the people I could get jealous of! Maybe it sounds crazy, but anytime I find myself thinking about a relationship it is always the very mundane or everyday/comfortable parts of a relationship that draw me in.

I do think asexuality stops me from pursuing a relationship a little bit. Often with my age group people have one thing on their mind with dating (sorry for the overt generalization but it has often proven true). I guess I am afraid of having to explain what I want from a relationship and facing what I often see as the inevitable rejection of that from the other person. I consider myself sex-positive and while I have no interest in it, I have not 100% closed myself off to the idea of having sex. I think I could be in a relationship with a sexual person if we had enough communication and respect. If they were respectful of my boundaries and goals for the relationship and I respected their needs, I believe it could work. It would be a lot of effort to keep up the communication!

What is your view about sex? Have you had sex before and if so, how did it make you feel? If you haven't, would you?

I consider myself a sex positive asexual. I know many people very close to me who are very sexual and I find nothing wrong with it. I'm very comfortable talking about sex as well, and I think dialogue about sex can be very healthy. Honestly, for a very sex centred culture, I think we don't have nearly enough honest, open conversations about sex.

I have not had sex myself. It is not something I have ever had any interest in. I have never wanted to have it. However, I think that if I was in a relationship where I felt safe and respected and it was something my partner wanted; I would be willing. It's not something I would look for or want in a relationship but if I was with someone I cared deeply about and who understood my feelings on it, I might do it for them.

Do you believe if a sexual person had a relationship with an asexual, it can work? And what do you think about it being fair or not?

I believe it can work between a sexual and an asexual person. It would take more work and communication since expectations would likely be quite different on both sides. Obviously this is coming from a more sex-positive ace. If someone was further on the spectrum and more sex repulsed it would become much more challenging. I'm honestly not sure if that would work not having any personal experience, I suppose it would depend on the people involved.

In terms of it being fair, I think it is fair as long as communication is clear. Obviously if expectations clash that will lead to problems, regardless of whether it is sex or any other expectation that was unclear. In my mind nothing is wrong with an asexual for not desiring sex in a relationship, and nothing is wrong with a sexual person for wanting it. If you both go in with your eyes open, even if things change or don't pan out, I think it is perfectly fair.

Asexuality is the lack of sexual attraction, as an asexual, what does this mean to you?

For me, I feel sexual attraction refers mostly to the act itself. Personally, I find a large distinction between looking at someone and thinking they are cute/attractive and sexual attraction or interest in having sex with them. So I guess for me sexual attraction has to do with interest in actually having sex. If I'm watching a movie and there is an attractive character I can see that. They pop up on screen and you think, "Wow they are really attractive!" But that's it. When my friend leans over and tells me all the things she can imagine them doing, I never get that. My mind just doesn't go there. And if it does end up going there thanks to a friend's creative imagination, it really doesn't appeal to me or makes me uncomfortable.

Do you believe sexual attraction and sexual desire are the same thing or different, please explain?

I think they are very similar, I suppose desire suggests stronger feelings, but yes I think they are two terms for feeling interested in someone sexually or wanting to have sex with them.

Do you think sexual arousal and sexual attraction are the same or different, please explain?

I think that sexual arousal is essentially a physical response that may or may not be tied to sexual attraction. The body can be a little weird so sexual arousal can occur without feelings of sexual attraction happening at the same time. To me arousal is a physiological response and only somewhat tied to emotions or feelings. Sex, solo or partnered, can be pleasurable for some people and you may be aroused to seek that out without specific sexual attraction for someone.

What's your view on living with someone?

Having never been in a relationship I don't think I have ever thought this far ahead! If I was in a committed relationship with someone who understood my needs in a relationship I would be willing to live with them. I would need to know that my boundaries would be respected.

Would you like kids and if so how many? And how do you hope to conceive these? If you already have kids, did you know before you had them that you are asexual and how did that impact your life?

I am not interested in having children, nor do I currently have any. The idea of having or raising children has just never appealed; I've never been drawn to children or gotten on with them very well. When I'm finished with my program I will have been in college for eight years and I definitely want to get out there and have a career, which would be challenging with a child. I know it's possible but given how disinterested I am in children it's not a sacrifice I'm willing to make.

What's your view on marriage? And if you were to get married, would it need to be with another asexual?

I am open to the idea of getting married; though having never been in a relationship and given where I am in life with school, such a commitment isn't something I've really given any thought to. I think that it might be easier to be married to another asexual, but if I was in a relationship with a sexual person who respected who I am and what I want out of our relationship, it could work as well.

What's your view on nudity? On porn? On masturbation? On BDSM and kinks?

I guess I will blanket answer this and say that I think anything done between consenting adults is absolutely fine. I think masturbation can be very good for both sexes, and doesn't have to be particularly sexual even; I'll do it if I have a headache since I find it helps! I don't want to be judged for my sexuality, I don't want to pass judgment on the sexuality of others. As long as there is consent, kinks and the like are great, and can add layers and intimacy to a relationship if mutual interests are shared.

How difficult is it for you to be asexual, in a sexualized world?

It is definitely a challenge, especially in your early twenties as everyone expects sex to be the only thing you think about really! People are very dismissive of asexuality as an identity, it is a label sadly sometimes slapped on the socially outcast. It is often used in a derogatory way about someone who that person believes could never get laid anyway. I personally have found some people my age simply can't wrap their heads around it, they assume you're just sheltered or prudish and once they run out of reasons they just label you as strange and move on. Actual acknowledgment of asexuality as an identity is hard. I find I don't tell people, and the list of people I'd be willing to tell is very, very, short. There are hardly any asexual characters on shows or in movies; we just aren't a 'thing'.

I think the way this has challenged me the most so far was just realizing what I was. You are constantly bombarded by sex as this holy grail that everyone judges you by; that is the mark of adulthood; that is the only real yardstick for what is a 'real' relationship. I spent so long thinking that there was something wrong with me; I didn't fit this sexual mould so I must be broken. It was really hard to try to fit into this idea that just wasn't me. I came across the term asexual online and started looking into it, and cried when I realized that there was a word for who I was and it was ok to be the way that I am. Even though most of the sexual world doesn't see it as real, it meant so much for me to have a name for myself. Thankfully, I do have some sexual people in my life who love and understand me the way I am.

Can you tell me about a time when you have had to deal with intrusive questions or a difficult situation due to your asexuality, and what happened?

I have had a very difficult time getting one of my roommates to understand what it means to be asexual. The first time I told her she just could not wrap her head around it so she drilled me with aggressive questions instead. She asked me if I just wasn't confident in my body and didn't want to be seen naked; told me I just had not met the right guy yet (she is straight), and was absolutely adamant that I could not know that I didn't want sex if I hadn't had it. That I think was the most frustrating thing, was that to her my whole sexuality was invalid because it 'didn't know what I was missing'. I felt really backed into a corner and didn't know how to defend my own identity. So I gave up and let her win after a while so she would leave me alone. I felt really empty after that, like she had invalidated a huge part of who I was. We went to the movies a few days later and during the film there was a sex scene. She leans over to me in the theater and starts interrogating me, about how she can't understand how this isn't attractive to me, and how crazy it is that I don't want that kind of sex in my life. I didn't say anything to that; I guess I was really startled and a movie theater isn't really the place for that kind of argument. We are still roommates and we get along fine but part of me has never forgiven her for her comments. The worst part is, I'm sure she didn't realize how offensive her comments were and likely doesn't even remember the conversation.

What are the positives about being asexual?

These are hard to put into words without sounding strange. I guess one positive is since I'm not interested in these sexual sorts of relationships I definitely have more time to put into my education. Which to some might sound sad but it is my passion and I love that I can dedicate myself to it as much as I can. I also think that we tend to look past the physical stuff when in relationships, be they platonic or otherwise, and I feel like you can develop very close relationships since you are focusing only on the person and their body doesn't come into it as much.

If you could have one wish about being asexual, what would it be and why?

It would be that asexuality was a better known and better understood thing. There are people, even people very close to me, who I have not told about my asexuality since it would be a difficult task to get them to understand. Not through any failing on their part but simply because they have never heard of this before.

If you were to look back at your life, what advice would you have given a younger version of yourself in regard to asexuality?

Realize earlier that it is ok! I thought for ages that I was just slow to develop the urges and interests everyone my age had and pushed myself to be a participant in sexual culture. I would tell my younger self that I'm fine the way I am and to find the confidence to participate in our sexually charged culture in an asexual way.

What advice would you give to others who are just discovering about asexuality and considering whether they are or not?

Don't force yourself into any boxes. Labels can really help you sort out who you are and help you see you are not alone. But the spectrum behind that label is so important too. For a while I felt that I wasn't truly asexual since I wasn't really sex-repulsed. I would say to explore the whole spectrum and if any part of it resonates with you then embrace that. There is no one correct way to be asexual.

Extra Info

What name would you like to go under for this book? Full name, first name, or alias?

Niki.

What country do you live in?

Ireland.

What age are you specifically? Or what decade age range are you – 20, 30. 40s?

Early twenties.

What nationality and ethnicity are you?

White, Canadian.

11. C.A. Oltmann's Story

When did you first discover you are asexual?

About two years ago; when I was twenty. I didn't really have an idea of just what that meant for me until recently though.

How did you discover you are asexual?

It was a gradual process; although I labeled myself asexual two years ago, I'd known I wasn't a "straight sexual" for a long time. Because I'd never known much about asexuality before then, I didn't know that it was a valid sexual orientation. I thought that maybe I had a low libido, or would have sex when I was ready, or was afraid of having sex, or would find the right person who would be the one I'd want to "lose my virginity" to.

From the sexual orientation soup, I first identified as bisexual because I seemed to like males and females equally. After that, I identified as homosexual because I didn't like the opposite gender, and then pansexual after I discovered non-binary folks because I seemed to like – or, more accurately, not like – everyone equally.

After some consideration, a realization that I had no desire to get sexual with anyone, and the discovery of the Asexual Visibility and Education Network's FAQ, identifying as asexual seemed the most viable option.

How do you identify yourself asexually?

I personally identify as an asexual panalterous aromantic – meaning I experience no sexual or romantic attraction but can be attracted to all genders in a not-quite-romantic, not-quite-platonic way – who loves cuddling and enjoys the occasional make out session. Straight up pecks, small kisses, are good always. As is nuzzling and casual touching – such as a stroke on the shoulder or a hand on the arm in passing.

Are you 'out' about being asexual? If not, why not? If you are out, to whom, and how did they react?

Yes, I'm out. I first came out to my sibling about two years ago; they weren't surprised and were supportive of my self-discovery, as they always are.

Just after that, I came out as asexual to a few of my close friends, who were all very supportive. Each time I came out to someone, it started a very interesting discussion about sexual orientation and social acceptance. One friend, when I came out to them, had a eureka moment that they were asexual as well.

A few weeks ago I came out to all my friends on Facebook, which included both sides of the family. There was an overall good response, though I didn't get a lot of likes so I'm not sure how many people actually read it.

What's your deepest fear, concern, or worry, about being asexual?

I've mostly come to terms with it all, and I don't date so there's no "acceptance from my partner" thing to get around, but there are times when I'm concerned that a sexual stranger will think I'm playing "hard to get" and try to harass or belittle me.

Why do you feel, in general, that society doesn't accept asexuality as a form of sexual orientation in its own right? And what can be done about this?

I don't actually understand that myself. It probably has something to do with how most people don't like – or even fear – what they don't understand, and it's very hard for anyone to understand what another person is experiencing. So, for a person who experiences sexual attraction regularly, it might be hard to understand living a life where you don't experience something as big as that. It also doesn't help that sexual relationships are so closely tied to romantic relationships and our basic human need for connection, to the point that when a sexual hears that anyone – celibates, asexuals, etc. – don't want sex, they might assume that a lack of sexual attraction, desire, or activity, is the same as a lack of desire for closeness with another human being – which, in most cases, is entirely inaccurate. Most asexuals desire human connection as much as sexuals, they just desire it in different ways.

As far as what can be done about this, I think it will be a very similar process to the queer acceptance movement – just bringing awareness to the general public about asexuality, and presenting it as a valid sexual orientation just like any other.

What's your view on love? Have you been in love before?

I believe love is possible between any number of individuals and groups. I also believe that our natural state is that of love, especially since it feels so bad to hate. Because of this, I have a hard time quantifying what the difference is between loving someone and being in love with someone. I love many people, and in the same way that I could never pick my absolute favourite movie, song, or artist, I could never tell you who I love the most – not because it would feel rude to pick favourites, or because I want to spare someone's feelings, but because I literally cannot tell you. I love a lot of people, and I love them a lot. When I try to compare my love for one person to my love for another, I get lost in just how much I love both of them. There is no comparison; both feelings are so strong; so beautiful; so lovely, that I cannot choose. It's impossible for me. In this way, I don't know what being in love means. From what I understand, it means loving someone so deeply you couldn't imagine not loving them, but – for me – love is always that way. Every "type" of love is that way for me. I cannot choose. None of my relationships are more important than any other relationship of mine; they're just different. They're as different as the people I have relationships with.

Are you currently in a relationship, and if so, is it with another asexual (if yes, do they identify the same as you or how do they identify), or is it a sexual person? And how is either working out?

No, I am not in a relationship – at least, not in the romantic context of "relationship". I have a lot of good friends instead.

If you are not in a relationship, would you like to be in one and if so, why, and what type of relationship – romantic? Platonic? What would your ideal relationship look like? And would you be in a relationship with a sexual person or not, and reason why?

I do not want to be in a romantic relationship with anyone, but I would certainly love being part of a tribe/constellation of close friends. Basically, I'd like to live in a community of people who are emotionally and/or physically close to each other, where there's a plethora of people available for cuddling and fun times (adventures, you perv), at any given time. I've always liked the idea of being part of a tight-knit, tribe-like community. Anyone in this community would be free to be as sexual or non-sexual as they please, so long as none of the sex happens with/to me.

What is your view about sex? Have you had sex before and if so, how did it make you feel? If you haven't, would you? Please explain.

I believe that everyone should be allowed to enjoy as much safe, sane, and consensual sex as they do or do not want.

I have had sex before, but it had nothing to do with passion on my part. It felt nice, but only in the same way that a reassuring pat on the shoulder would. Honestly, I mostly did it because they wanted to. I would have rather been cuddling or kissing; they were an excellent kisser, fantastic pacing and a luscious lower lip.

Do you believe if a sexual person had a relationship with an asexual, it can work? And what do you think about it being fair or not?

Certainly. Of course, every relationship works differently, because all people involved in any given relationship are unique. Sometimes that might mean a polyamorous relationship where the asexual has their friends, and the sexual has their friends and outside sexual partners, or perhaps the asexual doesn't mind, or even enjoys, having sex. There are also asexuals who experience sexual attraction in special circumstances, which may mean that they're sexually attracted to, and want to have sex with, their romantic partner.

There are so many ways that a sexual and asexual can work a relationship that I don't think fairness factors into it. All relationships are unique, since all parties involved in a relationship have unique desires and beliefs. There is always a way for things to work out, if all parties involved are committed to their love and willing to communicate and compromise freely.

Asexuality is the lack of sexual attraction; as an asexual, what does this mean to you?

It means I've never experienced sexual attraction. I know, academically, what it's supposed to feel like, and I can see it in others, but I've never looked at a person and burned to have sex with them. I've never even thought of having sex with someone when I look at them or think about them. I experience other forms of attraction instead. Mostly, instead of thinking of having sex with a person I'm attracted to, I admire them in a few different ways. I can recognize a beautiful person, or someone who could be considered "hot" or "smoking" – and I appreciate it, but more like anyone else would appreciate a well painted canvas: it's gorgeous but I wouldn't want to fuck oil paints and cotton. Gross.

There are also times when I look at a person and think that I'd love to get to know them, to learn all their deepest secrets and stay up until five in the morning snuggled together watching classics and eating ice cream while discussing philosophy and the psychology behind an actor's portrayal of a character.

And, occasionally, I might see a person and think that I'd love to be physical with them – that is, go hiking, camping, or biking – or just hug, share a moment of brief, mutual love, and then never see each other again.

Do you believe sexual attraction and sexual desire are the same thing or different?

I believe they're different concepts. Sexual attraction is looking at, or thinking of, specific people, and wanting or being willing to do sexual things with them. Sexual desire is the desire for sexual stimulation or acts, which doesn't have to be associated with any particular people, if at all. It's often linked to, or seen as a synonym of libido or sex drive.

Do you think sexual arousal and sexual attraction are the same or different?

Again, different concepts. As before, sexual attraction is wanting to perform sexual acts with another specific person or people. Sexual arousal is just the aroused state of a body; it's a physiological response, not necessarily a mental or emotional one. If you fondle genitals long enough, there will be a response in almost all people, no matter what the fondled thinks of the fondler or the fondling.

What's your view on living with someone?

I personally love living with people. I'm not actually sure I could live on my own without getting unbearably lonely or depressed. That being said, I don't believe anyone should be forced into living with someone they don't want to, no matter what their relationship. Romantic partners don't have to live in the same residence, just as "unattached" individuals don't have to live alone.

Would you like kids and if so how many? And how do you hope to conceive these? If you already have kids, did you know before you had them that you are asexual and how did that impact your life?

I don't want any kids.

What's your view on marriage? And if you were to get married, would it need to be with another asexual?

I believe marriage is a societal construct that's put in place for religious purposes or legal benefits for long-term partners. I believe it's unnecessary to get married to prove your love for one another, but sadly it is often seen as the last stepping stone to prove eternal love and find societal acceptance of a devoted relationship. In some cases, this preconception can have a very negative effect on a relationship, since it puts forever, "you're my one and only" strain into the mix; it implies that a short-term relationship isn't worth anything just because you don't think you'd like to spend the rest of your life with that one person.

I doubt I will ever get married, but if I did it wouldn't need to be with another asexual. I'd facilitate a polyamorous relationship instead, since there's no logical reason why one person should be expected to provide satisfaction for another person's entire set of needs and wants.

What's your view on nudity? On porn? On masturbation? On BDSM and kinks?

To each their own, basically. Personally, I believe nudity should be more widely accepted as a natural, non-sexual thing. I enjoy reading porn for the emotional side of it, but I don't enjoy watching it. I masturbate from time to time, but it's less to satisfy my libido and more for self-love and to do something fun. As for BDSM, I don't personally partake, but it's intriguing to watch the trust and relationship dynamics of a dom and sub at play. And I have my kinks, but wouldn't want to act them out with anyone. For me, sexual acts and desires are entirely personal and private.

How difficult is it for you to be asexual, in a sexualized world?

It's not so bad for me, since I don't find sexual concepts repulsive; I understand innuendo and can make a sexual joke or jab with the best of sexuals. I'm also lucky in that I don't crave or need any kind of romantic relationship or connection. For asexuals who identify as romantically inclined, this society is a definite downer so long as romantic relationships continue to be universally associated with sexual activities.

It's surprisingly difficult to explain having no desire for sex to sexual people. My favourite analogy is one posted on AVEN, where asexuals are likened to coming from Planet Asexual and dumped among earthlings as infants, to be raised in a culture and world where there's an entire earthling facet that we just don't experience; because we're aliens who don't know what this "sexual attraction" thing feels like. You don't know what it's like for your dog to hear and smell things that you can't (or don't want to) hear and smell, but that doesn't mean there aren't sounds and scents that you don't know about. You still understand that they experience sound and scent differently than you do. Same thing for asexuals – to varying degrees – but with sexual attraction instead.

Can you tell me about a time when you have had to deal with intrusive questions or a difficult situation due to your asexuality, and what happened?

I'm lucky in that I've never been grilled on asexuality, though I have been put in a few sexual situations I was uncomfortable with, before I knew I was asexual. The one time I had sex was one of those. Although not entirely unpleasant, it was an emotionally uncomfortable experience for me.

What are the positives about being asexual?

Because I also don't desire a relationship, being "single" is the best thing ever and also my perpetual state of being. I never feel a lack of sex or love and I'm freer to act however I wish.

I also have a lot more free time, I imagine, what with no romantic partner to take on dates, no sexual partner to make time for sex with, and no time spent looking for or trying to impress a suitable mate. That last point is my favourite; because I like my friends to like me for me, I never have to impress anyone. I wear, do, and own what I want, when – and wherever I want.

If you could have one wish about being asexual, what would it be and why?

I've always wished that platonic relationships were given more importance in the grand scheme of things. Friends are all I need and want, which is great because I can be friends with any plethora of people. However, there's always a chance that a good friend, who is unique and irreplaceable – as all people are – will enter into a romantic or sexual relationship that is nearly guaranteed to overshadow our friendship. It makes it harder to feel the same sense of security in a platonic relationship that most romantics would be provided in a romantic relationship. Of course, it is possible to be in a secure friendship, but still tricky to establish.

If you were to look back at your life, what advice would you have given a younger version of yourself in regard to asexuality?

It's alright to not have sex. You're not broken. You don't need medication. You're allowed to want love and affection without wanting sex or a romantic relationship. Just because it isn't common, doesn't mean it's not normal.

What advice would you give to others who are just discovering about asexuality and considering whether they are or not?

Remember that this is you you're defining; you're not gonna identify just like anyone else, because you're not anyone else, you're you. You're unique. Find a label that works for you, if you want a label at all, and use it if you want to. And if it takes you a while to find that label, so be it; it's not a race; it's a journey. You're on a guided safari, not fleeing hyenas alone, wishing you'd stayed at home. As long as you know who you are – whoever that is, – and are willing to communicate your needs and desires to the people that you love and care about, to the ones that matter, then don't worry about it. You'll be alright.

Do you have a story you would like to share or anything else you would like to say?

Just be you and you'll be excellent. Stay excellent!

Extra Info

What name would you like to go under for this book? Full name, first name, or alias?

C. A. Oltmann.

What country do you live in?

Canada.

What age are you specifically? Or what decade age range are you – 20, 30. 40s?

22.

What nationality and ethnicity are you?

Canadian Caucasian; includes French Canadian (French and likely some Canadian First Nations), Norwegian, British, German, and likely a lot of other European nationalities.

12. Victoria's Story

When did you first discover you are asexual?

I first discovered I was asexual the night someone told me I might be, I was 18 at the time.

How did you discover you are asexual?

I had recently been part a conversation, in which everyone described their sex-life, who they found "hot" and since when they had been sexually active. I felt so alien during that conversation, that I felt horrible all day. All the feelings I had stored up about being different, childish, or weird, started resurfacing. It got so bad that I got drunk and poured my heart out to a friend and basically asked what the hell was wrong with me. She suggested I might be demisexual. During this conversation I heard the word "asexual" and "asexual-spectrum" for the first time. The amount of relief I felt after this conversation is indescribable. After that conversation I spent about 2-3 weeks researching asexuality and trying to figure out where I fall on the asexual-spectrum. Ironically, it was after reading a demisexual's account of what sexual attraction felt like, I began to identify as fully asexual.

How do you identify yourself asexually?

I identify as a queer, bi-/panromantic asexual.

Are you 'out' about being asexual? If not, why not? If you are out, whom to, and how did they react?

I'm out to a lot of my friends and none of my family, although I intend on coming out to all of them at some point. I mostly only come out to people when the situation occurs organically. I usually won't go up to people and tell them I'm asexual. If the situation allows it, I come out. I've gotten the whole spectrum of reactions. From people telling me I'm confused or that I just haven't tried it with them yet, to people telling me it's just another regular orientation and being fine with it. Luckily I haven't had any bad reactions from close friends.

What's your deepest fear, concern or worry, about being asexual?

My greatest concern is that asexuality will remain invisible and that I will have to have hour-long conversations and answer rude questions for the rest of my life every time I come out to someone.

Why do you feel, in general, that society doesn't accept asexuality as a form of sexual orientation in its own right? And what can be done about this?

Our capitalist, patriarchal society, doesn't accept asexuality, because the whole system rests on the exploitation of people, especially women and women's bodies. Our society still has the notion that it owns women's bodies and that women are built to please men. By acknowledging asexuality, society would have to give up its ownership of women's/people's bodies. Additionally, sex is used to sell everything from beer to soap. Therefore it must seem desirable and more important than anything else. Acknowledging sex isn't the most importing thing in life would hurt the corporations. The most important step that can be done about this is to increase awareness of asexuality. Coming out to people, having asexuality awareness weeks, are all things that work towards inclusivity. And challenging sexnormativity, amatonormativity and heteronormativity, will also benefit the rest of society.

What's your view on love? Have you been in love before? Please explain.

I have been in love before. I believe moving away from seeing *romantic* love as the all-consuming, all-important thing that it's NOT; is something we as a society should be working on. Platonic and other types of non-romantic love are just as important as romantic love. Being able to fall in love has advantages and disadvantages. People tend to overlook the disadvantages in favour of the lovey-dovey feelings they have. As with all things, I think we, as a society, should take a step back and re-examine what love is and means.

Are you currently in a relationship, and if so, is it with another asexual (if yes, do they identify the same as you or how do they identify), or is it a sexual person? And how is either working out?

No.

If you are not in a relationship, would you like to be in one and if so, why, and what type of relationship – romantic? Platonic? What would your ideal relationship look like? And would you be in a relationship with a sexual person or not, and reason why?

At the moment I am fairly neutral on that topic. I don't need to be in a romantic relationship to be happy, nor do I have the desire to actively seek one out. Even if I have romantic feelings for someone I don't necessarily want to be in a relationship with them. However, I am not against being in a romantic relationship with someone. Given the right circumstances and person(s), I'd be inclined to try one. Ideally this person would be asexual, but I'd also try a romantic relationship with a sexual person. A sexual person can't help being sexual any more than I can help being asexual. So excluding someone based on their sexuality would seem unfair to me. I definitely would try it. This would probably result in an open/polyamorous relationship, as this would be the best way to meet our individual needs.

What is your view about sex? Have you had sex before and if so, how did it make you feel? If you haven't, would you?

I have never had sex before. I am moderately sex-repulsed, so in a perfect world I would never have sex. But I recognize that we live in an imperfect world. If my partner(s) and I had exhausted all other options, I would probably consent to very infrequent sex. In that situation though, I would only do the touching and not be touched. That is something I would not compromise on.

Do you believe if a sexual person had a relationship with an asexual, it can work? And what do you think about it being fair or not?

I believe it definitely can work, if certain factors are given.

1. Complete honesty about needs (on both sides).

2. Willingness to compromise.

If those factors are given, I believe two (or more) people can make it work. The asexual could compromise and have sex with their partner(s) or they could be in an open relationship and the sexual(s) could have their needs met by other people. It always puzzles me when people say asexual relationships are unfair to sexual people (in asexual relationships). After all they are getting a relationship out of it; a (presumably) deep connection with another human being. People tend to act as though sex is the most important part of a relationship, yet most couples break up for non-sex related issues. I think if all other aspects of a healthy relationship are given, the relationship can "survive" and flourish without sex, especially since the sexual(s) can meet their own needs/have them met by someone else.

People like to forget that aces can't help their lack of attraction and if they don't want to sleep with their partner(s), it is for a good reason (i.e. discomfort, repulsion, etc.) I think it's a lot more unfair for aces to be expected to put out (especially repulsed aces), than for sexuals to abstain from having sex with their (primary) partner.

Asexuality is the lack of sexual attraction, as an asexual, what does this mean to you?

To me it means that no one has ever turned me on. Whether that person was Brad Pitt, Shay Mitchel, or the person I was in love with.

Do you believe sexual attraction and sexual desire are the same thing or different?

Since I have never experienced either, this is a summary of what other people have told me it is. Attraction is being turned on by someone and wanting to sleep with them. Desire is the urge to act on that attraction.

Do you think sexual arousal and sexual attraction are the same or different, please explain?

Arousal is a physical phenomenon people with a libido experience, regardless of sexual orientation. Attraction is the desire to have sex with a certain person.

What's your view on living with someone?

I prefer living with people, although I don't mind living alone.

Would you like kids and if so how many? And how do you hope to conceive these? If you already have kids, did you know before you had them that you are asexual and how did that impact your life?

I don't want to have children. If I ever do change my mind (unlikely), I will adopt.

What's your view on marriage? And if you were to get married, would it need to be with another asexual?

Marriage is an out-dated concept, based on the ownership and entrapment of women. I don't want to get married. The only reason I'd ever get married is for tax benefits.

What's your view on nudity? On porn? On masturbation? On BDSM and kinks?

Although I prefer people clothed, I don't have a huge problem with nudity. I don't watch porn. It doesn't appeal to me. I don't have anything against people that do watch porn. I do have a problem with the porn industry, because it promotes an unrealistic image of sex and sexuality, contributes to the oversexualization of women, fetishization of women/people of colour, and focuses solely on male pleasure (this is of course a generalization).

I did masturbate at some point, but it always made me feel weird and the orgasms didn't live up to expectations. There are a number of things I prefer doing. I feel completely fine even though I don't masturbate. If my libido acts up I just expel my energy differently, go for a run etc.

I personally am not into BDSM nor do I have kinks (that I am aware of). I obviously don't mind it if other people have them.

How difficult is it for you to be asexual, in a sexualized world?

It really depends on what kind of people you surround yourself with. If you have understanding and accepting friends, it's not a huge issue. I have felt very alien at times, even though my friends are very accepting. And that is something that will probably always be the case. Having moments you remember you are wired differently, that for me is probably the worst part. Remembering how different I am from other people. I can deal with the occasional rude comment or question. I can also deal with some people not accepting me or thinking asexuality doesn't exist. That gets me really angry sometimes, but so do climate change deniers. Some people are idiots. That's not news to me. But being bombarded with sexual imagery as we are here in the west and realizing just how different I am, it is difficult at times, especially since I am the only asexual person in my friend group. I compare it to growing up in a world that revolves around colour as a colour-blind person. Or growing up in a country and slowly realizing you're a foreigner.

Can you tell me about a time when you have had to deal with intrusive questions or a difficult situation due to your asexuality, and what happened?

I came out to a guy who was interested in me. He did not take me seriously, asked invasive questions and tried to pressure me into going somewhere "more romantic" with him, insisting I just hadn't tried it with him yet, (#magic-dick-theory, #male-sense-of-entitlement); that we had a connection. I removed myself from the situation as soon as possible. During all this time I remained polite and apologetic.

What are the positives about being asexual?

Sometimes it seems aces are spared the drama that comes with sexual relationships. We get to lean back and observe the human mating ritual, which, lets be honest, is pretty hilarious. We also spend less time worrying about whom to sleep with and spend less time daydreaming about "hot" people. (But instead we have to worry about heteronormativity, etc.)

If you could have one wish about being asexual, what would it be and why?

I don't want to change anything about my sexuality, because it feels right to me. It feels like a part of me. I would not cut off my arm, nor do I want to change my sexuality. If I could change anything, I'd change society's view of asexuality and make it (and every other sexuality), as accepted as heterosexuality.

If you were to look back at your life, what advice would you have given a younger version of yourself in regard to asexuality?

It's okay you don't think anyone is "hot". One day you'll understand why you feel so alien in a group of your peers. You'll discover there are other people like you, a whole community. You won't feel so alone and alienated forever. You are not weird. You are not broken.

What advice would you give to others who are just discovering about asexuality and considering whether they are or not?

You don't have to label yourself. If you do choose to, you can always label yourself differently the next day. Sexuality is fluid, not static. It's hard to confine sexuality into one word/label. And that's not what labels are for. They're there to give you a sense of community. It's okay not to completely fit into one label. Most people don't. They're not there to define or confine you. If you don't experience sexual attraction, don't count on it coming in later life. The way you feel or don't feel, whether or not you experience attraction, or to what gender you experience it towards, is perfectly alright and fine. Everyone is unique in that way. And finally, if you have to ask genuinely "Am I asexual?", chances are you are on the ace spectrum.

Do you have a story you would like to share or anything else you would like to say?

If you are ace, surround yourself with people that accept and respect you. Don't waste your time and energy on people that don't accept you for who you are. Life is so full of amazing things to do that don't involve sex. Go out and enjoy them all!

Extra Info

What name would you like to go under for this book? Full name, first name, or alias?

Victoria.

What country do you live in?

Germany.

What nationality and ethnicity are you?

Caucasian.

13. Dee's Story

When did you first discover you are asexual?

There are two answers to this question. When I was 19-20 I discovered that I didn't particularly enjoy sex and would prefer a relationship without sex. It wasn't until I was 23 that I associated what I was experiencing with the word "asexual". I had thought asexual referred to someone who was uninterested in both sex and romance and thus hadn't thought that term applied to me.

How did you discover you are asexual?

I will also answer this question twofold, in parallel to the last. Realizing I wasn't interested in sex was kind of a steady process. I couldn't pinpoint the moment it happened. I always thought things would just click once I started having sex, which was first happening regularly at age 19. At some point I confidently realized that I was having sex because it was expected or because I was curious and not because of a physical urge.

In terms of discovering the label "asexual", as it applied to me, someone posted a comic on asexuality on Facebook for asexuality awareness week, and I started doing more research.

How do you identify yourself asexually?

I'm definitely heteroromatic. I'm a little wary to identify further, because I think I have a lot left to discover about my asexuality. Honestly, I prefer to say something like "I don't experience sexual attraction" than to use the label of asexuality.

Are you 'out' about being asexual? If not, why not? If you are out, whom to, and how did they react?

Mostly yes. Everyone important in my life knows, family, close friends, etc. I'll sometimes be uncertain about the right time to bring it up with new people in my life, especially if there are romantic undertones, though on the flip side it can be a fantastic way to ward off unwanted sexual advances. I am apprehensive about using the word "asexual", because I worry that if in the future I ever find myself interested in a sexual relationship, I'll somehow be betraying who I claimed to be. I don't want to put myself in a box or limit what I may want in the future.

All in all I've had positive responses. My mom likes to insinuate that it's a phase (i.e. recommending a movie that has several sex scenes and saying I should watch it because "I might get some ideas"), but she does this from a good-natured place, so I don't really mind. The only bad reaction was my last boyfriend, but I don't totally blame him, because I kind of blind-sided him with, "Oh and by the way I feel like I've been sleeping with you for all the wrong reasons and I'd like to stop".

What's your deepest fear, concern, or worry about being asexual?

The first would be that I'll end up in a sexual relationship that I don't want to be in because I'm afraid to stand up for myself. The close second (which is probably more scary because it's never happened, but definitely less scary in practice) is that I'll meet someone I really like, but no sex will be a deal-breaker for him.

Why do you feel, in general, that society doesn't accept asexuality as a form of sexual orientation in its own right? And what can be done about this?

Mostly I think it's a simple case of being skeptical of that with which you're unfamiliar. And arguably it's easier for asexuality to go under the radar than, say, homosexuality, because it's a *lack* of desire rather than a *presence* of a less conventional desire. I also think we've faced a problem where not having sex (particularly in women), is associated with oppression or puritanical ideals amongst the progressive folks who normally might usher in a non-heteronomative subgroup. I think this viewpoint in extremely harmful to sexual and asexual folks alike. Women should be empowered to be sexual when they'd like and to not be sexual when they'd rather not. Above all else, more awareness is going to help both of the issues. We're getting there. Slowly.

What's your view on love? Have you been in love before? Please explain.

I have loved many different men, and I have been in love once. As it were, the guy I was in love with is the only person I've ever felt what I would consider "sexual attraction" towards. I also never slept with him. There is an array of conclusions and implications that can be drawn here, but I'm hesitant to do so until I've fallen in love again and see what I do or do not feel sexually. I have slept with most of the other guys that I have loved and enjoyed it at times, from a 'I'm bringing pleasure to someone I love' perspective.

Are you currently in a relationship, and if so, is it with another asexual (if yes, do they identify the same as you or how do they identify), or is it a sexual person? And how is either working out?

This doesn't apply to me.

Would you like to be in a relationship? If you are not in a relationship, would you like to be in one and if so, why, and what type of relationship – romantic? Platonic? What would your ideal relationship look like? And would you be in a relationship with a sexual person or not, and reason why?

I would like to be in a relationship, contingent on the fact that I was really attracted to and excited about the person I was in a relationship with. In the meantime, I'm happy being single. Most importantly, I would want this relationship to be physically satisfying for both of us. This most likely means it could not be with a fully sexual person. It's hard for me to imagine a sexual person being happy in a sexless relationship, and it's hard for me to imagine being happy and physically satisfied in a relationship where I'm having sex. It's important to note that despite not having sexual needs, I do still have romantic, physical needs, and these are rarely met.

I am currently dating a guy (we've been on three dates), who I'm pretty damn sure is sexual. He doesn't know, though he has been very forward about making sure I'm comfortable with anything physical that happens (kissing included). Even so, it's hard for me to imagine things will work out.

What is your view about sex? Have you had sex before and if so, how did it make you feel? If you haven't, would you?

Oh, this is a complicated one. In many ways I'm enchanted by sex. I love the idea of it and thus can be extremely frustrated by my disinterest. Sometimes I'm really able to enjoy sex, usual from a place of, "Fuck yes! What an animalistic and awesome display of base instinct!" In short, I enjoy it from an academic standpoint. But this way of enjoying sex has caused far more pain and disconnect in relationships than anything else. I've now been sexless for about two years and can say I quite prefer this approach.

Do you believe if a sexual person had a relationship with an asexual, it can work? And what do you think about it being fair or not?

First of all, I'm certainly no authority on working relationships. In fact, asexuality aside, sometimes I doubt if any relationship can truly "work". But cynicism aside, I think it can work in cases. For one, every relationship has its sticking point and, as I understand it, sex drive mismatch is a common problem even amongst sexual folks. I think it's important that the sexual individual be very comfortable not having sex, or the asexual person be very comfortable with having it; ideally both.

Asexuality is the lack of sexual attraction. What does this mean to you?

Basically, it just means I don't want to sleep with anyone. When I see an attractive person on the street, I'm like, "Oh what a fine specimen!" and yes, perhaps my head turns, but there's nothing I want to do about it beyond stare (which is rude and I shouldn't do that). When I'm in a relationship with someone I want to be physical and close, but not in a sexual way. Sexual acts only seem to have meaning because they have meaning to so many of the people around me.

Do you believe sexual attraction and sexual desire are the same thing or different?

I've clumped them in my mind as more or less the same, but I'm sure someone with more experience with both, could draw a distinction.

Do you think sexual attraction and sexual arousal are the same thing or different?

Yes. Sexual arousal is a state in which your body can be. Sexual attraction is the desire to be sexual with another (specific) person. They often go hand in hand, but not always.

What's your view on living with someone?

I love living with people, but my experience so far has been roommates and family. I'll probably want to live with a romantic partner if I like them a lot, but it's hard for me to imagine not having my own bed or bedroom. At the very least, I think I would need some space in the house/apartment that was unambiguously mine. I think that might have to do more with my personality than with asexuality.

Would you like kids and if so, how many? And how do you hope to conceive these? If you already have kids, did you know before you had them that you are asexual and how did that impact your life?

Yes, but I'm unwilling to have them if the situation isn't right (both my personal situation and having a partner I can rely on).

I've learned from my divorced parents that having a child is by far the best way to interweave your future with someone else's forever. I would like two or three, because I think siblings are important. I think I'd be fine with being sexual for the purposes of procreation.

What's your view on marriage? And if you were to get married, would it need to be with another asexual?

I also think this is more my cynicism than my asexuality speaking, but I'm wary of marriage. I don't like the idea of making a promise I can't keep. In terms of marrying a sexual versus asexual, my answer is the same as it was on the relationship question: I try to be open to anything, but it's hard for me to imagine things working out if we weren't somewhat aligned on our physical needs.

What's your view on nudity? Or porn? On masturbation? On BDSM and kinks?

For everyone else, go for it!

For myself:

Nudity – I love being nude. I wish there were more opportunities to be nude in non-sexual situations and have been known to create such situations.

Porn – Sometimes watch it for intrigue purposes. Don't get arouse by it.

Masturbation – Not really my thing. I try sometimes.

BDSM/Kinks – When I was sexuality active, I was always a little drawn towards this (though I had pretty vanilla boyfriends), because it kept things interesting.

How difficult is it for you to be asexual, in a sexualized world?

Mostly it really doesn't matter. Probably creates undue anxiety. Sometimes I feel excluded from conversations or feel like if I include myself I'll be implying that I'm something I'm not.

Can you tell me about a time when you had to deal with intrusive questions or a difficult situation due to your asexuality, and what happened?

Well usually when people ask questions I'm quite enthusiastic because I like educating people and I don't have much of a sense of privacy. I don't like it when people ask if I've been sexually traumatized in response to hearing I'm asexual. I have been sexually assaulted, and I'm actually quite comfortable talking about it, but I worry that it will be perceived as invalidating my asexuality.

What are the positives about being asexual?

I never have to worry about satisfying a physical need. It helps weed out superficial romantic attraction (which can happen without sex but usually doesn't last long without sex). Similarly, I know someone I'm involved with isn't in just for the sex, because we're not having sex. It gives me a weird mythical status amongst sexual friends which sometimes is creepy but sometimes is kind of fun. I'd like to hope it makes me less threatening to other females in regard to their boyfriends, but I don't actually know if this is true.

If you could have one wish about being asexual, what would it be and why?

I wish my romantic partners wouldn't take it personally. It makes me really sad and guilty and makes a mutual understanding almost impossible.

I'm actually going to cheat and make a second, complimentary wish. I wish that myself and other asexuals wouldn't take being sexually attracted to as some sort of invalidation of our other qualities. My reasoning is basically the same as the first wish.

If you were to look back at your life, what advice would you have given a younger version of yourself in regard to asexuality?

Don't have any sex unless you're confident you want it.

What advice would you give to others who are just discovering about asexuality and considering whether they are or not?

Don't have any sex unless you're confident you want it. Also, don't feel the need to put yourself in a box, one way or the other. Also, related, just because you've done something before doesn't mean you need to do it again or do it with this particular guy.

Extra Info

What name would you like to go under for this book? Full name, first name, or alias?

Dee.

What country do you live in?

US.

What age are you specifically? Or what decade age range are you – 20, 30. 40s?

24.

What nationality and ethnicity are you?

American White Hispanic.

14. Hanalei Steinhart's Story

When did you first discover you are asexual?

I didn't particularly first discover it at any given point in time. Rather, it was more of a gradual realization of the factor that set me apart from the rest of my classmates. So if I was going to put a date to when I chose the label, it would be December of my freshman year in high school. However, for my entire life I've known I was just not interested, when my kindergarten friends were princesses waiting for their knights, I was galloping off on my own adventures on a horse made of fire.

How did you discover you are asexual?

So I'd always known that I was just not interested, but I was talking to a friend on a rafting trip this summer and she was openly asexual and it seemed like a good enough label so I sort of went with it. That same friend mentioned Aven in passing and when I got home I went online and made an account. And with every post I read about someone else's experience, I identified more strongly.

How do you identify yourself asexually?

I am an aromantic asexual, who enjoys completely platonic touching (hugs, etc.), with people I know well. I might be demiromantic, but as it hasn't happened yet I have no way of knowing. It is something I haven't experienced, but I don't think I'm completely aromantic. So would that be greyromantic then? I don't really care about the labels, but it is one of those things that is nice to know.

Are you 'out' about being asexual? If not, why not? If you are out, whom to, and how did they react?

Yes, I am out to all of my close friends, my sister, and have tried to come out to my parents. My friends just accepted it and moved on. The only difference is that they don't ask me about my sex / romantic life and don't send me pictures of guys they find attractive at 3am. My sister also accepted me and had a lot of questions as she had not known that asexuality existed previously and she identifies with graysexual a lot more than she did with her previous orientation. My parents have just told me that I need to find someone; that I need to have sex, to like it, etc. I wouldn't say that they were aphobic, just determinedly ignorant, but it still hurts.

What's your deepest fear, concern or worry, about being asexual?

It is probably never being fully accepted or ending up alone just because I am not interested in the same stuff as almost everyone else. I know there is nothing wrong, but the world sees it differently. The sheer amount of times someone has been surprised when I say that I don't find a model or an actor attractive and tried to convince me that they are "hot" is just saddening.

Why do you feel, in general, that society doesn't accept asexuality as a form of sexual orientation in its own right? And what can be done about this?

I feel that it is something most people don't even hear about unless they have a close friend or family member who is asexual. I also feel that the generation that is in their teens right now, is a lot more accepting of asexuality than say those in their 50's and 60's right now. I have yet to come out to anyone within ten years of my own age (16), who did not accept my sexuality. However, every person over the age of 50 has told me that I would discover sex eventually. So, I feel like we just need to spread awareness and over time it will become as commonplace for someone to consider themselves as asexual, as any other sexuality today. Then again, I don't live in a very conservative area and have never moved, so I cannot say much for the rest of the world.

What's your view on love? Have you been in love before?

Well, as an aromantic I have not been in love and don't really know what romantic love is supposed to feel like. I form close bonds with my friends but nothing that feels like romance. If you are talking about love in a platonic way, then I feel that a lot, but otherwise then no.

Are you currently in a relationship, and if so, is it with another asexual (if yes, do they identify the same as you or how do they identify), or is it a sexual person? And how is either working out?

I am in a queerplatonic relationship with someone, and the subject of sex has never come up, as it is a long distance relationship. We view each other more as extremely close friends who put each other before the world. I know that she is a strong supporter of all things LGBTQA (+anything I forgot) and so we've never felt the need to come out to each other. It is working out really well, and we just started writing a book together. We met at a summer camp two years ago and never stopped talking, and even with 90% of our interactions being over texts, we know each other inside out. We comfort the other when they've had a bad day, celebrate good test scores, anything.

What is your view about sex? Have you had sex before and if so, how did it make you feel? If you haven't, would you?

I have not had sex before, and am no way interested in it. Just having someone touch me in an even semi-romantic or sexual way repulses me.

Do you believe if a sexual person had a relationship with an asexual, it can work? And what do you think about it being fair or not?

It can absolutely work. It really depends on what one's views on fidelity are, how sex positive the asexual is, and how willing to compromise the allosexual person is. I would never ask a partner of mine to give up having sex, but I might suggest having occasional one-night stands, as I would be completely unable to fulfil his or her needs. It honestly would take discussion between the two people, the same with any other relationship. Think about a transgender person in a relationship that has not had sex reassignment surgery, they would need to discuss how they and their partner would handle that, and this should be no different. It might not be fair per se, but if you love someone for everything about them then there are ways to make it work. And not all of us are sex repulsed, so just because they are asexual does not mean that they will not have sex with you and enjoy it.

Asexuality is the lack of sexual attraction, as an asexual, what does this mean to you?

To me, I've never really separated out what sexual attraction and romantic attraction are supposed to be, as I experience neither. But for me, I don't look at anyone with the intent to have sex with them. I see people that I think are pretty or cute, but never hot or sexy. It means that I feel awkward about telling someone that I don't find them attractive. It means that I have something positive to say about almost everyone I meet, because there is usually something pretty about them. But, it is pretty the same way a garden or a cupcake is, nothing more than, "oh hey, that looks nice."

Do you believe sexual attraction and sexual desire are the same thing or different.

No, they are different, but to most people they are connected. Attraction is more of a, "I like your face" and is along the lines of aesthetic, etc. Desire is more of a, "I'd like to sleep with you." Desire is based off of attraction and at least my friends tell me it's a lot more intense. But not sure about the last part as I never really go beyond attraction.

Do you think sexual arousal and sexual attraction are the same or different?

I feel that arousal is completely physical, while attraction is being aroused or drawn to a specific person.

What's your view on living with someone?

I enjoy living with other people, as long as it is platonically. My zucchini and I have plans to move in together either during or after university. I like the company of another person or two, because I don't really like being alone and it's nice to have someone to come home to at night.

Would you like kids and if so how many? And how do you hope to conceive these? If you already have kids, did you know before you had them that you are asexual and how did that impact your life?

I would like to adopt a child or two at some point, or become a host parent for exchange students. I don't want to conceive my own children, especially with all of the children in foster systems or up for adoption. I feel that I'd have trouble bonding with a younger child but will probably want anywhere from one to three children once I have a steady life in which I could securely raise them.

What's your view on marriage? And if you were to get married, would it need to be with another asexual?

I am in favor of marriage for everyone who wants to get married, but I don't think that anyone has to get married to have their relationship be official. It would not need to be to another asexual as long as the other person understood that I would not be able to satisfy their sexual needs. At some point, if both of us end up unattached to others, my zucchini and I have agreed to get married for the sole purpose of being able to live in the same country and see each other every day. We haven't really discussed sexuality though, it was more of a "anything's fine, I won't judge", than a "I'm asexual", because I did not know the term when we had this conversation. But someday, we might end up married and living on an equestrian ranch with ten cats like we've been planning on doing for at least three years now. Personally, I have always wanting a wedding, but as I have no interest in the other person as anything more than platonic, it probably won't happen.

What's your view on nudity? On porn? On masturbation? On BDSM and kinks?

I attended the Oregon Country Fair and was on the swim team from age six to fourteen. Both of these and my parents influenced my views on nudity, which now stand as "everyone's got the same equipment, what is all the fuss about." I am personally not a fan of porn and have an extremely low to non-existent libido too. If anyone else wants to watch porn, masturbate, etc., then that is fine by me, I just don't want to be there. Same with BDSM and kinks, I don't care if you are into it or have them, but I don't want to watch you or hear the explicit, smutty details, of what you did last night. If you want to talk about the way it makes you feel, I'd gladly talk about it with you, as it seems like something I probably would have tried if I were allosexual.

How difficult is it for you to be asexual, in a sexualized world?

Quite, as one of my closest friends has a fairly high sex drive and is always going on about some male model, which just feels awkward and strange to me. Also, the magazines and advertisements don't seem at all appealing because they are focused on exposed stomachs and hinted genitalia. I can't associate with a lot of books, events in other people's lives, etc., because they are all focused on sex or romance, neither of which are part of my life. So in a rambly answer, it makes for an extremely awkward life at times.

Can you tell me about a time when you have had to deal with intrusive questions or a difficult situation due to your asexuality, and what happened?

Just the other day, a friend sent a handful of pictures of a shirtless actor to our group chat and they were exclaiming over how hot he was. Just before this, I'd been trying to find out where she was so I could meet up with her, and she included that in the message containing the images. So, my response was, "Thanks, I'll be there soon." However, they all started asking me why I wasn't commenting on the guy (I can't even remember anything about him now), and I had to deal with explaining that he just didn't appeal to me. I remember that he had nice eyes and mentioned them, but that was it. I felt really awkward because that led to me explaining that I have a very low to non-existent sex drive, which is just an awkward conversation to have with a mixed gender group of teenaged people.

What are the positives about being asexual?

I am not sure I have really found any personal negatives about being asexual, as everything but coming out has been good. It seems like I get more done and am far less distractible than all of my allosexual friends, I don't need to worry about finding someone, dressing up for them, etc., I can just be myself. And if I want to wear a baggy sweatshirt and sweats to school, why shouldn't I?

If you could have one wish about being asexual, what would it be and why?

It would be to feel what a heteronormative person feels for a day. I want to experience sexual and romantic desire for a short time, just to know what they feel like. I want to know what it is like to want to kiss someone, to feel the love that fills songs and stories from all history. However, I would not want to feel this all of the time as it seems like a huge distraction from accomplishing my goals.

If you were to look back at your life, what advice would you have given a younger version of yourself in regard to asexuality?

I don't have a whole lot of advice, but I would have steered myself to asexuality archive's glossary a couple of years sooner. I always had known I wasn't interested; it just took me a while to find a label that I was comfortable with.

What advice would you give to others who are just discovering about asexuality and considering whether they are or not?

If you want to identify with asexuality, do so! There is no consequence to changing your orientation, it just might get a bit confusing for those around you if you change it daily. And ask questions. The more you know, well, you either get more confused or things start to make more sense eventually. Also, ignore societal expectations. If you don't want sex, don't have it. Pretty simple. And create an Aven account, as everyone there is really nice and helpful.

Do you have a story you would like to share or anything else you would like to say?

Thank you for letting me contribute to your book! I can't wait to read it!!

Extra Info

What name would you like to go under for this book? Full name, first name, or alias?

Hanalei Steinhart.

What country do you live in?

United States.

What age are you specifically? Or what decade age range are you – 20, 30. 40s?

Physically sixteen. However, almost everybody tells me I seem at least five years older than that.

What nationality and ethnicity are you?

American and Caucasian.

15. Adelaide's Story

When did you first discover you are asexual?

I can't really define a time when I first discovered I was asexual. Throughout high school, I was never really interested in having a relationship with anyone. I would fake having crushes on people, and I figured everyone was faking, as it was considered "cool" to have a crush on someone. In about 11th grade, I figured out everyone else wasn't faking.

Even though I had sort of realized then that I was different, I didn't have the word "asexual" in my vocabulary. I spent many hours agonizing over what box to put myself in. I didn't "like" boys in that way so did that mean I was a lesbian? But I also didn't "like" girls in that way. Did that mean I liked them both equally? So was I bisexual? None of those labels really seemed to fit.

How did you discover you are asexual?

When I was in college, I finally added the word "asexual" to my vocabulary. I was talking to a friend, and to this day I cannot remember what we were talking about, when she stopped and asked the question: "Have you ever considered you might be asexual?" Of course, then I went home and Googled asexuality, and found that, finally, I had a label that fitted.

How do you identify yourself asexually?

I identify as an Aromantic Asexual.

Are you 'out' about being asexual? If not, why not? If you are out, whom to, and how did they react?

I am only "out" to a few people about being asexual, and those are my closest friends. I am not even out to my family. My friends reacted well; after a few surprise questions, they accepted it. I suppose that since I, at 21, had never been in a relationship or really shown interest in anyone in that way, it didn't really come as much of a shock to them. I am not out to my family because I don't really want to deal with the questions and all that.

What's your deepest fear, concern or worry, about being asexual?

My only real concern about being asexual is what I want to do in the future. I want to have kids and raise a family, but I don't really want to do it alone. However, this requires finding someone who is cool with being in an aromantic asexual relationship.

Why do you feel, in general, that society doesn't accept asexuality as a form of sexual orientation in its own right? And what can be done about this?

I feel like society doesn't accept asexuality for 2 main reasons:

The first reason is that society puts a lot of store by sex and re-lationships. Since they do, they feel like everyone needs to be in a relationship and having sex in order to be happy, and it is hard for them to wrap their minds around the fact that some people don't want that. So they have a misguided concern for the asexual individual and their welfare, as they are concerned that without wanting and having what everyone else wants, the individual won't be happy.

The second reason is fear of the unknown. Asexuality is a relatively "new" concept (although, as I figure it, we have always been around, but back in the pioneer days and whatnot when one needed 10 kids in order to survive, it just wasn't as much of an option). People don't know much about it and have never heard of it, so they fear it.

I think the solution to both of these problems is increasing awareness. The more people know about it and have heard about it, the less they will fear it.

What's your view on love? Have you been in love before?

I love my mom. I love my horse. I love my friends. As an aromantic asexual, I have never felt romantic love, but that is not the only kind of love in the world, and it is not the only one that is worth something.

Are you currently in a relationship, and if so, is it with another asexual (if yes, do they identify the same as you or how do they identify), or is it a sexual person? And how is either working out?

Nope.

If you are not in a relationship, would you like to be in one and if so, why, and what type of relationship – romantic? Platonic? What would your ideal relationship look like? And would you be in a relationship with a sexual person or not, and reason why?

I would like more of a "life partner," someone to do things with and raise a family with, but I don't need more. I would not be against being in a relationship with an allosexual person or an alloromantic person, but there would have to be some compromises being made, both on my side and theirs.

What is your view about sex? Have you had sex before and if so, how did it make you feel? If you haven't, would you?

I haven't and I can't say I ever really want to. It wouldn't be a deal-breaker in a relationship, but it would have to be under the right circumstances and a lot of compromises would have to be made.

Do you believe if a sexual person had a relationship with an asexual, it can work? And what do you think about it being fair or not?

I think it can, and I think it depends on the couple. Every couple will be different in their level of comfort with certain things and in their willingness to compromise.

Asexuality is the lack of sexual attraction, as an asexual, what does this mean to you?

It means I lack sexual attraction.

Do you believe sexual attraction and sexual desire are the same thing or different?

I do, I do not understand the difference.

Do you think sexual arousal and sexual attraction are the same or different?

I think they are different, but as I do not feel either, I do not feel qualified to comment on it.

What's your view on living with someone?

Living with someone is fine. It is something every couple, asexual or not, has to negotiate, same thing with roommates.

Would you like kids and if so how many? And how do you hope to conceive these? If you already have kids, did you know before you had them that you are asexual and how did that impact your life?

Yes, 2 or 3, and no idea. I figure that is something I will figure out in the future.

What's your view on marriage? And if you were to get married, would it need to be with another asexual?

To me, marriage is a piece of paper. If I were to get married, it would depend on the person, not their sexuality, and I would probably have to have a pretty good reason for getting married.

What's your view on nudity? On porn? On masturbation? On BDSM and kinks?

Whatever floats your boat. I personally am not interested in any of those things, but we are all individuals and with different experiences of life.

How difficult is it for you to be asexual, in a sexualized world?

I must say that, in my life, it doesn't come up much. I am not a sex repulsed asexual, sex just does not compute in my brain. Many people complain about advertising and TV and all that being over sexualized, but I mostly don't notice. I will say though, it gives me a different taste in books and movies than most of my friends, as I find romance and love scenes exceedingly dull.

Can you tell me about a time when you have had to deal with intrusive questions or a difficult situation due to your asexuality, and what happened?

I can't say it has ever really come up, mostly because I am not out to many people.

What are the positives about being asexual?

I can't say asexuality itself is contributing anything particularly to my life, but my life is not any less for being asexual. I still live a full life, full of friends and animals, and I don't feel like I am missing anything.

If you could have one wish about being asexual, what would it be and why?

I wish I could be out about it and not have to deal with annoying questions.

If you were to look back at your life, what advice would you have given a younger version of yourself in regard to asexuality?

I would have told myself earlier and saved myself years of agonizing about it.

What advice would you give to others who are just discovering about asexuality and considering whether they are or not?

It is a personal journey. It is okay to be asexual, it is okay to not be asexual, and it is okay to not know yet. Whatever camp you are in, just know that you will be supported and you are not alone.

Extra Info

What name would you like to go under for this book? Full name, first name, or alias?

Adelaide.

What country do you live in?

USA.

What age are you specifically? Or what decade age range are you – 20, 30. 40s?

20s.

What nationality and ethnicity are you?

Caucasian.

16. Sappho's Story

When did you first discover you are asexual?

I was about 13 years old when I first heard of asexuality, but it has taken me until very recently (the last six months or so), to really accept myself as asexual.

How did you discover you are asexual?

I was at a sleepover with my two best friends. They're both gay trans men, but at the time we were all young and questioning. We turned off the lights, and sat talking in the pitch black – we always found it easier to talk about the more 'taboo' topics that way – and we were talking about crushes. When it was my turn to spill the beans about my angsty teenage heartache, they were both shocked to hear that I'd never fancied anyone. One of them told me I might be asexual. I didn't even know what it meant at the time, but I looked it up and eventually decided it was a description that fitted me.

How do you identify yourself asexually?

I've never been sexually attracted to anyone, but I am curious about the idea of a sexual relationship, so I guess the sub-label of cupiosexual would fit me quite well. At the moment, however,

I'm not too worried about labels, so I don't think it's a label I would actively use unless explaining my asexuality in depth.

Are you 'out' about being asexual? If not, why not? If you are out, whom to, and how did they react?

Having seen the huge amount of mocking and phobia on social media, I'm not openly out. I have a few close friends who know that I'm asexual, who were all very accepting and normalising about it all, but for the most part I don't trust people to be as understanding, so I just don't mention it.

What's your deepest fear, concern or worry, about being asexual?

As someone who's not sex-repulsed, I think that my biggest concern about being openly asexual is that people won't want to date me because they'll think that I'm 'broken', or that I won't have sex with them, or that I don't 'fully' love them. For me, this is one of the biggest things I've had to tackle while coming to terms with my sexuality, (or lack thereof?!).

Why do you feel, in general, that society doesn't accept asexuality as a form of sexual orientation in its own right? And what can be done about this?

We live in a world that's obsessed with sex. Sex sells products; sex is what motivates people; sex is supposedly the key to a happy relationship. The main reason that asexuality is erased and ignored in modern culture is because people simply do not believe that it is real. To not be interested in sex, or to not be sexually attracted to anyone, is unimaginable to many people.

Growing up in this society has given rise to generations who believe they are supposed to be hypersexual in order to meet the media's portrayal of adult life, and anything less can be difficult to understand. Asexuality, then, is a completely alien concept to so many, and with no compulsory LGBTQ education in schools, this is going to be very difficult to change.

I think that the best platform we have right now is that of the LGBTQ+ community. We are already included in the acronym (it stands for asexual/aromantic, not ally!), so I think that if the whole community could be more accepting and supportive, we could really use that platform to spread awareness and educate people.

What's your view on love? Have you been in love before?

I don't think I've ever been in love before, and I've had a total of two crushes in my life. I'd love to experience being in love with someone, but I'm quite worried that they will struggle to love me in return after learning that I am asexual, as I feel like many people think that it means that I don't 'really' love (which is totally untrue!).

At the moment I have a painful crush on a girl who's quite a bit older than me, who I just want to kiss a lot! I'm not in love though, and I never have been.

Are you currently in a relationship, and if so, is it with another asexual (if yes, do they identify the same as you or how do they identify), or is it a sexual person? And how is either working out?

I've never been in a relationship.

If you are not in a relationship, would you like to be in one and if so, why, and what type of relationship – romantic? Platonic? What would your ideal relationship look like? And would you be in a relationship with a sexual person or not, and reason why?

I would love to be in a romantic relationship eventually. I spent the last couple of years in a queerplatonic 'relationship' of sorts, (an intense, usually 'same-gender' friendship that borders on a relationship), which was wonderful while it lasted. I think that I would have liked to have been romantically involved with her, but she wasn't interested in me that way. When we parted ways, she told me, "If you weren't asexual, I would have fallen in love with you", which hurt a lot and is part of the reason I'm reluctant to come out to others.

My ideal relationship would look like anyone else's, I guess, just loving and supportive. I wouldn't mind dating someone who was asexual or not, as long as we were both happy!

What is your view about sex? Have you had sex before and if so, how did it make you feel? If you haven't, would you?

I haven't had sex before, but I'd definitely like to at least once, mainly because I'm so curious about it! Masturbation doesn't do much for me, so I suppose I'm hoping that full-blown sex is the 'missing puzzle piece' of my personal sexual enjoyment. And, of course, I want to see what all the fuss is about!

Do you believe if a sexual person had a relationship with an asexual, it can work? And what do you think about it being fair or not?

I think that, more than in any other kind of relationship, communication is key here. The most important thing is that both members of the relationship feel content and satisfied. Whether this means being in a trusting open relationship, being polyamorous, the asexual person agreeing to sex despite a lack of interest, or anything else, as long as both people within the relationship are happy, that is the way to make it "fair".

What's your view on living with someone?

Personally, I'm not sure where I stand on this. I definitely don't want to spend my life alone, but I'm not sure how any future relationships are going to work out due to my lack of sexual attraction and potential lack of interest in sex. As I've never been in a relationship, I don't know how it feels and don't know if, ultimately, I would like to live with a significant other.

Would you like kids and if so how many? And how do you hope to conceive these? If you already have kids, did you know before you had them that you are asexual and how did that impact your life?

Again, this is a weird one for me, because I can't imagine myself having kids, but I also want to lead quite a conventional life, which would probably involve me having them at some point! If I were to have children biologically, I would probably conceive by sex.

What's your view on marriage? And if you were to get married, would it need to be with another asexual?

Marriage is another thing I'm personally unsure about, but I think I will probably end up married (if I find anyone!) because I am set on living a 'conventional' life.

What's your view on nudity? On porn? On masturbation? On BDSM and kinks?

Nudity doesn't bother me at all, because it's just people. I've never seen a naked person as any more than that: a person who has no clothes on.

I find porn pretty boring, but it is the only way I can get aroused, so I suppose it's good for something!

From personal experience, masturbation doesn't interest or particularly stimulate me, but I still try it from time to time in the hope that something will be different and I'll finally see what all the fuss is about.

Kinks are a funny thing for me, because from quite a young age I've always had – in some capacity – a couple of my own. I've always been fixated by the idea of hurt/comfort, but it doesn't have a specifically sexual facet, just an urge to kiss and touch.

How difficult is it for you to be asexual, in a sexualized world?

At the moment, as a teenager, I'm finding it very hard. Kids are cruel, and hormonal kids are worse. Even at a very accepting college such as my own, I don't feel particularly comfortable broadcasting my asexuality, and this can be very frustrating.

Can you tell me about a time when you have had to deal with intrusive questions or a difficult situation due to your asexuality, and what happened?

Being as I'm not really openly out, I haven't had too many experiences like this, but I know a lot of people who have been accused of having been abused as children. It's an awful thing to suggest to someone who's asexual, and it really demonstrates how pervasive sex is in society, if the only way that someone will believe that you don't experience sexual attraction is if you have had a horrible and traumatic experience in your life.

What are the positives about being asexual?

I feel like the main thing asexuals have that is positive, is we don't waste so much of our time! I was absolutely amazed to realize just how much time some sexual people spend thinking about sex.

If you could have one wish about being asexual, what would it be and why?

My one wish would be that people would be better educated. Most asexuals are not Sheldon Cooper, or Spock, or a spotty, socially inept teenage boy who plays Dungeons and Dragons and 'can't get any'. These stereotypes, and bad media portrayal, perpetuate people's ignorance and are harmful.

If you were to look back at your life, what advice would you have given a younger version of yourself in regard to asexuality?

Stop worrying about labels; just go with it. It's something I still have to remind myself of every so often.

What advice would you give to others who are just discovering about asexuality and considering whether they are or not?

Take your time, especially if you're young. Asexuality is such a huge spectrum, with a vast wealth of identities. You might find yourself in one of them, you might not, and if you don't, that's okay too.

Do you have a story you would like to share or anything else you would like to say?

If you're a writer, write beautiful, complex asexual characters who are completely ordinary, and who are completely extraordinary, and who are everything in between. Keep talking about asexuality. Keep tweeting, reading, and learning.

Extra Info

What name would you like to go under for this book? Full name, first name, or alias?

Alias: Sappho.

What country do you live in?

England.

What age are you specifically? Or what decade age range are you – 20, 30. 40s?

17.

What nationality and ethnicity are you?

White British.

17. Zoe's Story

When did you first discover you are asexual?

I was 11 years old the first time I got an inkling I was different from other girls. I was in grade 6, (just finishing primary school), when a couple of girls told me a boy in our class "liked" me. This was a foreign concept to me; I did not understand attraction. I wondered if I was supposed to like him back; I felt quite neutral about him, as I did all the other boys (and girls) in class.

At the end of the year, we had a party for our graduating class. A boy, (different from the one mentioned above), asked me to dance, and kept asking only me throughout the evening. The other girls were giggling, saying we liked each other, and teasing me with the kissing song ("Zoe and xxxx sitting in a tree, k-i-s-s-i-n-g!"). I was mortified and felt an overwhelming need for them to understand I did not like this boy "that way". I admit, I felt flattered by his attention (coming as I did from an emotionally abusive background), but I felt no attraction to him.

At the start of the next school year (age 12, grade 7), I returned from summer break to find all my friends (girls), had changed. They talked about hair and clothes, wore make-up and nail polish. I felt like my world had done a 180-degree turn without first advising me. What had happened to all of them over the summer? Here I was saying, "Hey, let's play skipping rope, dodgeball, hopscotch" (just as we'd done a mere 2 months prior), and they were having none of it. They wanted to walk past the boys, talk to the boys, hang around the boys, watch the boys play sports. When had boys ceased to be the evil-must-be-avoided-at-all-costs entities of our childhood?

Next came high school. I couldn't even fathom that a term like asexuality existed (this was in the 70's and I'd had a very isolated childhood), but the fact that I was different was cemented for me over the next 4 years. I never had a crush on a boy (or girl, at that time), never had a date, never wanted to go to school dances, never wanted to be around boys or even have one as a friend. I felt no physical, sexual attraction to the male of the species, a glaring opposite to what seemed like every other girl's situation. In fact, I considered boys alien entities because I just couldn't figure them out.

Hindsight being 20/20, I would say age 11 is when my asexuality started to assert itself, though I was unaware of what was going on at the time.

How did you discover you are asexual?

In my 40's (can't remember my exact age), I came across an article in the newspaper. The first word of the headline read "Asexuality". The moment I read that word, I knew. Finally, a word to verbalize what was *my* normal. I read that article and everything clicked into place. I was elated! The article also mentioned Aven's website. Unfortunately, I didn't get an Internet connection until many years later, (financial restrictions), so I couldn't check it out at the time, (I didn't dare use someone else's computer). Even when I did eventually get Internet, I initially only visited Aven as a guest, still too afraid to step out of the shadows and into asexuality (afraid of rejection, ridicule, …).

How do you identify yourself asexually?

These labels are still so new to me that I find it difficult to categorize correctly. I am an asexual who doesn't like or want sex, but who needs human affection, (hugs, an arm around my waist, holding hands, cuddling). As for kissing, a kiss on the cheek and the lips is ok, but I don't need French kissing.

As to orientation, it is difficult for me to state because I feel no sexual attraction to either gender. I feel attracted to the person who is inside the human shell. Most of the time, I gravitate towards women. Does that make me gay, even though I've never had a sexual relationship with a woman? Hard to be sure, but all things are pointing to that. (I don't really like men, even just as friends, because I find most of them have a condescending, chauvinistic mindset towards women). I did have a squish (I just recently learned this term), on a woman a few years ago. She was a temp at my workplace, and I felt a connection to her, though I only approached her as a friend, not on a romantic level. When she found a full-time job elsewhere, I gave her my personal email address and said I wanted to keep in contact, (this is the first person I'd ever said that to). She wholeheartedly agreed, and that made me happy, thinking this could evolve into something (at the very least, a new friend). However, she never answered any of my emails, so after a few months I stopped sending them. I was crushed; I really thought she liked me.

Are you 'out' about being asexual? If not, why not? If you are out, whom to, and how did they react?

Both yes and no. I'm out on the Internet (through Aven and Pinterest), and I recently confirmed my asexuality to my psychologist, whom I've been seeing for the past 17 years. I felt no misgivings on her part, either through words or demeanor. Also, I'm out in the sense that I wear a black ring on my middle finger, right hand. I know very few people yet know the meaning of a black ring worn this way, but it validates me and my decision to stand proud.

I am not out to my father, (my only family member) who lives with me. He is 83 years old and he would not understand this concept at all, (I know he would worry about the state of my mental health). It would only create uncomfortable feelings between us were I to tell him. As well, I am not out to my friendly acquaintance (whom I've known for 22 years), also for the same reasons as stated for my father. This saddens me because neither of them will ever completely know the "real" me.

That said; the very concept of "coming out" peeves me. Straight people never have to stand on a soap box yelling "I'm hetero!", so why should I have to state to the world "I'm asexual!". (Same applies to gay, lesbian, bi, etc.)

What's your deepest fear, concern or worry, about being asexual?

Never having a special someone in my life, because she will want or need sex and I never want to experience sex again. Ever.

Why do you feel, in general, that society doesn't accept asexuality as a form of sexual orientation in its own right? And what can be done about this?

I think the term is too alien for them. They cannot relate to this concept, therefore it cannot exist. If you have no *sex*, then you cannot have a *sex*ual orientation.

I think this term should be added to any sex education and human biology taught in schools (if not already done so). Children and teenagers need to hear it from a young age, so they will grow up with it and know it is a valid concept, and that it can be applied to them, as the case may be, without fear of ridicule or rejection or misunderstanding.

As for adults, exposure is needed. Visibility through media attention, newspaper articles, Internet, books, TV, movies, documentaries, etc., so that the term asexuality becomes commonplace, valid, understood, and accepted, not just a passing fad.

It should also be added to the curriculum for medical students. Doctors also need to realize asexuality exists, that it is valid, and that their asexual patients are normal in this sense. They do not have a low sex drive, are not inhibited, frigid, prudish, and they most certainly do not "need to relax!" (I wonder if it shows I've had experience with this type of narrow-mindedness?)

People know and believe the term asexual when applied to plants and amoebas; why is it so difficult to believe it also applies in the human realm? I think it is because people are always afraid of what they don't know or understand. If you are asexual, you must be a freak, and freaks scare people.

What's your view on love? Have you been in love before?

I wonder if love actually exists or if it's an illusion we are all chasing. I've never been in love or even infatuated; the closest I've come to any type of romantic feelings are squishes.

I believe in the idea of love, of having a soulmate. I would like to be in love.

With the 2 sexual relationships I've had, I felt obligated to answer "yes" when the men first approached me and asked me out on a date. I was not physically attracted to them, but they did not repulse me, so I felt I had no good reason to say no. After all, that was what adults did, right? They paired up with the opposite sex to have relationships, right?

My relationships made me feel like a fraud, like I was playing at being a grown-up. I didn't really want them, but that was what everybody else was doing, so I had to do the same so I could appear 'normal'. I did care about my partners, but only as human beings. I did not love them; was not physically or sexually attracted to them.

(Aside: Isn't it sad that my criteria for accepting a date from a man was that he did not "repulse" me? Not "I like him, he's funny, kind, cute, generous, etc.")

Are you currently in a relationship, and if so, is it with another asexual (if yes, do they identify the same as you or how do they identify), or is it a sexual person? And how is either working out?

Not currently in a relationship.

If you are not in a relationship, would you like to be in one and if so, why, and what type of relationship – romantic? Platonic? What would your ideal relationship look like? And would you be in a relationship with a sexual person or not, and reason why?

I would like to be in a relationship. Even though I've been solo for years and like my own company, I do get quite lonely sometimes.

My ideal partner would be my best friend, confidant, companion, love of my life, soulmate and absolutely asexual. (Never again will I have a relationship with a sexual; never again will I be in a situation where I am coerced to have sex in order to keep a relationship.)

Like me, my partner will want and need the same type of affection as I do (see my answer to the 3rd Question for details of affection). My ideal partner will also be an introvert, like me. This is important because I need someone who understands when and why I need a break from "peopling". My last relationship was with an extrovert and we had many arguments about my being "anti-social". My ideal partner will also be understanding about mental health issues, and will know to give me time and space when I am in one of my down cycles in my bipolar depression. And I will gladly return the favor, if needed.

What is your view about sex? Have you had sex before and if so, how did it make you feel? If you haven't, would you?

I have had sex with men. I think I hate sex because I was emotionally coerced into having it. I never enjoyed a man's body, (too sweaty, stinky, hairy, ugly). Sex was never something I wanted, but I grew up with the message that you have to give a man sex (as much as he wants, and any kind that he wants), if you want to keep him. And, of course, you want to have a man because no woman wants to be a spinster, an old maid.

(Aside: What a bunch of horseshit!!! That a woman is nothing without a man is a horrible message to drill into young girls' heads.)

Sex made me feel used, like I'd put my body through something that was unnatural.

Do you believe if a sexual person had a relationship with an asexual, it can work? And what do you think about it being fair or not?

I've had 2 sexual relationships with men. My reluctance to have sex/lack of pleasure in having sex was the primary point of contention. I did not understand why I had to do this even once a month, let alone several times a week. Many disagreements and emotional extortion ensued. At the time, I did not know the term asexuality and therefore could not adequately explain my reticence towards sexual activity nor understand their need to have so much of it. In my second relationship, which was a live-in that lasted almost 5 years, my partner was unfaithful to me; his reason being that he was not getting enough sex at home. (What hurt me most about this was his forming an emotional attachment to someone else; I felt rejected as a person.)

Personally, I find it difficult to believe that a romantic relationship between an asexual and a sexual could work in the long run. The sexual may say he/she understands, but eventually will feel an overwhelming need for their sexual urges to be properly met. At this point, the unfairness to both parties becomes apparent. The sexual will want more than masturbation and feel denied if it isn't forthcoming, and the asexual will feel pressured to provide sexual intercourse/oral sex when they truly don't want it.

Asexuality is the lack of sexual attraction, as an asexual, what does this mean to you?

That someone's physical body holds no allure for me; does not "turn me on". That my own physical body holds no allure for anyone else. The latter is not said in a self-deprecating manner; I simply think I do not send out any sexual vibes because I do not feel sexual vibes.

Do you believe sexual attraction and sexual desire are the same thing or different?

From my own experience, I am attracted to the person on the inside, (their mindset and all that it entails), not their physical body or appearance. I suppose if someone feels sexual desire, the urge could be satisfied with just about anyone, not necessarily someone they are attracted to as a person, as evidenced by the number of "one-night stands" and "bar hook-ups" that are so regretted the next morning (ex: "I don't know what I saw in him/her, but I was horny/drunk, so it happened").

Do you think sexual arousal and sexual attraction are the same or different?

I'd have to say not the same, based on the fact that people will get aroused by watching porn. They do not know the person they are watching; have not perceived them in the real world. How could they be attracted to someone they've never met "in the flesh" (no pun), or even spoken to?

What's your view on living with someone?

That everything would be perfect if it weren't for sex rearing its ugly head, (absolutely no pun intended).

Would you like kids and if so how many? And how do you hope to conceive these? If you already have kids, did you know before you had them that you are asexual and how did that impact your life?

Even though I didn't know about asexuality at the time, I knew when I was 14 that I didn't want to marry a man or have children. I made the mistake of saying as much to my mother and had to endure the usual, "You will one day", "You're just a late bloomer", "You'll meet the right person and change your mind", and "Everybody has children" retorts.

I am 54 and never once changed my mind or regretted my decision. One thing I feel very strongly about is that if people have children it should be because *they* really want them, not because they feel pressured by family, their spouse, friends, co-workers, society, for appearances' sake, or whatever other reasons.

Giving birth has always struck me as a completely unnatural thing. A female pelvis having to "crack open", and a vagina having to enlarge to so many times its size, is torture to the soul as well as the body. This may be my asexuality speaking; I've always felt repulsed by anything that disturbs my vagina/genital area, (my credo is, "leave me alone!").

What's your view on marriage? And if you were to get married, would it need to be with another asexual?

I won't get married unless it is to another asexual, (fear that a sexual person would eventually demand sexual activity and reject me when it is not provided).

I've never been married (except for the quasi-marriage that was my 5-year live-in relationship). I would marry if I could find the love of my life/best friend/soulmate. My marriage deal-breaker is monogamy, both physical and emotional. This is what I want to give my partner and I would want it reciprocated.

What's your view on nudity? On porn? On masturbation? On BDSM and kinks?

I don't like male nudity because I associate it with sex, which I dislike, and because male genitalia is truly fugly. I don't mind female nudity because it is more aesthetically pleasing to me (except for the porn poses; only gynaecologists could like those!).

As for masturbation, I never enjoyed doing it to someone else (no sexual appeal/pleasure for me), but was always made to feel I had to do it. After my last relationship ended, I did masturbate but very infrequently (+ 2-3 times a year). It was simply physical manipulation to achieve an orgasm (no fantasies associated with it, no sexual appeal). After menopause, which for me came early, (started at 39 and by 45 it was all over; never used hormone replacements), I very rarely feel the need for physical release and couldn't ascertain if I masturbate even once a year.

I wish porn didn't exist because it is extremely hurtful to women. No matter what people may delude themselves into thinking, the majority of the women in the porn industry don't enjoy what they do; many have physical/emotional abuse in their past and/or problems with alcohol or drugs. Porn wounds the soul. Same goes for BDSM and kinks.

How difficult is it for you to be asexual, in a sexualized world?

It's difficult in that I feel I am still hiding part of my true identity. Many people perceive me as strange because I don't flirt; don't engage in telling ribald jokes; don't have a partner in my life; don't go gaga over so-and-so "hot" celebrity; don't wear shirts that put most of my breasts on display for everyone else's viewing pleasure. They feel something is "off" about me, but they can't pinpoint what. I won't deny being an asexual if someone asks me, but no one has.

This is another difficulty; I don't have anyone in my life who would understand asexuality.

Also, I'm fed up with all the overtly sexual messages in our society that are so negative for women. From fashion, movies, TV, print media, billboards, etc., the message is still that a woman's only validity is for sex (which thereby *in*validates me). Boobs and butts; that's all a woman is good for. As a woman and a human being, this message is insulting; as a consumer, it does not make me want to buy those products. It's the 21st century and young girls are still being given that damaging message, (dresses must be this short, shoes must be this high, make-up must be plastered on, all for you to be acceptable enough to step out your door and into public view).

Can you tell me about a time when you have had to deal with intrusive questions or a difficult situation due to your asexuality, and what happened?

Most of my uncomfortable moments:

- When someone asks me about my personal status, (are you married? Do you have a boyfriend?) and feels awkward when I reply no; they've no idea how to continue the conversation with someone who is out of their comfort zone (i.e. not fitting the "normal" mould); that makes me uncomfortable and I (or they), usually just end up walking away.

- During events geared more towards couples (Christmas party at your workplace when spouses are invited to accompany you; Valentine's Day; New Year's Eve when everyone seems to have someone to kiss; going on holidays solo; going to the restaurant solo; going to the theatre solo). These seem to make my "weirdness" all the more apparent, which makes me uncomfortable, which is why I rarely do these things.

- Refusing to date men. If someone tells me they have the perfect guy for me and can they set up a blind date, they always end up looking at me as if I've sprouted 2 heads when I answer no. (Them: "What do you mean 'no', I thought you weren't seeing anyone?" Me: "I'm not." Them: "Then why don't you want this blind date?" Me: "Because I don't feel like it." Them: "Why not?"). People just don't get how a woman could not want to date a man nor be part of a couple with a man.

163

What are the positives about being asexual?

Freedom! Emotional and physical freedom. No more living a life of pretence, of trying to conform to someone else's standards and appear "normal" by having a partner and/or children the way society demands that you do. (Which the lack of either will earn you a barrage of, "Why aren't you married?" "Why don't you have a boyfriend?" "When are you going to have kids?" "Have I got a blind date for you; you'll love him!")

No more fear of emotional extortion/coercion, of feeling that I have no choice but to have sex in order to keep a relationship. No more feeling as if I'm allowing my body to be abused and have no control over stopping it.

If you could have one wish about being asexual, what would it be and why?

I wish it would be easier to find a special someone who is also an asexual. Asexuals get as lonely as anyone else.

If you were to look back at your life, what advice would you have given a younger version of yourself in regard to asexuality?

Dear Younger Self:

You are not weird because you are not attracted to anyone, because you do not bounce from person to person every few months forming superficial attachments, because you do not like dating, because you've never had a crush on someone, because you never talk about boys/girls.

You are an asexual. I know you have never heard this term before, but it is a real thing. It simply means that you do not experience sexual attraction. There is nothing wrong or broken about being like this; it is simply the way you/your brain developed.

I know the road ahead of you will be difficult because you will come across many people who will not understand you. Because of this lack of understanding, some people may sever their ties with you, may think you are mentally unstable, may be afraid of you, may shake their heads and walk away, may think you are saying this just to get attention. None of this, I repeat NONE of this, is in any way a reflection of you or your validity as a human being. It is their shortcomings, and I know it hurts.

Never feel obligated to have sex with someone in order to keep them in your life. Anyone who makes such a demand of you doesn't deserve you.

You may feel tremendous loneliness at times, but please never waiver away from beliefs and feelings; they are as important as anyone else's, and once you are older you will thank yourself for being true to yourself first and foremost.

You are beautiful.

Signed,

Your Older Self

What advice would you give to others who are just discovering about asexuality and considering whether they are or not?

That there are many people just like them. To go on asexual websites and read all they can about this orientation. To get all the information they can find. To read it and let it simmer on the back burner, if need be. All the answers don't need to be figured out exactly right now. That it takes time to learn about asexuality and discover how it applies to them. That the asexuality spectrum is very wide and that all of this is a learning process that cannot be rushed.

Do you have a story you would like to share or anything else you would like to say?

I hope there is never another person who has to endure the emotional/physical horrors of sex in order to maintain a relationship.

I wish society/media would change the negative message they send to women/girls, every single day.

I wish men would respect women more.

I wish there was more openness and education about asexuality so the younger people would know about it sooner and realize they are all ok.

Extra Info

What name would you like to go under for this book? Full name, first name, or alias?

Zoe.

What country do you live in?

Canada.

What age are you specifically? Or what decade age range are you – 20, 30. 40s?

54.

What nationality and ethnicity are you?

Canadian Caucasian.

18. Anonymous's Story

When did you first discover you are asexual?

I first discovered I was asexual in my late teens when I found out about the term 'asexual.' Not sure exactly what age I was. Late teens.

How did you discover you are asexual?

Not really sure what led up to it. I probably heard about the term "asexual" somewhere, decided to look it up, then I had the revelation of, "Wait a minute… this describes me perfectly." I've identified as being asexual since.

How do you identify yourself asexually?

Aromantic Asexual. I like girls and I would like to have a romantic relationship with an ace girl but I just don't experience any romantic or sexual drives (I think being physically romantic could be fun although I have no drive for physical romance).

Are you 'out' about being asexual? If not, why not? If you are out, whom to, and how did they react?

I've only told a few of my friends and a former co-worker. My friends were accepting but the co-worker, who is homosexual, asked me a whole lot of questions, such as if I'm asexual because I came from a conservative family; if I'm secretly gay, and if I was ever sexually assaulted or raped. I told him that I am not gay and jokingly responded by asking, "How do you know that you're not into girls?" I also told him that I was never sexually victimized. He ended up telling me that I should see a doctor and stopped talking to me. I forgive him though. I feel like some members of the LGBTQ community transfer the hatred that they have received in their lives onto asexuals. I want members of the LGBTQ community to know that I accept them for who they are. I hope they can accept asexuals too.

What's your deepest fear, concern or worry, about being asexual?

I don't really feel like I have many fears or worries about being an asexual, although I fear not being able to find an asexual girl to get married to. Dating is hard as an asexual, although I've had far more success than most asexuals I'm sure, since I've dated three asexuals within a year and have the phone numbers of many more. I don't fear discrimination at work or in public.

Why do you feel, in general, that society doesn't accept asexuality as a form of sexual orientation in its own right? And what can be done about this?

Well the problem with this question is that I'm being told that I feel that society doesn't accept asexuality as a form of sexual orientation. That isn't how I feel at all. I feel that most people are accepting of it but they just don't vocalize their acceptance. I feel like others just don't understand it. Those are the people who I think aren't accepting of it.

What's your view on love? Have you been in love before?

I honestly feel like I've never been in love. That may sound horrible and reinforce the harmful stereotype that asexuals are incapable of love but that's how I am. It's difficult for me to connect emotionally with others. I consider myself very good at reading social cues such as flirting but when a girl flirts with me, I simply don't care and rarely reciprocate. When I do, it feels like I'm acting. It doesn't feel genuine to me. Similarly, I consider myself good at reading facial expressions and body language but I just don't feel the emotion that most people do. I never felt sad when someone told me about someone being sick or that someone dear to them has passed away. I do care for people and believe that people should be treated fairly and with respect. I just never felt the passion of being "in love" but I feel like I can love others in the sense that I care about the wellbeing of others. I guess the best way of putting it is that I do develop feelings for girls but I can only love them like a sister... not like a romantic partner.

Are you currently in a relationship, and if so, is it with another asexual (if yes, do they identify the same as you or how do they identify), or is it a sexual person? And how is either working out?

No, I am not currently in a relationship.

If you are not in a relationship, would you like to be in one and if so, why, and what type of relationship – romantic? Platonic? What would your ideal relationship look like? And would you be in a relationship with a sexual person or not, and reason why?

I think it would be nice to be in a relationship. I'd like to be in a relationship with a girl but I'm indifferent to whether it's a romantic or platonic relationship since I'm aromantic and lack romantic drives, but I'm not opposed to being romantic. Not sure what my ideal relationship would look like. I wouldn't mind being in a relationship with a sexual person although I'd prefer to be in a relationship with an asexual girl. With a sexual girl, well... they'd expect sex at some point which would be impossible since my body's not wired for sexual arousal so the relationship probably wouldn't last too long. It would just end up being a waste of time.

What is your view about sex? Have you had sex before and if so, how did it make you feel? If you haven't, would you?

I never had sex. I never fantasized about sex. Never had a sex dream. I imagine that sex would be boring. My body isn't wired for sexual pleasure. I'm pretty sure that I have what psychologists would consider a sexual disorder or a sexual dysfunction in addition to my asexuality, since I've heard that asexuals can function sexually. I just can't get sexually aroused. I also never felt sexual attraction or sexual desire. I wouldn't mind trying sex though. I'm not sex-repulsed. I'm just not sure if I would be physically able to have intercourse.

Do you believe if a sexual person had a relationship with an asexual, it can work? And what do you think about it being fair or not?

I think it can work but I don't think that it is likely to work. I think it can only work if the asexual person is willing to have sex... but what if the asexual person isn't into sex? What is that? It seems like consensual rape to me. Grey-asexuals may fare better with a relationship with a sexual person if they can enjoy sex, but I'm fairly certain that for asexuals (mostly females), they'll unfortunately have a significantly higher chance of being raped than sexuals. I hope that all asexuals can find partners who truly love and respect them for being asexual, but that's not always how things work out. Do I think it's fair? Not at all. No one deserves to be raped.

Asexuality is the lack of sexual attraction, as an asexual, what does this mean to you?

It means that when I look at an attractive girl, I can admire how aesthetically beautiful she is and may even want to pursue a relationship with her but I would not feel the need to have sexual relations with her.

Do you believe sexual attraction and sexual desire are the same thing or different?

Not sure. I've never experienced either as far as I'm concerned. I think sexual attraction is based more on appearance and sexual desire is based more on an individual's sex drive from what I've heard.

Do you think sexual arousal and sexual attraction are the same or different?

I'm sorry. I'm not sure. I've heard about both but I'm not sure how to explain. I've never experienced either. Maybe a grey-sexual can provide some insight.

What's your view on living with someone?

I live with my mom, my stepfather, and my siblings, so I think it's nice to live with someone to have some company although I do like to be alone sometimes.

Would you like kids and if so how many? And how do you hope to conceive these? If you already have kids, did you know before you had them that you are asexual and how did that impact your life?

I think it would be cool to have a biological son but I don't think I would be physically able to reproduce since I never experienced sexual attraction or sexual arousal.

What's your view on marriage? And if you were to get married, would it need to be with another asexual?

I think that marriage is something that I might pursue eventually since it's expected from my family. I would like to get married with another asexual of course.

What's your view on nudity? On porn? On masturbation? On BDSM and kinks?

I'm indifferent to nudity. I'm comfortable enough with my body to walk around naked if I had to or if I really wanted to. I'm also comfortable with seeing others naked. As for porn, my friends showed me some porn when I was in college; I didn't feel anything from looking at it. I feel like it's degrading to women though since I imagine that it has caused a lot of women to be critical of their appearance. As for masturbation, I cannot masturbate. My body is incapable of doing so. I've never felt sexual arousal. I probably couldn't masturbate successfully even if I tried. I never tried to masturbate.

How difficult is it for you to be asexual, in a sexualized world?

Being an ace guy is fairly easy in our sexualized world. I think I fit in just fine. The girls that I talk to on the various dating apps that I have, or the girls that I have dated recently, probably think I'm taking things slow by not making sexual comments. I compliment them on aspects of their personality instead. I think that I gain a lot of respect from women who are into serious relationships rather than hook-ups for being like that.

Can you tell me about a time when you have had to deal with intrusive questions or a difficult situation due to your asexuality, and what happened?

When I told my former co-worker that I am asexual he asked me a lot of questions about possible causes such as rape, religious views, hormone problems, and the like. I've never been raped or sexually victimized so I have no problem with answering such personal questions. As for other factors, I told him that it's possible that hormones or biology may influence my asexuality but I told him that I'm sure those things affect sexual people too and that such things shouldn't disqualify me from being asexual. He eventually stopped talking to me soon after we had this conversation. So far, he's been the only one to show hostility towards me because of my asexuality. I found this weird since he's gay and I told him that I accepted his sexuality regardless. I'm very open to answering very personal questions so I've never felt offended by someone asking questions about my asexuality. As for being in a difficult situation because I'm asexual, thankfully I've never been in a difficult situation because of my asexuality.

What are the positives about being asexual?

I'm sure that there are those who dehumanize asexuals but I feel like there's some advantages to being asexual. We've all heard the saying that "love is blind." I think it's more accurate to say, "lust is blind." I think that when sexuals lust over someone they oversee their shortcomings until later on when the sexual feelings probably die down. I think with asexuals, we are more likely to see a potential mate for who they are as a person and accept them more for who they are regardless of their shortcomings. That's been my experience anyway. I also imagine that another benefit is that asexuals can devote their time that most sexuals would spend watching porn or getting laid on more meaningful activities.

If you could have one wish about being asexual, what would it be and why?

I wish the girls on the asexual sites weren't so shy or fearful of men. I've dated three asexual girls since I first signed up on Asexualitic almost a year ago. In a year, I've acquired about eight phone numbers of ace girls who live within an hour of me. Only a few ever saw me in person. I had some asexual girls tell me that they're too nervous to talk to me or meet me in person. I think a part of it has to do with the possibility that some ace girls are afraid of men because men have victimized them in the past. I had one girl that I met at a meet-up that I organized; admit she thought the other ace guy and myself would end up being rapists instead of asexuals. I feel like a lot of asexual girls have the same fear. I'm sure they all have valid reasons though. A member of the asexual Facebook group that I made researched the prevalence of abuse among asexuals. Although it wasn't a published study, it was found that asexuals are twice as likely than those in the general population, to have experienced sexual abuse/assault. As such, I'm sure that there is a significant amount of asexual girls who have been victimized by men in the past. I'm sure others were too shy. I'm also sure that some just weren't interested in meeting me. Regardless, I wish there was something I could do to make those asexual girls who may be fearful of men (or just really shy), more comfortable with me.

If you were to look back at your life, what advice would you have given a younger version of yourself in regard to asexuality?

I honestly wouldn't change a thing.

What advice would you give to others who are just discovering about asexuality and considering whether they are or not?

To those who are considering whether they are asexual or not, I'd tell them to take some time to think about it and to not feel pressured to have to stick to a sexual orientation. To those who just discovered that they are asexual, I'd tell them to make an effort to become an active part of the asexual community.

Do you have a story you would like to share or anything else you would like to say?

Yes. Here is my story…

I am an aromantic asexual. I don't experience sexual attraction or sexual desire. I can't experience sexual arousal. I've never had sex or masturbated. I am indifferent to breasts on women, which I heard is rare even among ace guys. I never had a sex dream. Most people would never suspect that I'm asexual. I believe I blend in with everyone else.

In May of 2015, I was bored and interested to talk to and meet other asexuals... so I decided to sign up to Asexualitic so I can start dating. I considered myself asexual for a few years before that point. Within a month, I dated the first asexual girl that I ever met. We stopped talking so I made accounts on AVEN and Acebook. Dated two more ace girls in July but I honestly didn't feel any kind of connection with them. A month later, in August, I organized an asexual meet-up in my region. Only three aces showed up, an ace girl, another ace guy, and myself.

A few months later, I founded a Facebook group for asexuals. We have about 60 members so far. I then organized another meet-up. With each asexual person I talked to, I found out more about asexuals. I found out that many asexuals seem to have some kind of social anxiety. I've also noticed that some of the girls are a bit wary of meeting people from the Internet. Specifically, some girls seemed to be fearful of men. I suspect that a significant amount have been victimized by men. I remember at the first meet-up that I hosted, the only ace girl to show up made a comment about how she thought that the ace guys that showed up (the other ace guy and myself), would turn out to be rapists instead of asexuals.

With this revelation that a lot of girls are fearful of meeting guys from the Internet or just extremely shy, I decided to try sexual dating for the first time back in January (of 2016), just to expand my options and since I didn't appreciate the feeling that ace girls may be fearful of me. I made dating accounts on a lot of dating sites and apps. I hit it off with a 49-year-old girl from a cougar dating site and we were going to go out for drinks, but after talking for a while I realized that things probably wouldn't work out so I decided not to date her. As for sexual girls my age, things were a lot different. I talked to a lot of sexual girls at once as opposed to only talking to one or two asexual girls on asexual sites.

I ended up talking to so many sexual girls that I ended up forgetting about a few of them and many of them ended up texting me first. Needless to say, things were a lot different with sexual girls. I only dated two sexual girls since January though.

Right now, I'm in the process of dating sexual girls while I wait for one asexual girl to overcome a severe illness that has prevented her from dating me and for another asexual girl to feel comfortable enough to date me. She's the one who I met at the meet-up that I hosted and said that she initially thought that the ace guys there would be rapists. She has said that she wants to meet in a group setting so we have to work something out. I think it would be really nice to see her again.

As I am not cupioromantic, I'm aromantic, I'd prefer a relationship with an aromantic girl but I don't think that's likely to happen so I leave my options open. With 9 out of 10 asexual girls that live near me being romantic, I feel like I don't have much of a choice. I know that cupioromantic people want a romantic relationship despite not feeling romantic attraction. I'm open to the idea of having a romantic relationship. I think a romantic relationship could be fun because I see that so many others enjoy being romantic. This is just me being optimistic about my situation (I'm an optimist), since the only aromantic asexual girl near me is the one that I think is fearful of men. I think an aromantic relationship would be more fun and allow me to be true to myself. If there were a lot more aromantic asexual girls in my age range near me, I'd definitely pursue them first and pursue the romantic asexual girls as a last resort. I guess my philosophy is that I feel I shouldn't limit myself and that I should be adaptable. There's also this thing called "casual dating" so I don't understand why people think that aromantics can't/don't/shouldn't date. Dating is fun after all. Unfortunately, not too many asexual girls near me seem to think so.

My hope for asexuals everywhere is that we all come together as a community. I feel like the asexual communities that we have at the moment aren't all that great. No one seems to actively participate. I also hope that by coming together as a community that we can spread awareness about asexuality and expand on the current community to allow aces an environment where they can talk about asexual issues and talk to people like themselves.

Extra Info

What name would you like to go under for this book? Full name, first name, or alias?

Anonymous.

What country do you live in?

United States.

What age are you specifically? Or what decade age range are you – 20, 30. 40s?

23.

What nationality and ethnicity are you?

I am American. I am Caucasian. As for my sex and gender, I am a male.

19. Caryn Purdy's Story
Author of Asexual Book – "The Lonely Ace of Hearts"

When did you first discover you are asexual?

I may have suspected that I was asexual many times throughout my life, but always connected it to something else. Long story short, it wasn't until 2014, when I was 30, that I discovered (thanks to the Internet!), that I am not alone in how I feel, (technically, "don't feel"), and it was a major turning point for me.

How did you discover you are asexual?

Actually, I remember encountering it when I was 17, when I enjoyed studying a psychology textbook for fun. This is always dangerous when you find something that fits you – I related to the definition of asexuality but wasn't comfortable with the way it was described as a sexual disorder. So I brushed it off at that time.

I don't really think anything in specific prompted me to Google "asexual", but when I did (and discovered AVEN/the community/ a definition treating asexuality as an orientation instead of a disorder), I was more willing to explore it further than several years ago, when it was defined as a sexual disorder.

How do you identify yourself asexually?

Heteroromantic asexual. Mostly sex repulsed, but more willing when there is a strong emotional bond. And I'm jaded too so in other words – s*** out of luck LOL.

Are you 'out' about being asexual? If not, why not? If you are out, whom to, and how did they react?

I'm neither out nor in. I don't broadcast or tell everyone – but if it's relevant (such as potentially dating a person), I will explain this part of myself. And I have told a few friends.

What's your deepest fear, concern or worry, about being asexual?

I'd like to say I have none, because it was a huge relief to "accept and embrace" this piece of clarity about myself. Buuuu-uut... there are times when I wish I wasn't this way, because it would make the prospects of dating so much easier. I honestly don't mind the single life at all, but would like to feel hopeful that it doesn't have to be a life-long lifestyle. The grass is always greener... right?

Why do you feel, in general, that society doesn't accept asexuality as a form of sexual orientation in its own right? And what can be done about this?

Honestly, I don't think that society in general has a problem accepting asexuality as an orientation. There are individuals who have strong opinions – some roll their eyes at the million and 5 different "special snowflake" labels/identities... but even then it's just because they don't understand how important it is for some people to relate. It's not that we are trying to be different, it's that we are trying to connect with others who can relate to us on different levels.

In other words, anyone who challenges asexuality as an orientation is only doing so because they don't understand what it actually is. It has nothing to do with sex drive – it's about who you are attracted to sexually. (In our case, nobody.) Which can contradict who we are attracted to romantically.

What's your view on love? Have you been in love before?

I have been in love, and hurt, many times. I would like to feel love like that again someday, but only with the right person.

Are you currently in a relationship, and if so, is it with another asexual (if yes, do they identify the same as you or how do they identify), or is it a sexual person? And how is either working out?

No. My last relationship was my marriage, which ended 6 years ago. I have talked to/dated a few people since, but have been incredibly picky and just haven't met anyone worth building a new relationship with, yet!

If you are not in a relationship, would you like to be in one and if so, why, and what type of relationship – romantic? Platonic? What would your ideal relationship look like? And would you be in a relationship with a sexual person or not, and reason why?

Yes, I would love to be in a relationship. Ideally, it does not need to be with another asexual (though this would probably be best), but it should be somebody who does not need physical affection to feel loved and appreciated. It would be somebody who is understanding and respectful, somebody who is compatible with me. We don't need to be identical, just a right fit for each other.

And there are many other expectations I'd have, but that's what's relevant.

What is your view about sex? Have you had sex before and if so, how did it make you feel? If you haven't, would you?

I'm cautious about bringing this up because it should not be confused as a correlation with asexuality – but I have a history of sexual abuse. This is why I have an aversion; it does not feel good to me at all when I do have sex – even if I'm in a relationship with someone. Quite the opposite actually.

However, if I am in a strong and healthy relationship, with someone I trust, who is respectful and understanding, I am more willing to have sex to satisfy their needs. With that being said, it's more ideal that I be in a relationship with someone who doesn't need that as much because it becomes a problem. There's no compatibility when someone "needs" you to do something that makes you feel uncomfortable, you know?

Do you believe if a sexual person had a relationship with an asexual, it can work? And what do you think about it being fair or not?

Absolutely! Asexuality is more about experiencing sexual attraction. The conflict happens based on how that person feels about having sex. For somebody like me, who has an aversion or even a lack of interest in sex, it's going to be a bigger struggle to have a healthy relationship with a more sexual person. It can work sometimes, on a case-by-case basis.

Asexuality is the lack of sexual attraction, as an asexual, what does this mean to you? Do you believe sexual attraction and sexual desire are the same thing or different?

There are different kinds of attraction; sexual; romantic; aesthetic, etc. I think it's important for others to understand these differences, because asexual means not experiencing sexual attraction to any person, in the same way that a homosexual means experiencing sexual attraction to the same sex. This definition can't be changed, but each person who relates to asexuality (because they may be attracted to people romantically and aesthetically, but not in a sexual way), will often add to/elaborate what it means with their own personal differences.

Not at all. Sexual attraction is who you are attracted to in a sexual way. Sexual desire/drive is a completely different thing, though they can be related.

Do you think sexual arousal and sexual attraction are the same or different, please explain?

I don't know what it feels like to be sexually aroused by a person because you're attracted to them, but I assume they can be similar. However, sexual arousal is also different because it can occur as a reaction to something – a kiss on the neck, whisper in the ear, etc.

What's your view on living with someone?

I used to say that if you can live with someone for a year and still get along – marry them!

I still say that's a solid approach. Don't ever marry somebody until you've lived with them for a year, because this is when it all comes out. How well can you share daily responsibilities, how well can you communicate, etc.

Would you like kids and if so how many? And how do you hope to conceive these? If you already have kids, did you know before you had them that you are asexual and how did that impact your life?

Yes, I have 2 boys. I did suspect I was asexual before, but I was also married at the time.

What's your view on marriage? And if you were to get married, would it need to be with another asexual?

I was married for 5 years. I'm not opposed to ever getting married again, but I'm not in a rush or planning on it either. A healthy and happy relationship will be enough for me.

What's your view on nudity? On porn? On masturbation? On BDSM and kinks?

They don't bother me, but they also aren't my interests.

How difficult is it for you to be asexual, in a sexualized world?

It used to be a lot harder, before meeting others (online) who I can identify and relate with.

Can you tell me about a time when you have had to deal with intrusive questions or a difficult situation due to your asexuality, and what happened?

Since I only really bring it up when (potentially) dating someone, there's the standard, "Do you masturbate?" (And I don't talk to them anymore because they are not my type). But on the other hand, sometimes you can always tell who actually wants to know more because they will ask "the right" questions...

What are the positives about being asexual?

For me, personally, it's easier to be single and enjoy being alone. It seems like sexual people will just bounce from one relationship to another without ever really working on themselves. (On the other hand, I spend too much time working on myself! LOL.)

If you could have one wish about being asexual, what would it be and why?

That there'd be others; so it would be easier to find a compatible partner.

If you were to look back at your life, what advice would you have given a younger version of yourself in regard to asexuality?

That I'm not broken, there's nothing to "fix", and it's okay.

What advice would you give to others who are just discovering about asexuality and considering whether they are or not?

There are a LOT of labels out there, and it can be confusing or overwhelming. It might even scare you off. If you find a few that fit, you'll understand yourself better. For everything that doesn't fit, don't worry about it. Just be yourself and enjoy understanding yourself a little bit better than you did before.

Do you have a story you would like to share or anything else you would like to say?

I published a book (The Lonely Ace of Hearts: A Journey to Embracing the Asexual Identity), which was written specifically to help guide you through the common struggles of coming to terms with the ace identity. There is also a chapter just for friends, family, or partners to help THEM understand better, sparing you from having to explain it all or answer the intrusive/misinformed questions. Check it out on Amazon.

Extra Info

What name would you like to go under for this book? Full name, first name, or alias?

Caryn Purdy, Author of "The Lonely Ace Of Hearts".

What country do you live in?

USA.

What age are you specifically? Or what decade age range are you – 20, 30. 40s?

30s.

What nationality and ethnicity are you?

Caucasian.

20. Geeske Van Der Poel's Story

When did you first discover you are asexual?

In 2005, when I saw a documentary about asexuality on the Discovery Channel, I recognized myself in the stories told by the asexuals who had been interviewed for that documentary.

How do you identify yourself asexually?

I identify as a heteroromantic asexual.

Are you 'out' about being asexual? If not, why not? If you are out, whom to, and how did they react?

I am out to my parents and my best friends. My parents were very concerned when I came out. They wanted me to see a doctor and to take hormone injections. (Unfortunately, when I came out in 2009, most information about asexuality was negative. My parents found an article on the internet about a sexologist who claimed that asexuals suffer from hormone insufficiency, and that they therefore need hormone injections.) Now, my parents are happy to see me happy with my asexual boyfriend. My friends all reacted in a positive way. I have only found one friend who cannot wrap her mind around the concept of asexuality.

What's your deepest fear, concern or worry, about being asexual?

That people who judge asexuality in a wrong way, find out about my sexual orientation. I know, for example, that there are asexuals who have lost their jobs once their employers knew about their asexuality. I do not want this to happen to me.

Why do you feel, in general, that society doesn't accept asexuality as a form of sexual orientation in its own right? And what can be done about this?

Because society in general treats asexuality in a different way, there are double standards. For instance, many people see asexuality as 'unnatural', a 'disease', because it is an orientation that is not 'pro conception'. So is homosexuality, for example, but that does not seem to be a problem.

What's your view on love? Have you been in love before?

Love is a deep feeling of connection towards someone who is kind and loving. I am in love with my boyfriend, who loves me for who I am, and I love him for who he is.

Are you currently in a relationship, and if so, is it with another asexual (if yes, do they identify the same as you or how do they identify), or is it a sexual person? And how is either working out?

I am currently in a relationship with an asexual man (and I have been in a relationship with him for 4 years and 2 months). He identifies the same as me. It is working out well. We love each other and have the same sexual need (=none...).

What is your view about sex? Have you had sex before and if so, how did it make you feel? If you haven't, would you?

I am a sex-positive person. I feel that everybody has a right to enjoy sex (with mutual consent). Sex just doesn't suit me. I do not need sex as a way of confirming my bond with my partner. I can love him without having sex with him.

Do you believe if a sexual person had a relationship with an asexual, it can work? And what do you think about it being fair or not?

It could work and it could be fair. However, both partners will have to compromise as far as sex in concerned, or the sexual partner should be allowed to search for sex outside of the relationship. In the first case, neither of the partners has the sex life they dream of, and in the second case, the sexual person does not like seeking sex outside of the relationship, as he/she, only wants to have sex with his/her partner. In other words it can work, but it is difficult.

Asexuality is the lack of sexual attraction, as an asexual, what does this mean to you?

It means that I do not feel sexually attracted to other people.

Do you believe sexual attraction and sexual desire are the same thing or different?

Most people will only feel sexual desire for people they find sexually attractive. In that sense they are the same. On the other hand, there are people who have a very strong sexual desire and who would satisfy that desire with whomever is available, regardless of that person's degree of sexual attraction. In that sense, they are different.

Do you think sexual arousal and sexual attraction are the same or different?

For most people they are the same, I think. Sexual attraction can lead to sexual arousal. However, for many asexuals, they are different. One can be sexually aroused without having feelings of sexual attraction. For instance, one can just masturbate because it feels good, without having any sexual fantasies involved about sexually attractive people.

What's your view on living with someone?

I love sharing my life with someone I love and who loves me. There are only a few things that we do not share (such as our genital parts...).

Would you like kids and if so how many? And how do you hope to conceive these? If you already have kids, did you know before you had them that you are asexual and how did that impact your life?

I would not like to have kids.

What's your view on marriage? And if you were to get married, would it need to be with another asexual?

I do not need marriage to show love for my partner. Yes, it would. I do not feel like compromising between the sheets.

What's your view on nudity? On porn? On masturbation? On BDSM and kinks?

My view on nudity: we were all born naked, so nudity is not a bad thing.

My view on porn: there is a lot of abuse in the porn business. That is why I am more negative towards porn.

My view on masturbation: it is a good way of relieving stress.

My view on BDSM: it is not my cup of tea, but I would like people who like it, to enjoy it.

My view on kinks: see the previous answer.

How difficult is it for you to be asexual, in a sexualized world?

It is difficult to live in a world where asexuality is neither widely known, nor accepted. However, the more asexuality is covered by the media/research, the more acceptance there will be. As far as I can judge, there is already more acceptance of asexuality now than 5 years ago.

Can you tell me about a time when you have had to deal with intrusive questions or a difficult situation due to your asexuality, and what happened?

A friend of mine told me she could not believe asexuality exists. After all, if there are asexuals who masturbate, they are per definition not asexual, but sexual! I explained that asexuality is the lack of sexual attraction much more than about sexual behavior.

For instance, there are children who masturbate, just because it feels good, without having feelings of sexual attraction tied to that behavior. Explaining helps...

What are the positives about being asexual?

I will not get an STD, and I do not need to buy condoms...

If you could have one wish about being asexual, what would it be and why?

I would like asexuality to be discussed in SexED courses. That is the best way to inform young people (sexual and asexual alike), about this sexual orientation.

If you were to look back at your life, what advice would you have given a younger version of yourself in regard to asexuality?

Asexuality is not wrong, just be who you are. You should not feel guilty for not giving your parents any grandchildren, either.

What advice would you give to others who are just discovering about asexuality and considering whether they are or not?

I would advise them to read the Aven website, as it offers a lot of information on asexuality.

Do you have a story you would like to share or anything else you would like to say?

I hope my answers were helpful...

Extra Info

What name would you like to go under for this book? Full name, first name, or alias?

Alias: Geeske Van Der Poel.

What country do you live in?

I live in Germany.

What age are you specifically? Or what decade age range are you – 20, 30. 40s?

35.

What nationality and ethnicity are you?

I am Dutch and Caucasian.

21. Molly's Story

When did you first discover you are asexual?

When I was 21.

How did you discover you are asexual?

I had asexual friends and when I told them I never felt sexual attraction, they told me I might be asexual.

How do you identify yourself asexually?

I am an aromantic asexual; I don't like sex. I don't like kissing more than on the cheek.

Are you 'out' about being asexual? If not, why not? If you are out, whom to, and how did they react?

I am out to my family and friends and some people in my community. There were shocked and tried to convince me to just try sex, get my hormones checked...but slowly they are coming to terms with it.

What's your deepest fear, concern or worry, about being asexual?

I want to have committed loving friendships and I feel like in a society where romantic and sexual relationships are prioritized over friendship, this can be hard.

Why do you feel, in general, that society doesn't accept asexuality as a form of sexual orientation in its own right? And what can be done about this?

People think that sex is so important, that you can't love people without having sex. Education and visibility can help teach people that love can be nurtured without sex.

What's your view on love? Have you been in love before?

I've never fell in love. I have had passionate friendships, I love my friends a lot, but it's all platonic. Romance isn't my thing.

Are you currently in a relationship, and if so, is it with another asexual (if yes, do they identify the same as you or how do they identify), or is it a sexual person? And how is either working out?

I have many friendships. Some with sexual people and some with LGBTQ+ people. I come out to my friends at the very beginning of our relationships so they and I are on the same page. I like to communicate to my friends that I am aromantic and asexual and constantly discuss our comfort zones in the relationship regarding sex and romance.

I have one close friend who is aromantic and asexual like me and that friendship is very special to me. It's less complicated but sometimes gets very intense in a good way.

What is your view about sex? Have you had sex before and if so, how did it make you feel? If you haven't, would you?

I had sex once and felt uncomfortable most of the time. Some sensual parts were a bit enjoyable but the good sensations were fleeting. As things continued, I grew more and more annoyed and uncomfortable. I don't want to have sex again until I am ready to have kids.

Do you believe if a sexual person had a relationship with an asexual, it can work? And what do you think about it being fair or not?

It really depends on both parties' comfort zones. It can work.

Asexuality is the lack of sexual attraction, as an asexual, what does this mean to you?

I make friends based on what our common interests are or just based on their personality. Sex is really not a consideration when making friends.

Do you believe sexual attraction and sexual desire are the same thing or different?

Different. Sexual attraction determines if someone is asexual mostly, though lack of sexual desire can also make one asexual I think.

Do you think sexual arousal and sexual attraction are the same or different?

I don't feel sexual attraction but I can get aroused sexually when intimate.

What's your view on living with someone?

Once I finish my college degree I'd like to marry another aromatic asexual and start a family.

How many kids would you like?

I want a few children, maybe 2 or 3.

What's your view on nudity? On porn? On masturbation? On BDSM and kinks?

I don't feel the need for masturbation so I just don't do it. I have a very low sex drive; sex is off my radar most of the time, unless someone brings it up. I've watched porn and found it weird that people would do sexual things and actually enjoy it. I think the human body is a beautiful thing and don't really see it as something that is only sexual.

How difficult is it for you to be asexual, in a sexualized world?

I feel like I don't get jokes. I feel like I am missing out on a sensation and passion that many people have. But I love my life and I am happy I am asexual, I get less distracted by sexual things than sexual people.

Can you tell me about a time when you have had to deal with intrusive questions or a difficult situation due to your asexuality, and what happened?

People ask me if I masturbate; if I was abused or have imbalanced hormones. I respond differently depending who asks but I usually send people to asexuality.org if they have more questions.

What are the positives about being asexual?

Less distractions. I love people for who they are, not because of sex.

If you could have one wish about being asexual, what would it be and why?

To have meaningful friendships void of sex and romance.

If you were to look back at your life, what advice would you have given a younger version of yourself in regard to asexuality?

Coming out is a process. Take time to get comfortable with yourself and your orientation before coming out.

What advice would you give to others who are just discovering about asexuality and considering whether they are or not?

Take your time, if asexual describes you, use it, and enjoy our awesome community.

Extra Info

What name would you like to go under for this book? Full name, first name, or alias?

Alias: Molly.

What country do you live in?

USA.

What age are you specifically? Or what decade age range are you – 20, 30. 40s?

20's.

22. Jamie James's Story

When did you first discover you are asexual?

I was 11 years old.

How did you discover you are asexual?

I saw arguments between my mum, stepdad, and brother and girlfriend, who wanted a relationship, and I saw people having sex always argued. I didn't want it so I was told I wasn't normal.

How do you identify yourself asexually?

When I saw the word asexuality, it made me feel not so different after all, but it wasn't until I was 28 that it seemed to exist. Back then I classed myself as aromantic because I was anti-men full stop. These days I'm okay to be alone and no longer angry but more on the romantic asexual term now.

Are you 'out' about being asexual? If not, why not? If you are out, whom to, and how did they react?

I no longer have a family and I have one true friend; we met in 2008, he thought it was crap until I explained it, but still thinks there's got to be some sex in a relationship. I'm happy not to have a sexual relationship and I'm also happy staying single these days.

What's your deepest fear, concern or worry, about being asexual?

I do have a concern but it's not about being asexual, it's more of a fear inside myself because of other things that happened, but happened after I felt different.

Why do you feel, in general, that society doesn't accept asexuality as a form of sexual orientation in its own right? And what can be done about this?

It's the same as everything else out there; anything new people are skeptical about, all we can do is be ourselves. Why do we have to make people believe, we know we exist, just like gays, lesbians, black, white, yellow and green people, we are who we are, we're not breaking any laws, we have just as much right to be us as everyone else.

What's your view on love? Have you been in love before?

Yes, I have actually got married, had kids, and now on my own. My view on love is neutral, I'm not looking for love but never say never, I guess just don't hold your breath, lol.

Are you currently in a relationship, and if so, is it with another asexual (if yes, do they identify the same as you or how do they identify), or is it a sexual person? And how is either working out?

Single.

If you are not in a relationship, would you like to be in one and if so, why, and what type of relationship – romantic? Platonic? What would your ideal relationship look like? And would you be in a relationship with a sexual person or not, and reason why?

I'd like to never say never. In an ideal world I'd love a relationship, but realistically I have a doubt in my mind about the trust side of things. So if I stay single I stay safe, if I'm in a relationship I'm happy, catch 22, you can't win either way.

What is your view about sex? Have you had sex before and if so, how did it make you feel? If you haven't, would you?

Yes, I've had 2 kids. I wasn't fussed to have sex; I can live without it. I'm not saying that it isn't enjoyable, but I'd rather leave it than have it.

Do you believe if a sexual person had a relationship with an asexual, it can work? And what do you think about it being fair or not?

I'm guessing it could work but it depends on the person. Nine out of ten times probably not, but on rare occasion it could, I don't see a problem with it and the fairness is on perception. As an outsider looking in, I could say fairness doesn't matter, but if you're in that relationship, although you'd believe in your beliefs, you wouldn't want to hurt your partner so you'd also want his beliefs met.

Asexuality is the lack of sexual attraction, as an asexual, what does this mean to you?

Sexual attraction is looking at someone and wanting to have sex with them.

Do you believe sexual attraction and sexual desire are the same thing or different?

Sexual attraction and desire are two different things. Attraction is to look at something; desire is to want something. You can look at a banana and like the look of it without wanting to eat one, after all you may not be hungry

Do you think sexual arousal and sexual attraction are the same or different?

Sexual attraction is liking the look of someone and arousal is getting turned on by someone; again, one is looking at and the other is participating in

What's your view on living with someone?

If you'd asked me that when I was 19, it was my escape, and when I moved in with my partner I was comfortable with him, nowadays I'm more reluctant on trust.

Would you like kids and if so how many? And how do you hope to conceive these? If you already have kids, did you know before you had them that you are asexual and how did that impact your life?

Yes, I did know before I had kids I wasn't the same as others, although asexuality back then was unheard of; that was 1991. The problem with my past is each situation had a knock on effect to the next.

What's your view on marriage? And if you were to get married, would it need to be with another asexual?

I was married for a whole year. I wont say I'd never get married again; it would be nice to say I would, but yeah, if ever I did, it would be with an asexual.

What's your view on nudity? On porn? On masturbation? On BDSM and kinks?

Back in the day, even sexual jokes made me angry never mind anything else. These days BDSM I think is bull, I don't believe in it whatsoever. I don't watch TV past the 9 pm watershed because there's rubbish on TV and sometimes adult channels. I'm not a prude but no, I don't overly like nudity either.

How difficult is it for you to be asexual, in a sexualized world?

Quite easily, I have mobility problems; I'm alone; no friends; that way is the easy way, but to find a relationship and have the trust there with an asexual is hard to find. And the fact that many men in the world are sexual, it's believing that person is not sexual.

Can you tell me about a time when you have had to deal with intrusive questions or a difficult situation due to your asexuality, and what happened?

Yes, my only friend said I was lying and asexuality was BS and it didn't exist. I explained what it is then he thought otherwise, though the way it was said made me feel awkward, being called a liar.

What are the positives about being asexual?

The positives are I get left alone; I can be me; I can stay safe.

If you could have one wish about being asexual, what would it be and why?

In an ideal world, a relationship with a male asexual that was asexual.

If you were to look back at your life, what advice would you have given a younger version of yourself in regard to asexuality?

Don't doubt yourself. Don't trust others so willingly and trust your instincts and beliefs.

What advice would you give to others who are just discovering about asexuality and considering whether they are or not?

Trust in what you believe in, stick to it, don't doubt yourself, you are who you are and don't let anyone tell you otherwise.

Do you have a story you would like to share or anything else you would like to say?

Now to fill in the blanks, that will now make sense. I was mentally abused as a kid. "Why can't you be more like your brother, get off your ass lazy and come and help." On the next breath, "You're useless, you might as well not help at all". I felt useless and no one wanted me. My dad left my mum and at age 11 she was with a new partner for a few years – now I think it was, I don't remember. I do remember I didn't like him. He was always getting me into trouble with my mum like my brother also did. At 12, he sexually abused me, which sent my head up my ass because I was told I wasn't normal for not wanting sex. I decided to get into a relationship to get out the house when I was 16, because of what happened. So because I wasn't normal, I had sex to try to prove I could be a better mum than my mum. I left at 16; got with a partner; got pregnant, and the first-born was terminally ill so I wasn't planning anymore. One night whilst I was still recovering from a C-section, my partner decided to help himself, after he was asking for a second the night before and I said no. (He raped me, result being kid number two). Then my partner told me, "It's not mine". He stole bill money for fags, yet I went without cigarettes so he could have them if I had any spare money. I left, l had had enough, and he even tried to rub it in my face that he'd got his son back, which only lasted a week before social services took him. He left a vacuum plugged in with my son crawling across the floor, the stairgate was open and there was a saw and bench at the top of the stairs, both could have been deadly towards him, say no more.

I had my first son in November 2000. February 2002 was the second son's birthday. I had the C-section with both. So the mental abuse made my decision to leave home early and changed my mind on things. I didn't realise back then my mum was screwing with my head, it took me until I was 21 to realise the head games people were playing with me. By the time I was 22, in 2002, my head was so screwed up I'd had enough, yet I still gave my kids to his mum to look after rather than them go into care, even though social services tried to say they took the kids off me. If that were the case, I'd have no saying where my kids would go. Since then, I have been diagnosed with PTSD, which I can pinpoint as having dreams when I was a kid to. So trust your instinct and follow your heart and head.

Extra Info

What name would you like to go under for this book? Full name, first name, or alias?

Jamie James.

What age are you specifically? Or what decade age range are you – 20, 30. 40s?

35.

What nationality and ethnicity are you?

British.

23. Fiorya's Story

When did you first discover you are asexual?

I was 20 years old.

How did you discover you are asexual?

A couple of guys had recently asked me out, and even though I felt some emotional attachment to them, I couldn't bring myself to date them. There was just something... missing. I was so confused because I didn't feel anything physically for them, even though people had always told me I should feel that. But I've never felt that way for anyone, ever. And I thought maybe I was broken somehow. That's when I searched online to see if other people have felt the same, and I found AVEN. I've known I was asexual ever since.

How do you identify yourself asexually?

I identify as a heteroromantic asexual, but I am not romantically inclined – meaning, even though I do have crushes, I don't actually feel a 'pull' to be in a relationship with the people I have crushes on. Romance doesn't appeal to me.

Are you 'out' about being asexual? If not, why not? If you are out, whom to, and how did they react?

I've come out to my older sister and my two best friends.

The day after I discovered I was asexual, I told my sister that I've never been sexually attracted to anyone, just to see what she would say. And she told me I might be asexual. But when I actually came out to her as asexual, a couple of weeks later, she was skeptical and told me I just haven't met the right person yet. It was kind of disappointing, because I thought for sure that she'd be more accepting, especially since she herself suggested I might be ace.

My best friends took it well. I told them over text, and they responded quickly and said they accept me no matter what my sexuality is. Afterwards, one of them even asked me questions about asexuality, to learn more about it.

What's your deepest fear, concern or worry, about being asexual?

Even though my asexuality sometimes makes the world confusing (especially when my friends talk about sex and I just can't share in their enjoyment of it, like I could for movies or books), I'm constantly afraid of one day discovering that I'm *not* asexual. It's been such an enlightening experience to learn more about myself as an asexual, that I hope I don't someday realize I'm actually straight, and lose that confidence I've gained in myself.

Why do you feel, in general, that society doesn't accept asexuality as a form of sexual orientation in its own right? And what can be done about this?

I think it's mostly because people don't understand how someone can base a sexual orientation on the *lack* of wanting sex. It seems contradictory. And also, they don't understand that someone can go through life without desiring sex at some point, even if it's just in some small way. To most people, wanting sex, at least subconsciously, is a natural part of life. I think the best way for asexuality to become accepted is for asexuals to tell their families and friends about their experiences.

What's your view on love? Have you been in love before?

I haven't been in love, but I've been close to it, with one of my best friends. But I've begun to see that I'm not interested in romantic love. I prefer the kind of love that binds families together, the kind that friends share when they're talking late at night, about everything and nothing at all. The kind of love you have with someone that allows you to sit in a room with them in complete silence; just their presence is enough. That's the kind of love I seek.

Are you currently in a relationship, and if so, is it with another asexual (if yes, do they identify the same as you or how do they identify), or is it a sexual person? And how is either working out?

I'm not.

If you are not in a relationship, would you like to be in one and if so, why, and what type of relationship – romantic? Platonic? What would your ideal relationship look like? And would you be in a relationship with a sexual person or not, and reason why?

Even though I'm heteroromantic, I don't actually want to be in a romantic relationship. Cuddling, kissing, and even holding hands make me uncomfortable. And most gestures of love seem empty to me. I prefer friendships much more than other relationships, and I think if I ever *did* develop a romantic relationship, it would be after I had been close friends with the person for a long time.

As far as whether the person is sexual or not, I wouldn't mind either way, as long as they go into it knowing that they may never, or very rarely, be able to be intimate with me.

What is your view about sex? Have you had sex before and if so, how did it make you feel? If you haven't, would you?

I haven't had sex, but I think I would, either to have children, to see what it's like, or to please my partner. But I don't have any innate desire to have it.

Do you believe if a sexual person had a relationship with an asexual, it can work? And what do you think about it being fair or not?

I think the partners would have to be very patient with each other. You'd have to understand what's okay and what isn't. I've heard of some aces allowing their sexual partners to satisfy their needs in other ways, such as by watching porn or having friends with benefits. I think you'd have to find a system that works for you.

Asexuality is the lack of sexual attraction, as an asexual, what does this mean to you?

I don't like using the term 'sexual attraction' because it's so vague, and many sexuals don't even know what it means, haha. To me, sexual attraction is the innate desire for partnered sex, as that's the one thing that aces seem to consistently lack. I usually make things simpler, and just describe asexuality as not having any desire to have sex with someone else.

Do you believe sexual attraction and sexual desire are the same thing or different?

Yes, in the sense that 'sexual desire' means a desire for partnered sex. Some people also use the term 'sexual desire' to refer to sex drive, but many aces do have sex drives. However, they don't feel the need for partnered sex.

Do you think sexual arousal and sexual attraction are the same or different?

No, I don't think they're the same, or at least not for asexuals. Aces can be aroused by someone, but it's just a physical response, and not connected to any sort of desire for the person they're aroused by.

What's your view on living with someone?

I've had a lot of roommates, and we made many good memories together. But I prefer living alone, just because it makes life a lot simpler. I wouldn't mind living with a significant other, though, if I ever have one.

Would you like kids and if so how many? And how do you hope to conceive these? If you already have kids, did you know before you had them that you are asexual and how did that impact your life?

I'm not sure if I want kids. If I do have them, I want to have at least three. I know that sounds like a lot to many people, but I would prefer a larger family to a smaller one. As for how I'd have kids, I wouldn't mind conceiving them through sex.

What's your view on marriage? And if you were to get married, would it need to be with another asexual?

Marriage is for some people, but not necessarily for everyone. Right now, I'm not sure I want to get married. (But if I do date someone, marriage would probably be the end goal.) And no, the person wouldn't have to be asexual.

What's your view on nudity? On porn? On masturbation? On BDSM and kinks?

Nudity – This might sound weird to some people, but I seriously love being naked. Some days I'm alone, I'll just strip and walk around in my birthday suit. And I don't really mind if I see naked people. Unless they're having sex, because eww.

Porn – I'm not really a fan.

BDSM – I can see why people are into it, but my kinks are a bit different.

Kinks – I actually have a few of them. Some of them are weird, but most aren't. They usually involve roleplaying superheroes or literary characters... but not in a sexual fashion, just in a cute / romantic way.

How difficult is it for you to be asexual, in a sexualized world?

I don't find it that difficult. It doesn't bother me that everyone else likes sex, and that they talk about it often. It's like how I love and talk about my favorite books. Sometimes it annoys me when I see sex scenes in movies, but not to the point that I feel offended by it.

Can you tell me about a time when you have had to deal with intrusive questions or a difficult situation due to your asexuality, and what happened?

This isn't entirely related to the question, but I was browsing the AVEN website one day, and my twin sister happened to see it on my phone screen. She was shocked and asked me, "You're not looking at that website for yourself, are you? Is it for a friend?" Since then, she has subtly brought up asexuality into our conversations. I've had to find ways to skirt around it. I'd come out to her, but I can't tell if she would take it well or not.

What are the positives about being asexual?

People have told me that they wish sexual attraction wasn't such a distraction for them, so I guess one positive thing is that I don't have to deal with that.

If you could have one wish about being asexual, what would it be and why?

I wish that I knew more aces in real life.

If you were to look back at your life, what advice would you have given a younger version of yourself in regard to asexuality?

I wouldn't have given myself any advice. My younger self never thought about such things, and I prefer it that way. I think it was good that I didn't realize I was asexual until college. That way I had some time to explore friendships/relationships, and came to the realization that I was ace through those.

What advice would you give to others who are just discovering about asexuality and considering whether they are or not?

I would say, don't get too caught up in trying to label yourself. Just do what feels right. If you're not comfortable with sex and don't desire it at all, you could very well be asexual. But whatever you are, the important thing is that you know yourself. You're not just a label; you're a human being, with thoughts and emotions. You're more than your sexuality.

Do you have a story you would like to share or anything else you would like to say?

Umm... It's kind of funny; people have suspected I was lesbian in the past, because I didn't express any interest in guys. I've heard other aces say that too! Interesting, right?

Extra Info

What name would you like to go under for this book? Full name, first name, or alias?

Fiorya.

What country do you live in?

United States.

What age are you specifically? Or what decade age range are you – 20, 30. 40s?

21.

What nationality and ethnicity are you?

German American.

24. Joelle's Story

When did you first discover you are asexual?

About 2 years ago I learned what asexuality was and that it best described how I felt.

How did you discover you are asexual?

I was house sitting for a friend, trying to find something to watch on TV when I stumbled upon (A)sexual, a documentary about asexuality. The longer I watched, the more I had in common with the people featured in the movie. By the time it was over I Googled AVEN and never looked back!

How do you identify yourself asexually?

I identify as Panromantic Asexual.

Are you 'out' about being asexual? If not, why not? If you are out, whom to, and how did they react?

I never really understood coming out. To me, asexuality is no sexuality (a lack of sexuality, essentially), so there would be no reason to "come out" as asexual, as there would be to come out as anything you're not. I'm not sexual, so there should be no need to come out as anything, right? But there are quite a few people I have mentioned my asexuality to in passing. I try to keep the "bomb drop" as casual as possible. It's not really anyone's business, so I don't make it a point to bring it up. But I'm lucky enough to work in the LGBTQA community already, so they are accepting of my asexuality. When I dropped the "A" bomb on my friend Brian (who identifies as Bisexual), his response was, "Oh, really? I read about that online." It was the best reaction I could hope for, a non-reaction. Just accepted it without question.

What's your deepest fear, concern or worry, about being asexual?

I don't look forward to trying to explain to, or more precisely, to argue with, people who will tell me things like I just haven't found the right guy/girl yet, or that I just need to try sex and I'll like it. It's not a new flavor of ice cream, not an acquired taste for me to adjust to. As a woman, I admit there is a fear that some man will decide that it is his duty to (forcibly) show me what I'm missing. Unfortunately that is par for the course for any woman of any sexual preference in this world.

Why do you feel, in general, that society doesn't accept asexuality as a form of sexual orientation in its own right? And what can be done about this?

Scientifically speaking, humans and dolphins are the only mammals who have sex for pleasure, so it makes sense that non-asexuals would have a hard time accepting that there would be people born who don't have any sexual desire or drive; no need for sex. There are also people who feel that it is something chemical, a flux of hormones or brain chemicals that any doctor could fix with the right pill. It's no different than those who think anything other than heterosexuality can be "fixed" and will dissipate with time and visibility.

What's your view on love? Have you been in love before? Please explain.

I've been in love before. Love exists! My parents are about to celebrate their 50th anniversary and still act like they are a couple of teenagers sometimes.

Are you currently in a relationship, and if so, is it with another asexual (if yes, do they identify the same as you or how do they identify), or is it a sexual person? And how is either working out?

I am technically single, but I have been talking to another asexual for almost 2 years; now developing something of a relationship. We are both busy people so this has been a great way of connecting with someone without the pressures of traditional dating.

If you are not in a relationship, would you like to be in one and if so, why, and what type of relationship – romantic? Platonic? What would your ideal relationship look like? And would you be in a relationship with a sexual person or not, and reason why?

I'm not entirely sex averse, so the possibility of developing a sexual relationship is not entirely out of the realm of possibility for me. My preference would be for a romantic asexual relationship, but I wouldn't avoid sexual people as potential relationship material. There is so much more to the world of sex outside of penetrative hetero intercourse that accommodations could be made to satisfy a partner who isn't entirely asexual.

Do you believe if a sexual person had a relationship with an asexual, it can work? And what do you think about it being fair or not?

I think it can work if both people are open and honest. Romantic asexuals could be great partners for polyamorous people who can satisfy their sex needs through other relationships. Again, honesty and open communication can make almost any relationship work.

Asexuality is the lack of sexual attraction, as an asexual, what does this mean to you? Do you believe sexual attraction and sexual desire are the same thing or different?

I can see attractiveness in people; I can understand why one person would be more attractive than another for whatever reason. I personally don't feel what others describe as "wanting to jump their bones"; I don't ever feel like I need to have sex just because I haven't in a while. The only difference between sexual attraction and sexual desire, would be desire seeming to mean a stronger pull but are essentially the same thing.

Do you think sexual arousal and sexual attraction are the same or different?

Entirely different! Sexual attraction is feeling the pull towards someone you want to have sex with; sexual arousal is the body's natural response to stimuli. Asexuals are still capable of sex/masturbation, you play with it and you will get aroused!

What's your view on living with someone?

It can help save on bills and there is safety in numbers.

Would you like kids and if so how many? And how do you hope to conceive these? If you already have kids, did you know before you had them that you are asexual and how did that impact your life?

I'm too old for kids now, but may some day adopt or foster kids. If I had decided to have children I would have done whatever I needed to in order to become pregnant. Women struggling with fertility are willing to do whatever it takes to have a baby, and I'm no different. If I had to, I would happily have sex if having a baby was my goal.

What's your view on marriage? And if you were to get married, would it need to be with another asexual?

Marriage is nice but not needed. I just want the big party and my fancy dress! As long as I love the person, they could be any sexuality.

What's your view on nudity? On porn? On masturbation? On BDSM and kinks?

I am a modest person by nature but I hold nothing against anyone for their personal sexual preference as long as it doesn't involve kids or animals. What consenting adults do with their bodies is for them to decide!

How difficult is it for you to be asexual, in a sexualized world?

It's frustrating at times. Sex certainly does take up a majority of people's lives in more ways than just the act of having it. I guess I have adjusted to dealing with it after all these years so I don't think about it much anymore.

Can you tell me about a time when you have had to deal with intrusive questions or a difficult situation due to your asexuality, and what happened?

The time my mother and best friend sat me down in a fast food restaurant to tell me all about how much fun sex is and how I just needed to give it a try because I would love it. I wasn't out or even identifying as asexual at this point, but WOW, was that an uncomfortable conversation! A lot of, "Just find a guy and jump on him! You don't need to like him, you just need to get it over with."

What are the positives about being asexual?

Never needing birth control, never needing to get tested for STDs. No wondering if I might be pregnant! Those are the fun ones, but mainly not having sex in my life keeps things far simpler.

If you could have one wish about being asexual, what would it be and why?

Acceptance. I want asexuality to be as "normal" as heterosexuality; just accepted as being real and not questioned or doubted.

If you were to look back at your life, what advice would you have given a younger version of yourself in regard to asexuality?

I would have told myself about it and not worried so much about what was "wrong" with me.

What advice would you give to others who are just discovering about asexuality and considering whether they are or not?

Don't feel like you have to define your sexuality in absolutes. You are not required to decide that you will forever and always like one thing. This week you might be interested in a boy, next time a girl, sometimes nobody, and other times everybody. You don't have to label yourself with a permanent marker. Sexuality, like life, is fluid. You may have hated broccoli as a kid and love it now, or you may never like it. Don't force yourself into a box you can't get out of if you change your mind!

Do you have a story you would like to share or anything else you would like to say?

There are asexuals who have sex or masturbate. There are gay men who don't like penetrative intercourse. There are hetero married people who come out as gay. There are men who feel they are women, women who feel they are men. Everyone's journey is different; everyone has different baggage to carry through that journey. No one fits neatly into one simple definition of any form of sexuality, so stop comparing and just accept your sex isn't my sex, isn't their sex...

Extra Info

What name would you like to go under for this book? Full name, first name, or alias?

Joelle.

What country do you live in?

United States.

What age are you specifically? Or what decade age range are you – 20, 30. 40s?

39.

What nationality and ethnicity are you?

I'm more mixed than a bag of Chex.

25. Adair Gearhart's Story

When did you first discover you are asexual?

I was 19.

How did you discover you are asexual?

I was attending a LGBTQA group when another member mentioned that they were asexual. I asked them about it and what it meant. They explained it to me and all sorts of bells and whistles went off in my head. I had previously thought that maybe I was just gay, but since I hadn't come out yet I was still trying to pretend to be heterosexual. I thought I just wasn't attracted to the gender I was forcing myself to have sex with and my lack of experience with other genders was the explanation for my lack of desire.

How do you identify yourself asexually?

I am a panromantic asexual.

Are you 'out' about being asexual? If not, why not? If you are out, whom to, and how did they react?

I am out to everyone who needs to know. I do not discuss my

sex life with most of my family. So I haven't bothered to tell any of them. Most partners I've told didn't believe me and/or thought they could change my mind.

What's your deepest fear, concern or worry, about being asexual?

My deepest fear about being asexual is that I will never find a solid lifelong partnership. In a world obsessed with sex, I'm an oddball. There aren't a lot of us out here.

Why do you feel, in general, that society doesn't accept asexuality as a form of sexual orientation in its own right? And what can be done about this?

Society seems to think asexuality is a disorder that needs to be cured. It's different; so it must be fixed or otherwise eradicated. Most people enjoy and desire sex...so we must all, right? If we don't, we are broken and should be taking a pill or something.

I don't think this is an issue that can be fixed with mere education. The world rejects those who are different. Until we learn to embrace that not every person is going to fit any particular mould (and that's okay!), there will always be issues with us "weirdos" finding acceptance.

What's your view on love? Have you been in love before?

I have never been in love. I think the idea is lovely and it works well for a lot of people, but I do not think it is something I will ever experience. That's due, in part, to my asexuality and the difficulty of finding an accepting partner, but not entirely.

Are you currently in a relationship, and if so, is it with another asexual (if yes, do they identify the same as you or how do they identify), or is it a sexual person? And how is either working out?

I am currently single. I have been for a few years. It's really working out. I think I'm the one.

If you are not in a relationship, would you like to be in one and if so, why, and what type of relationship – romantic? Platonic? What would your ideal relationship look like? And would you be in a relationship with a sexual person or not, and reason why?

I would like to be in a romantic relationship with another asexual person. The ideal would be all of the regular cutesy relationship stuff...without any of the sexual activities. From personal experience, I couldn't have this with a sexual person, as there will always be that need I will not be able to fulfill for them.

What is your view about sex? Have you had sex before and if so, how did it make you feel? If you haven't, would you?

I've had sex several times. It nauseates me most of the time. If I'm not nauseated, I am going to be very disgusted afterward and deeply resent the person I engaged with. I feel as if I've done something very wrong or have somehow let myself down by giving in to another person's desire.

Do you believe if a sexual person had a relationship with an asexual, it can work? And what do you think about it being fair or not?

I think anything is possible. All people are different. What they choose to do is up to them and not for me to decide what's fair and what isn't.

Asexuality is the lack of sexual attraction, as an asexual, what does this mean to you? Do you believe sexual attraction and sexual desire are the same thing or different, please explain?

I think every person defines it as they see fit. For me, personally, I do not feel sexual attraction or sexual desire. I don't know if they're technically the same or different... but I don't feel them, regardless.

Do you think sexual arousal and sexual attraction are the same or different?

I think a person can be aroused without being sexually attracted to another person. Arousal is a physical response to stimuli to prepare for copulation. It can happen whether or not you "want" the person you're about to engage with.

What's your view on living with someone?

I live with someone, a roommate. It's fine. It works for him because he doesn't have a roommate that has loud, obnoxious sex. Lol. I don't see anything wrong with living with another person, romantic or otherwise. It just makes good financial sense sometimes.

Would you like kids and if so how many? And how do you hope to conceive these? If you already have kids, did you know before you had them that you are asexual and how did that impact your life?

I have a son already. I knew I was asexual before he came into this world. However, he was not conceived consensually. My sexuality made no difference to the person that impregnated me. Having a child has made declaring my sexuality more difficult because it seems to discredit me a bit or give people an excuse to not believe me when I tell them.

What's your view on marriage? And if you were to get married, would it need to be with another asexual?

I am adamantly opposed to marriage for myself for political reasons, but I do not see anything wrong with other people wanting to do it. If, for some reason, I were to change my stance on marriage, I would only marry an asexual person. I can't even imagine the nightmare it would be trying to maintain a lifelong relationship with someone who "needs" sex.

What's your view on nudity? On porn? On masturbation? On BDSM and kinks?

I despise pornography. I have friends that are adult film performers and am supportive of them doing what makes them happy, but I do not watch it. I am uncomfortable with nudity that isn't artistic. I do not like to be naked anywhere but in the shower. I don't masturbate as I have no desire or need to. I do have several kinks, but, of course, none of them result in sex. For me, BDSM is a cathartic experience...much like I imagine sex is for other people. I walk away from it feeling renewed and cleansed.

How difficult is it for you to be asexual, in a sexualized world?

I can ignore most of the sexualization in the world. The only part that really bothers me is trying to date.

Can you tell me about a time when you have had to deal with intrusive questions or a difficult situation due to your asexuality, and what happened?

In college, my sexuality got mistakenly brought up at a volume loud enough for a group of people nearby to hear it. I didn't know the people, all young men, but they were *very* curious…so they had to ask 20 questions. It was pretty humiliating because it turned into them offering to demonstrate their sexual prowess in an effort to "fix" me. I just sat there quietly, laughing uncomfortably, before I darted out of the building. I did my best to not return to that area for the rest of the quarter.

What are the positives about being asexual?

I think I'm less distracted than a lot of people. I don't have that nagging thing in my head that sends me looking for sexual encounters. I don't fall for the whole "sex sells" bit. I can see through a lot of things and keep a level head when someone is trying to cloud my vision with sexual images.

If you could have one wish about being asexual, what would it be and why?

That I wasn't. I didn't ask for this. I don't enjoy it, but it is what it is and I can't change it. Trust me, I've tried.

If you were to look back at your life, what advice would you have given a younger version of yourself in regard to asexuality?

Stick with it. You know what you are and know what you don't want. Don't lose yourself in trying to appease people who couldn't care less about you or how you feel.

What advice would you give to others who are just discovering about asexuality and considering whether they are or not?

Just do you. If it feels right, run with it and don't let other people dictate your sexuality. It's difficult, but being honest with yourself is always worth it. Forcing yourself into uncomfortable situations only results in resentment and disgust.

Extra Info

What name would you like to go under for this book? Full name, first name, or alias?

Adair Gearhart.

What country do you live in?

United States of America.

What age are you specifically? Or what decade age range are you – 20, 30. 40s?

30.

What nationality and ethnicity are you?

Native American.

26. Anon's Story

When did you first discover you are asexual?

I discovered it applied to me in 2015. I didn't have a set time for an epiphany; it just slowly connected the dots for me. During the summer of 2013 I watched a documentary about sex and it touched upon asexuality which sounded a lot like me, but I pushed it aside and continued thinking I'm straight. After looking through stuff on DeviantArt I became comfortable with this identity. Before this point I'd say I'm straight, but it wouldn't exactly feel honest.

How did you discover you are asexual?

Through my boyfriend. In the beginning of our relationship, it was all about the romance. We'd kiss and make out, hold hands, and for me it wasn't connected with going further. I thought this was normal. But he slowly developed feelings I didn't have after about a year. I could sense the difference between us. After heavy kissing I would listen to his heartbeat and his breathing and both were elevated. But for me my physiological processes never changed like that beyond slight physical arousal not connected to any desire. My heart rate was at resting point and my breathing was slow. He'd want to go further and I didn't really care for that. I wanted to stay as we were. I didn't understand why we were so different. For the longest time I thought I was just waiting for marriage until it dawned on me that this isn't the case. I'm not abstaining. I'm asexual.

How do you identify yourself asexually?

I am asexual and somewhere in the gray aromantic area. An alternative to gray aromantic is calling myself demiromantic, since that's how my first and so far only relationship started out as. However, I have experienced other gray area romantic feelings, mostly undirected towards anybody, so I mainly identify as gray aromantic or arospec.

Are you "out" about being asexual? If not, why not? If you are out, whom to, and how did they react?

I am out to a select few in real life. Online I don't mind being a little more out. In real life, I told my boyfriend because he deserved to know what was happening and to a few coworkers. One of my coworkers was fine with it and she had heard of it before. Another coworker, a former shift leader at work, was fine but she had a few questions, including the hormone stereotype, but it wasn't condescending. Those who know at work were just curious about it. My boyfriend is still with me but I think he thinks it'll change because his online friend's girlfriend was asexual until she craved her guy sexually. I am mostly not out, because I don't see any point in people I don't see on a personal level knowing. And my family doesn't know because I am not close to them. My mother especially would not be accepting of it.

What's your deepest fear, concern, or worry about being asexual?

I'm not sure to be honest. I would think it would be that it prevented me from being able to please my boyfriend if we ever do have sex. Other than that I don't really have any worries about it.

Why do you feel, in general, that society doesn't accept asexuality as a form of sexual orientation in its own right? And what can be done about this?

I feel like this is the case because society doesn't hear about people never having sex or craving it. We are the 1% and even in this 1% we may have never heard of this being possible. We are so unheard of and misunderstood that it's only natural for society to bash that which it doesn't recognize. So when somebody declares the inability to see others "in that way", it's only natural for those who can, to say something is wrong with this person. "Oh you can't fall in love? You never have urges? There's a pill for that." Even though we may not see ourselves as a problem other than in romantic relationships with an allosexual. I think visibility and communication can help combat this. Such as what this book will do. We speak up; we can change the world. Just because we are 1% doesn't mean we don't have a voice to be heard.

What's your view on love? Have you been in love before?

My view on love is that it takes many forms. Romantic love is thought of, as the meaning of love, but there can be many different loves even to the same person. For example, I love my boyfriend. I mulled over what sort of love I feel towards him. But I think it's a mix of love types. There's a mutual feel to it like we're best friends. But there's also feelings of what could be family related besides a little bit of romance involved. To me, love in its basic definition means a feeling of caring and adoration towards someone. I'm not sure if I've ever been in love before. Someone could say I'd be in love the moment I met someone. Another could say I'm in love once I become close enough to someone. So my answer to the second question is, I don't know.

Are you currently in a relationship, and if so, is it with another asexual (if yes, do they identify the same as you or how do they identify), or is it a sexual person? And how is either working out?

I am currently in a relationship that has lasted since October 26, 2013. We had a rough patch that lasted from August 2015 to January 2016, but other than that we mostly get along. He is most certainly not asexual. He is heterosexual. Other than him trying to get me into sex we are great together for the most part. We have a best friends aspect to us and I enjoy intimate non-sexual moments. As for the non-penetration sexual acts he tries with me, I don't care for it but I compromise on it. I don't hate it but I'm more apathetic about it. He assumes my physical arousal is me being turned on even though I feel nothing in regard to sexual desire.

If you are not in a relationship, would you like to be in one and if so, why, and what type of relationship-romantic? Platonic? What would your ideal relationship look like? And would you be in a relationship with a sexual person or not, and the reason why?

These questions do not apply to me since I am in a relationship. However, if I were single I would want a romantic relationship because I have an undirected romantic drive. My ideal relationship would be with another asexual or heterosexual, both possibilities male only, around my age, who understands my boundaries. I would not reduce my availability to only a small fraction of the 1%, which is why I'm not picky about my man's sexual orientation.

What is your view about sex? Have you had sex before and if so, how did it make you feel? If you haven't, would you?

I'm neutral on sex. I don't like it and I don't hate it. It's something that exists in life and as of this point I don't really have much to do with it. I have not had penetrative sex but I have compromised on other sexual acts with my boyfriend. I could feel everything physically but internally I don't care for it much. It's just something that happens. If I absolutely had to I probably would go all the way with penetration and if it wasn't a necessity to my partner I would not. My only fear would be the pain involved with vaginal sex for the first time and the awkwardness of it.

Do you believe if a sexual person had a relationship with an asexual, it can work out? And what do you think about it being fair or not?

Obviously it can work out if two people communicate effectively and are willing to work something out. If the asexual is willing to have sex, or if the sexual is willing to give it up, then great for them. Or having a polyamorous relationship if both are willing. But if neither can budge then I don't think it would work. I think an asexual and sexual pairing is only unfair if the two see it as unfair. Nobody else's opinion matters to the two in a relationship.

Asexuality is the lack of sexual attraction, as an asexual, what does this mean to you?

It means my desire for my partner and how I see individual humans, is different from my partner's desire for me and how he sees females. We have different instinctive feelings in regard to what most consider the biggest part of romance. That's all it means to me.

Do you believe sexual attraction and sexual desire are the same thing or different?

I have no clue. I've heard that sexual desire without attraction is described as going to a store hungry but not finding any of the food appetizing. I have no libido and no attraction of that regard so I have very little I can contribute to this question.

Do you think sexual arousal and sexual attraction are the same or different?

Most certainly they are different. During my intimate moments with my boyfriend my body responds like it should sometimes. But the physical arousal has nothing to do with desires to do anything with it. I have the ability to be aroused but the inability to be attracted. So I know for a fact that they don't always go hand-in-hand.

What's your view on living with someone?

If two or more people are compatible enough to spend a lot of time together and sharing the responsibility of bills, mortgage, etc., then I'd say they should go for it. As for me, once I and someone else are capable of supporting ourselves, I'd love to have a roommate, be it friendly, romantic, or what have you.

Would you like to have kids, and if so how many? And how do you hope to conceive these? If you already have kids, did you know before you had them that are asexual and how did that impact your life?

I do not have kids currently. I'm not sure if I want any. If I marry my boyfriend then yes I am considering strongly eventually conceiving them naturally. If this were the case I wouldn't want more than 2. However, if he and I split off the romance I would not want any kids in the future. If the future holds me having any then I would be open to them being of other orientations than straight and I'd let them show their pride in that.

What's your view on marriage? And if you were to get married, would it need to be with another asexual?

Marriage is beautiful if the couple involved is willing to stick through good times and bad to remain together. It is my hope that marriage for me would be like this. Just like with dating, I don't need to get married to an asexual if the male I'm compatible with is not asexual too.

What is your view on nudity? On porn? On masturbation? On BDSM and kinks?

Tasteful nudity is alright. It is often a subject in art. I find it awkward seeing the nude body on male or female since I am not used to it but I believe the human body can be a beautiful art piece. I stay away from porn, masturbation, and BDSM/kinks.

How difficult is it for you to be asexual in a sexualized world?

I don't find it too difficult in my area. Mostly the people I'm in contact with keep sex to a private status. It is most difficult between my boyfriend and I. I have gotten people thinking I'm strange for not checking guys out, my mother being the biggest in this. She jokingly said she did something wrong in raising me for me being this way. If only she knew...

Can you tell me about a time when you have had to deal with intrusive questions or a difficult situation due to your asexuality, and what happened?

When I came out to my boyfriend in October it was a very nervous time. I had no idea how he'd react or if he'd believe me, or if he'd even want to be romantic with me again, (it was during our difficult time in the relationship). It was through a texting app, I was talking to an online friend about it, who happens to be gay, and he helped encourage me to come out to my guy. I introduced the topic by sending the text to my guy: "I've realized this for a while. But I think I'm asexual." It led to me explaining it then showing him a video by Swankivy on YouTube about what it even is. He understands it, sort of. But I get the thought that he thinks it'll change. I was absolutely nervous and scared to see his reaction after that first text was sent.

What are the positives of being asexual?

We prove love can exist in all different forms, even in previously unfamiliar ways. We are a different breed that offer a unique presence and perspective to this thing we call life. And to be honest, it's kinda cool being able to say I belong to the 1%. Like we're the redheads of the sexuality world.

If you could have one wish about being asexual, what would it be and why?

My wish would be for others to understand that we're perfect the way we are and we don't need to be changed or fixed. There are many of us and we aren't broken. We are good romantic partners and some are still willing to have sex even without attraction.

If you were to look back at your life, what advice would you have given a younger version of yourself in regard to asexuality?

"You don't have to be attracted to guys if you don't feel it. There's an orientation you haven't heard of called asexuality. It means you don't feel sexual attraction to a man or woman. And nobody cares who dates whom. Don't worry about finding a romantic partner in high school, focus on your life and if someone does happen to catch your heart, go with him. Don't throw him away."

What advice would you give others who are just discovering about asexuality and considering whether they are or not?

"If you feel this is you, then this is you. If you don't think it's you, then it's not. I can't tell you what you feel or don't feel, but if this is you, then welcome to our community. And don't feel rushed in discovering a label; feelings first, label later."

Do you have a story you would like to share or anything else you would like to say?

Yes. Asexuals are ace-some!

Extra Info

What name would you like to go under for this book? Full name, first name, or alias?

Anon, cis female.

What country do you live in?

USA.

What nationality and ethnicity are you?

I am White/Caucasian. European descent.

Links to your website/social media.

My Aven account is @cetasoul.

27. David's Story

When did you first discover you are asexual?

It's difficult to pinpoint exactly, I am quite sure in saying that by the age of 13, I remember having no interest in sex and feeling that it wasn't a phase or something I would grow out of.

How did you discover you are asexual?

It was more of a gradual awareness/realization rather than any 'light bulb moment'. I don't like the word but I had a 'crush' on someone at school and although I liked her it never manifested itself in thoughts of a sexual nature at all. While everyone in my peer group was full of bravado about who they would 'like to 'do'', that just didn't occur to me. In my head when I thought about asking the girl out or us 'being together' it was just about being in her company and having conversation.

How do you identify yourself asexually?

First and foremost, just plainly 'asexual'. I would probably lean towards saying heteroromantic as I do have attraction to the opposite sex, but not necessarily romantic inclinations which probably leaves me somewhere between hetero- and a- romantic.

Are you 'out' about being asexual? If not, why not? If you are out, whom to, and how did they react?

I'm not, for a few reasons. I don't think it's particularly relevant or necessary for anyone to know, I feel no need to declare or announce it to anyone. If during conversation I was explicitly asked, I think I'd be honest but it's not important to me that anyone knows. I have told one friend, who being particularly liberal I knew would be aware of asexuality already. If in the future I was more open about it, I know it would mean a lot to him that I had chosen to confide in him first.

What's your deepest fear, concern or worry, about being asexual?

None particularly. I suppose 'being alone' is the obvious one but I've accepted that as more of a likelihood than a fear. It's dispiriting to see friends couple up and move in together knowing I will probably never have that.

Why do you feel, in general, that society doesn't accept asexuality as a form of sexual orientation in its own right? And what can be done about this?

I think society at large is just unaware of it rather than unaccepting. But I think any sort of 'asexual pride' movement could do more harm than good as people become desensitised – 'Oh, look, here's another group who wants special attention'.

What's your view on love? Have you been in love before? Please explain.

Having realized I probably could be considered 'aromantic' was disappointing to me, as I 'love' love! I'm all for romance in general and love to see two people who are right for each other en-joy all that it brings, despite knowing that I won't ever be the one who turns up on a doorstep with a bunch of flowers. When I was younger I thought I had been in love, I believed I *would* be in love, but I think it would be more accurate to say that I 'fall in af-fection'. If I like someone, the goal for me is to make them happy. If I can get them to smile then that is like hearing 'I love you' and it's enough for me. Love needs to be reciprocated.

Are you currently in a relationship, and if so, is it with another asexual (if yes, do they identify the same as you or how do they identify), or is it a sexual person? And how is either working out?

I'm not, and have never been.

If you are not in a relationship, would you like to be in one and if so, why, and what type of relationship – romantic? Platonic? What would your ideal relationship look like? And would you be in a relationship with a sexual person or not, and reason why?

It was answering this question online in conversation with an-other asexual that made me realise that my perfect relationship would be exclusively platonic. I would like to have that one per-son to be with, who wants to be with me but where emotional closeness wouldn't necessarily require physical closeness.

What is your view about sex? Have you had sex before and if so, how did it make you feel? If you haven't, would you?

My view on sex is 'to each their own'. And my own is 'not inter-ested!' I haven't had sex and don't feel any curiosity about doing so in the future.

Do you believe if a sexual person had a relationship with an asexual, it can work? And what do you think about it being fair or not?

Like any relationship it would depend entirely on the people involved. Being an optimist (and as far as other people go, a romantic!), I would like to believe that there are cases where it could, although it may be more difficult for the sexual half, but in reality I think it's unlikely. It would be fair if entered into knowingly and with acceptance.

Asexuality is the lack of sexual attraction, as an asexual, what does this mean to you?

Well as a definition, it explains itself. To me it means I can notice someone and find them attractive but have no interest in them beyond that. I can have a conversation with someone who is single, pretty, intelligent, whatever else that appeals but not have any thoughts of it being any more than that.

Do you believe sexual attraction and sexual desire are the same thing or different?

I wouldn't say that they're the same, but in many cases one would lead to the other. Attraction is more subjective, conscious and desire is more instinctive, biological.

Do you think sexual arousal and sexual attraction are the same or different?

I think they're different, I would expect sexual arousal to occur prior to, or in anticipation of, a sexual act, whereas sexual attraction is more of an acknowledgement of potential.

What's your view on living with someone?

If I was with someone who I was compatible with, and we shared the same thoughts on it, I would happily live with someone. When I was younger and first considered my asexuality and what it might mean for the future, I came to the conclusion that I'd just have to find someone else 'like me', as I wanted the 'normal' life of falling in love and living with somebody.

Would you like kids and if so how many? And how do you hope to conceive these? If you already have kids, did you know before you had them that you are asexual and how did that impact your life?

I wouldn't like kids, whether that's a fortunate coincidence as an asexual or as a result of being one, I don't know.

What's your view on marriage? And if you were to get married, would it need to be with another asexual?

I'm very supportive of marriage. If I did get married I am very sure it would mean my partner was asexual also.

What's your view on nudity? On porn? On masturbation? On BDSM and kinks?

(Kinks? Waterloo Sunset is a masterpiece!)

Nudity, to me, just... is. If I see a topless woman in the paper I'll have a look, but it neither disgusts me nor fascinates me.

I have no use for, or interest in, porn. I have seen some out of curiosity, and to confirm that 'yes, this isn't for me, thanks'.

BDSM/Kinks; fine for other people. Again, 'to each their own'. I find it as odd as someone into BDSM probably finds asexuality, nothing wrong with that. People are different.

Masturbation, I do find myself doing but it's a perfunctory task.

How difficult is it for you to be asexual, in a sexualized world?

Not difficult at all, I just accept that I'm a minority not being catered for. I don't feel hard-done by or put out by it in the slightest.

Can you tell me about a time when you have had to deal with intrusive questions or a difficult situation due to your asexuality, and what happened?

This is not something that has happened, people tend to be heteronormative, so more often than not the question is, "Are you seeing anybody?" To which I can honestly answer no and the conversation moves on.

What are the positives about being asexual?

I think I am a more self-sufficient person as a result of being asexual. I am comfortable with my own company. Potentially as an asexual you can be less concerned how you come across to other people – you're not competing with anyone, you don't feel pressured to look or act better than anyone else.

If you could have one wish about being asexual, what would it be and why?

I think I have too readily equated being asexual with being alone – I would like it to be easier to connect with other asexuals, for conversation or companionship.

If you were to look back at your life, what advice would you have given a younger version of yourself in regard to asexuality?

'Confront' is maybe the wrong word, but face it sooner – realise that it is a part of who you are and don't wait so long to find out about it or to embrace it.

What advice would you give to others who are just discovering about asexuality and considering whether they are or not?

If you feel even a small possibility that you might be, don't shy away from it, don't get cold feet, there is so much information out there now - look into it.

Extra Info

What name would you like to go under for this book? Full name, first name, or alias?

David.

What country do you live in?

England.

What age are you specifically? Or what decade age range are you – 20, 30. 40s?

30.

What nationality and ethnicity are you?

White British.

28. Elle Hardwick's Story

When did you first discover you are asexual?

When I was 18.

How did you discover you are asexual?

I met an asexual, and after they described and explained things to me, it all seemed to make sense.

How do you identify yourself asexually?

Biromantic asexual.

Are you 'out' about being asexual? If not, why not? If you are out, whom to, and how did they react?

I'm out to some more of my accepting friends who were lovely about it, one of them even coming out as asexual themselves. I've also come out to my parents who were not so accepting and told me asexuality wasn't real.

What's your deepest fear, concern or worry, about being asexual?

Not finding anyone romantically who accepts my need to not have sex.

Why do you feel, in general, that society doesn't accept asexuality as a form of sexual orientation in its own right? And what can be done about this?

We, as a society, place a lot of esteem on sex, *sex sells etc.,* and not having that same regard is seen as odd or unnatural. A greater media representation would go a long way to normalising asexuality.

What's your view on love? Have you been in love before?

I'm not aromantic so I like the idea of being in love. I've been in love once before with a man who accepted my asexuality.

Are you currently in a relationship, and if so, is it with another asexual (if yes, do they identify the same as you or how do they identify), or is it a sexual person? And how is either working out?

I am not in a relationship. Although I was previously in a relationship with a sexual person, it worked out for five years until he had to move away to another country for a job.

If you are not in a relationship, would you like to be in one and if so, why, and what type of relationship – romantic? Platonic? What would your ideal relationship look like? And would you be in a relationship with a sexual person or not, and reason why?

I would like to be in a romantic relationship again, although I'm in no hurry. My ideal relationship would look like a normal relationship with all of its ups and downs, just without the sex. I would be in a relationship with another sexual person, provided they either do not have sex with me or we can come to some kind of compromise.

What is your view about sex? Have you had sex before and if so, how did it make you feel? If you haven't, would you?

Sex for me is an endurance rather than an enjoyment. I've had sex before and I didn't feel good, I felt like I'd gone along with something I didn't want to for the sake of someone else and it's not something I want to repeat. It's not the best for my mental health.

Do you believe if a sexual person had a relationship with an asexual, it can work? And what do you think about it being fair or not?

I think it can work definitely. I always had a little low-lying guilt over not giving him what he wanted when he was giving me what I wanted but other than that it was fine. Looking back it doesn't really seem fair and I should probably have compromised a little more for his sake, even if it wasn't actual sex.

Asexuality is the lack of sexual attraction, as an asexual, what does this mean to you?

Something completely normal. This is a very true statement for me and I identify strongly with it.

Do you believe sexual attraction and sexual desire are the same thing or different?

I'm not sure. Having never felt either I can't tell the difference.

Do you think sexual arousal and sexual attraction are the same or different?

I think these two can be different. You can become aroused without being around someone you're sexually attracted to.

What's your view on living with someone?

Probably a little different from some others. I love living with someone but it doesn't have to be romantic. I prefer living with friends.

Would you like kids and if so how many? And how do you hope to conceive these? If you already have kids, did you know before you had them that you are asexual and how did that impact your life?

I would like kids one day but I'm going to adopt.

What's your view on marriage? And if you were to get married, would it need to be with another asexual?

My view on marriage is apathetic but I don't think this has anything to do with my asexuality. If I were to get married it wouldn't *need* to be with an asexual but that would certainly be my preference. No low-lying guilt.

What's your view on nudity? On porn? On masturbation? On BDSM and kinks?

It's fine for people who like it and it's consensual but it's not for me.

How difficult is it for you to be asexual, in a sexualized world?

I find it difficult to watch the sex scenes on television mostly because I don't understand it. I just don't get why people like it and it confuses me. I also find it hard to persuade people that asexuality exists.

Can you tell me about a time when you have had to deal with intrusive questions or a difficult situation due to your asexuality, and what happened?

Coming out to my parents. They told me asexuality didn't exist and made me feel like my feelings were invalid.

What are the positives about being asexual?

Sex doesn't complicate things. When making relationship decisions or dealing with people who I imagine I'd find sexually appealing if I could, I can make clear-headed decisions.

If you could have one wish about being asexual, what would it be and why?

That it was universally known and accepted. It would make life so much easier.

If you were to look back at your life, what advice would you have given a younger version of yourself in regard to asexuality?

It's okay; *you're not broken.*

What advice would you give to others who are just discovering about asexuality and considering whether they are or not?

Take your time in exploring your sexual identity, don't rush things and never do anything you don't want to do.

Extra Info

What name would you like to go under for this book? Full name, first name, or alias?

Elle Hardwick.

What country do you live in?

United Kingdom.

What age are you specifically? Or what decade age range are you – 20, 30. 40s?

24.

What nationality and ethnicity are you?

British White.

29. Katie's Story

When did you first discover you are asexual?

At 18 years old; first semester of my Freshman year at college.

How did you discover you are asexual?

I had a boyfriend at the time, and our relationship was getting to a point where it was becoming more physical. He could probably sense my aversion, so one day he broached the topic. We had a very open discussion, where I told him that I wasn't sure I could go any further. It was he who actually brought up the term "asexual," which I had never heard of before. As soon as I started doing the research, I realized it explained *exactly* how I felt.

How do you identify yourself asexually?

I am a biromantic, sex-repulsed asexual.

Are you 'out' about being asexual? If not, why not? If you are out, whom to, and how did they react?

I am out of the closet to all of the friends I have met since I discovered that I'm asexual, but have not had a coming out to many of my old friends and family members. I have only experienced positive responses from those I have told about my orientation, and I am not worried about the responses of those I have not told. The only major reason I have, is that I think it would not matter to those who have known me for years, because most of them probably already suspected it in the first place.

What's your deepest fear, concern or worry, about being asexual?

I'm worried the most about my future; I'm scared of ending up alone. I want to eventually find a partner, get married, maybe even have kids, but I feel inept when it comes to maintaining relationships.

Why do you feel, in general, that society doesn't accept asexuality as a form of sexual orientation in its own right? And what can be done about this?

I think the issue stems from a lack of information. I think if more people learn that asexuality exists, and what exactly it is, then we would find more support than we may think. Visibility is key.

What's your view on love? Have you been in love before?

Love is complicated for me. I know I love certain members of my family. I know because I experience a sense of loss when we are separated for long periods of time, and then subsequent happiness at reunion. However, I have never felt such strong emotions toward any of my romantic partners; I've often responded to their absences with indifference, or even relief that I might finally have some solitude.

Love, for me, is not strengthened with any kind of physical expression. Rather, the physical expression of a hug or a kiss is the by-product of a bond formed through years of shared hardships and shared victories.

Are you currently in a relationship, and if so, is it with another asexual (if yes, do they identify the same as you or how do they identify), or is it a sexual person? And how is either working out?

I am not currently in a relationship. Up until recently, I was in a relationship with someone who was sexual. We ended on good terms, and I think there were multiple factors that caused our breakup, not just our mismatched needs.

If you are not in a relationship, would you like to be in one and if so, why, and what type of relationship – romantic? Platonic? What would your ideal relationship look like? And would you be in a relationship with a sexual person or not, and reason why?

I would love to be in a serious romantic relationship with another asexual, with all of the aspects of a stereotypical relationship, minus the sex.

What is your view about sex? Have you had sex before and if so, how did it make you feel? If you haven't, would you?

I don't mind the idea of sex, and I don't mind when people talk about it. When it comes to me, however, I don't know that I ever want to actually have sex. Unless it was with someone I had known for a very long time, I would not even consider it. As it applies to my life, I see sexual intercourse as a tool for maybe having children someday, but nothing else.

Do you believe if a sexual person had a relationship with an asexual, it can work? And what do you think about it being fair or not?

Yes, I think a situation like that could work. It really comes down to how honest the people are about their needs and what they can compromise on. If they could meet in the middle, they would definitely find a solution.

Asexuality is the lack of sexual attraction, as an asexual, what does this mean to you?

Sometimes I wish I understood what sexual attraction feels like. I never quite understood what my friends meant when they thought someone was "hot," but I went along with it anyway. I find certain people aesthetically pleasing, but it does not make me want to have sex with them.

Do you believe sexual attraction and sexual desire are the same thing or different?

Yes, I think they are two separate things, and they may not necessarily be aligned with one another. I believe that a person can experience being attracted to someone sexually, but not want to actually have sex with the person. If that happens, then I don't believe they would qualify as asexual; they would only be categorized as sex-repulsed.

Do you think sexual arousal and sexual attraction are the same or different?

Yes, they are two separate things. Someone who is sexually attracted to someone will probably feel arousal at the thought of them, but a person can feel aroused without an object of attraction. Arousal is a bodily response that can be triggered by many different things.

What's your view on living with someone?

I would love to share an apartment with a close friend. I put up a big show of being an introvert, but I actually would get lonely if I did not have someone around that I like to talk to.

Would you like kids and if so how many? And how do you hope to conceive these? If you already have kids, did you know before you had them that you are asexual and how did that impact your life?

I would love to have kids in the future! Unless I am in a long-term relationship with a person I trust, I would not do this through sex. Instead I would have it done artificially with a sperm donation.

What's your view on marriage? And if you were to get married, would it need to be with another asexual?

I want to get married eventually, or at least find some kind of close friend I can share my life with. I would want it to be with another asexual, but it does not have to be, depending on the person.

What's your view on nudity? On porn? On masturbation? On BDSM and kinks?

To each their own. As long as people are having fun and no one gets hurt, it doesn't bother me in the slightest.

How difficult is it for you to be asexual, in a sexualized world?

Honestly, I never noticed how sexual the world was until I realized how asexual I am. I was completely blind to it for a long time. Now, I get annoyed sometimes, but I try not to be bothered too much. I don't find it too difficult, except when it actually comes to forging relationships.

Can you tell me about a time when you have had to deal with intrusive questions or a difficult situation due to your asexuality, and what happened?

I can happily say that I haven't had any negative situation of the sort.

What are the positives about being asexual?

Apparently advertisements don't work on me. I also don't have to deal with as much relationship drama.

If you could have one wish about being asexual, what would it be and why?

I wish I'd find someone to love and share my life with someday.

If you were to look back at your life, what advice would you have given a younger version of yourself in regard to asexuality?

I would have told myself that it existed. It would have saved me from a lot of teen angst and awkward relationship moments.

What advice would you give to others who are just discovering about asexuality and considering whether they are or not?

Be confident in yourself. Embrace who you are and know that everything will turn out alright somehow.

Extra Info

What name would you like to go under for this book? Full name, first name, or alias?

Katie.

What country do you live in?

United States.

What age are you specifically? Or what decade age range are you – 20, 30. 40s?

18.

What nationality and ethnicity are you?

Caucasian.

Links to your website/social media.

My AVEN username is Waywardheroine.

30. Kali's Story

When did you first discover you are asexual?

I'm not sure exactly, but I would have been 18 or 19, athough I didn't actually accept that it applied to me until I was 21.

How did you discover you are asexual?

A friend from high school mentioned the term in passing in conversation. I had no idea what it meant, but I didn't ask because I didn't want to appear ignorant. So, when I got home that evening I Googled and it was an answer to a question I had been avoiding asking for years. I didn't actually use the term to describe myself for a couple of years though.

How do you identify yourself asexually

I'm an aromantic (technically cupioromantic) asexual.

Are you 'out' about being asexual? If not, why not? If you are out, whom to, and how did they react?

I'm out to some people and not others. Most people I met before I started actually identifying as ace don't know because it seems like an awkward thing to just bring up randomly. A few old co-workers know, because they outright asked if I was asexual and I'm fairly open about it now that I've moved away from home. Everyone I've told has reacted positively fortunately for me.

What's your deepest fear, concern or worry, about being asexual?

All of my friends getting married and forgetting about me, leaving me to be lonely forever.

Why do you feel, in general, that society doesn't accept asexuality as a form of sexual orientation in its own right? And what can be done about this?

I suspect that it is because asexuality does not fit the general view of sexual orientation the way it is taught. It is taught as being who you are sexually attracted to and no one is not regarded as a valid answer except for in children. So people see it as something abnormal, something that needs to be fixed. In my view all that can be done is educational efforts. Until people learn about asexuality alongside the other sexual orientations, it won't be widely accepted as just another form of sexual orientation.

What's your view on love? Have you been in love before?

I've never been in love before, but I think it's one of the most beautiful things in the world. Love, pure love, is a precious gift and deserves to be sheltered in a relationship that all involved parties work to protect.

Are you currently in a relationship, and if so, is it with another asexual (if yes, do they identify the same as you or how do they identify), or is it a sexual person? And how is either working out?

No.

If you are not in a relationship, would you like to be in one and if so, why, and what type of relationship – romantic? Platonic? What would your ideal relationship look like? And would you be in a relationship with a sexual person or not, and reason why?

I would like to be in a relationship in the future though I do not see it as particularly likely. Ideally that relationship would be a romantic one, but I would also be happy in a dedicated queer platonic relationship. My ideal relationship would be one where we live together, laugh together, talk about our lives and the world, cuddle together, etc.

I don't think I could be in a relationship with a sexual person because I am extremely repulsed even by the idea of myself engaging in sexual intercourse. If I did end up in a relationship with a sexual person, it would have to be an open relationship so that they could have their sexual needs met elsewhere.

What is your view about sex? Have you had sex before and if so, how did it make you feel? If you haven't, would you?

I have not had sex and would not have sex. My view on sex in general though, is that I really don't care what anyone else does as long as everybody involved is consenting and they don't try and drag me into it.

Do you believe if a sexual person had a relationship with an asexual, it can work? And what do you think about it being fair or not?

I do think it can work, but I also know it adds another layer of complications. I know people who make it work and I think as long as both parties are open and up-front about what they need and what they will and will not do, then it is completely fair.

Asexuality is the lack of sexual attraction, as an asexual, what does this mean to you?

I think the best way I've ever heard it explained (and the way I usually explain it to others), is that the feeling that you (general you), get when you see someone you think is good looking and you would like to get to know them on an intimate level – well, I've never felt that feeling.

Do you believe sexual attraction and sexual desire are the same thing or different?

I think for most people they are, but not necessarily. In my mind I mostly understand sexual attraction as something that is inspired by a person, whereas sexual desire can just be a general feeling of wanting to be sexual with someone in general. So a person can feel sexual desire directionlessly, but sexual attraction always has a target so to speak.

Do you think sexual arousal and sexual attraction are the same or different?

Definitely different. Similar to the difference between sexual attraction and sexual desire you can feel sexual arousal without needing to feel sexual attraction. Many, if not most asexuals, can feel sexual arousal (aka: libido), but still not have sexual attraction (or, at least, that's my understanding). Arousal is a physical thing, whereas sexual attraction I've always seen as more of a mental thing – although with a physical element probably.

What's your view on living with someone?

I would always want to live with someone. I'm not an overly social person, but a home with just me in it would be too quiet and would make me feel exceedingly lonely.

Would you like kids and if so how many? And how do you hope to conceive these? If you already have kids, did you know before you had them that you are asexual and how did that impact your life?

I don't want kids and I never have. I'm not opposed to considering adoption if I end up in a relationship with someone whom kids are very important to, but it's not something I have any particular desire for.

What's your view on marriage? And if you were to get married, would it need to be with another asexual?

I like the idea of marriage. Some of the more traditional parts of a wedding can be kind of sexist, but usually you can get rid of those nowadays. Marriage itself is not a huge deal to me. If I ended up in a serious relationship then it is something I would want, but only time will tell.

As I said before, I would be open to a relationship with a non-asexual person but they would need to get their needs met elsewhere. The same applied to marriage.

What's your view on nudity? On porn? On masturbation? On BDSM and kinks?

When it comes to nudity it's not a thing I'm personally comfortable with. I'm not exactly secure in any kind of self-confidence or self-image, so the idea of anyone seeing me nude is panic worthy. As for my seeing other people nude, I'm just kind of ambivalent. I mean, I would rather not, but I don't think I would run away screaming or anything.

Porn is very much something I just don't care about at all. I tried watching it a handful of times when I was trying to convince myself that I wasn't ace, but I just found it boring. Everything I know about it tells me it's a problematic industry that could use reforming, but that's about as much as I know.

Masturbation is just a thing. Lot's of people (including aces) do it too. I don't. Like porn it's something I've tried, found to be boring and a waste of time, and moved on.

As far as BDSM and kinks I am exceptionally supportive. I have never engaged in any of that personally, but I have friends who have, and honestly, I can see the appeal. Generally too sexual for me to ever try anything out, but I can see why people would be drawn to something like that.

How difficult is it for you to be asexual, in a sexualized world?

I've been exceedingly lucky actually. Even before I was ace I never seemed to gravitate to the type of people as friends who were particularly sexual/sex obsessed, so the fact that I wasn't into that was never a big deal. And most of the people in my close circles of friends nowadays, know about my asexuality and are completely fine with it.

Can you tell me about a time when you have had to deal with intrusive questions or a difficult situation due to your asexuality, and what happened?

I've only had to deal with such a situation once. I was at an LGBT conference in Toronto and the last night there was a nice dinner. Everyone was sharing coming out stories and the like, and then they asked me and I told them I was ace. I had to explain asexuality, which was fine, but then one of the guys started getting really intrusive. He was asking me all these questions about whether I had ever had sex, how I could know I was ace without having sex, did I masturbate, etc. It was extremely awkward, but everyone else at the table was backing me up and eventually he just gave up.

What are the positives about being asexual?

I feel like this question has a lot of dependence on how you identify. For instance, as a sex repulsed asexual one of the perks is that I don't have to worry about pregnancy or STIs, but that would not apply to an ace who was in a sexual relationship for whatever reason.

I think one of the main positives for me personally, is that I'm more objective about things that have to do with dating and such, so people find me good to come to for advice.

If you could have one wish about being asexual, what would it be and why?

Mostly I just wish that everyone knew what it was. Having to explain it all the time gets tiring and it means that a lot of people think you're making something up so that you look special.

If you were to look back at your life, what advice would you have given a younger version of yourself in regard to asexuality?

It's okay to not like anyone like that. You don't have to pretend that you do. There's nothing wrong with you. You're perfectly fine just the way you are.

What advice would you give to others who are just discovering about asexuality and considering whether they are or not?

If you want to tell people, tell people. If you don't want to tell people, then don't. There's no need to decide right away, but if you think you are ace then come join in and chat with us. We're not scary and we get it.

Do you have a story you would like to share or anything else you would like to say?

For several years I wouldn't admit I was ace even to myself. I'm not sure why I was so afraid, it's not like I was ever afraid of being different in any other way, but I was. I hope that as we go forward there will be fewer and fewer people who feel like I did.

Extra Info

What name would you like to go under for this book? Full name, first name, or alias?

Kali.

What country do you live in?

Canada.

What age are you specifically? Or what decade age range are you – 20, 30. 40s?

24.

What nationality and ethnicity are you?

Canadian – Caucasian.

31. Ari's Story

When did you first discover you are asexual?

I first started to question my sexuality around the time I turned sixteen. I was trying to figure of if I was bisexual, because I was in love with a girl but didn't want to have sex with her. I hadn't thought over the idea that I didn't want to have sex with boys either yet. I'd dated a few boys because I didn't know how to turn them down and each time I just thought it was that specific boy I wasn't sexually interested in, not sex in general. I eventually took everyone's word for it that I was just a "late bloomer" and concluded I had more important things to worry about. By the time I turned seventeen I felt entirely confirmed in my suspicion that regardless of what adults said, I was never going to hit that part of puberty any day now. I was eighteen or nineteen when I first heard the label "asexual."

How did you discover you are asexual?

I saw the term described somewhere on the Internet, not AVEN itself. I instantly connected with it. It was this feeling of; "Oh, here are words to more elegantly and efficiently explain the concepts I figured out about myself when I was sixteen."

How do you identify yourself asexually?

Asexual biromantic.

Are you 'out' about being asexual? If not, why not? If you are out, whom to, and how did they react?

I'm out to people who follow me on Tumblr, which is mostly my Internet friends, but a few people I know offline. My offline friends have never commented on it, and I'm perfectly happy with that state of affairs. The only other person who gets to have an opinion on the subject is my significant other... My current partner presumably knows from reading my Tumblr, but we've never talked about it. I'm too embarrassed to bring it up directly, and he's never pushed me for sex in the few months of our long-distance relationship.

I'm definitely not out to my parents. They complain all the time about me not being married and providing them grandkids. They can at least comfort themselves with the thought I date and don't tell them about it, or maybe they suspect I'm keeping it a secret because I'm gay. They'd be awful if I tried to convince them asexuality is a legitimate sexual orientation. It would be all, "We just want you to be happy and not alone and destitute in your old age" and "Can't you try even if someone isn't absolutely perfect?"

What's your deepest fear, concern or worry, about being asexual?

I worry that my asexuality will make me incompatible with someone I want to be dating. They'll like me as a friend, but eventually they'll want a sex partner and I won't be willing/able to be that for them, so we'll drift apart and they'll break up with me. Or that I'll try to force myself to try out sex to make my partner happy and have a panic attack and hurt them in my need to get away.

Why do you feel, in general, that society doesn't accept asexuality as a form of sexual orientation in its own right? And what can be done about this?

I'm not sure. I get the impression most people really want to be having sex, and while they can vaguely understand some people want to have sex with different people than they do, or the "wrong" people; not being interested in having sex as a general statement is totally outside their experiences. Plus the social pressure that there must always be a romantic subplot, that a person isn't a real adult until they're having sex and in a relationship.

What can be done about it? Again, I don't know. Representation would help. Showing people we exist and it's just a way some people are and it's not these various negative stereotypes. Even within the LGBT community, I know a lot of people haven't heard of asexuality. Showing people that there are asexuals who remained asexual their entire lives and were happy and fulfilled anyway.

What's your view on love? Have you been in love before?

I'm not aro. I fall in love. Love is... really nice. Love is caring for someone more than yourself, wanting to protect them but also wanting them to go out there and grow as a person, being there for them in any way you can, enjoying your time together, thinking of them at random moments even when you're apart.

I've been in love four times in my life so far. I've always been good about differentiating a momentary crush from genuinely being in love. I don't think of myself as ever really falling out of love, we just move apart, don't see each other anymore or keep up a long-distance thing, and I accept I have to move on even if we never quite had the closure of breaking up. Falling in love with someone has never made me develop a sexual interest in them, which was confusing at first, but I've definitely been in love.

Are you currently in a relationship, and if so, is it with another asexual (if yes, do they identify the same as you or how do they identify), or is it a sexual person? And how is either working out?

Currently in a relationship, for the last four months. My boyfriend isn't asexual, as far as I know. It's working out well. I like hanging out with him and talking and taking time aside to spend together. I'd like to live closer to him instead of usually talking over the Internet and hope to move to the same city when I need a new job in a few months. But I do worry having a long-distance relationship has allowed us to push off talking about sexual issues. I'm entirely happy with how things are now and don't want anything else/more. He does like things like cuddling more than I do, though he doesn't push past what I'm comfortable with, and presumably would like a more physical relationship at some point. I don't know how that will work out.

If you are not in a relationship, would you like to be in one and if so, why, and what type of relationship – romantic? Platonic? What would your ideal relationship look like? And would you be in a relationship with a sexual person or not, and reason why?

My ideal relationship would be with another asexual person, but I like my boyfriend.

What is your view about sex? Have you had sex before and if so, how did it make you feel? If you haven't, would you?

Sex is perfectly fine for other people, I suppose, but I don't want to have it or hear about it. I've never had sex or done much more than kissing with anyone. I would consider trying sex with my partner if they wanted to, but I can't say I find it very appealing. It sounds messy, uncomfortable, and involving physical contact. Even non-sexual, benign physical contact sets off my fight-or-flight response bad.

In previous relationships, the people I've liked haven't been that attracted to me sexually. A couple of people I dated because I didn't know how to turn them down, I barely tolerated them while at arm's length, and refused any attempts at physicality with extreme prejudice. I was totally uninterested in popularity in junior high and high school, so I never felt any urge to look sexy or to date to gain social approval. I was much older before I ever entertained the thought something might be "wrong" with me, because something was so clearly wrong with everyone else. I have very little sex drive too; so sexual arousal was never very intrusive in my life.

Do you believe if a sexual person had a relationship with an asexual, it can work? And what do you think about it being fair or not?

I like to think it can. I don't have a lot of asexual friends or role models to point to such a relationship, but I hope so. I think it would come down to if the people could find a compromise to their mutual satisfaction. Is the asexual person willing to occasionally have sex with their partner? Is the sexual person willing to accept never having sex with their partner? I don't think it's a matter of fairness, (that sounds like blaming the ace person for maliciously denying their long-suffering partner the sex they deserve) but compatibility. If a sexual person really wants a sexual partner as well as a romantic partner and the asexual person isn't comfortable with sexuality, then they should break up. It's not a matter of whose at fault; it's just incompatible orientation.

Asexuality is the lack of sexual attraction, as an asexual, what does this mean to you?

I think of it as a lack of interest in having sex with someone else primarily. I also tend to associate it with a lack of interest in having sex as a general statement and the whole subject of sex.

I'm uncomfortable with some of the definitions I see of asexuality. I see they try to be inclusive of everyone in a very broad range of "asexual spectrum." Because I feel they're so wide, they're grouping in people who have nothing to do with me and sound like exactly the opposite of me. I generally think of asexuals as not being interested in seeking out sex, not lusting after particular people, and not finding sex more compelling than "yeah, that was fun" if they have it.

Do you believe sexual attraction and sexual desire are the same thing or different?

I don't differentiate between those two terms.

Do you think sexual arousal and sexual attraction are the same or different?

Sexual arousal I think of more as having a sex drive, and sexual attraction as wanting to have sex with a given person. I think of the former as more of a hormonal thing that happens at random moments for no particular reason, and feel it in a way that's completely detached from the latter.

What's your view on living with someone?

I like living alone. I like privacy and space and being able to take time to myself whenever I need it and not being answerable to anyone around the house. I don't get lonely. On the other hand, I enjoyed living with the handful of good roommates I had in college and would consider doing so again.

Would you like kids and if so how many? And how do you hope to conceive these? If you already have kids, did you know before you had them that you are asexual and how did that impact your life?

I don't have kids and don't want them. I think you should really, really want kids to have them, because of how much of your life will need to center around them for the next eighteen years at least. If I ever changed my mind about wanting them, hopefully I'd have a girlfriend who wanted to give birth to them with a sperm donor, because I still wouldn't want to be pregnant. Or adoption, but I hear that's prohibitively difficult and expensive.

What's your view on marriage? And if you were to get married, would it need to be with another asexual?

I think there's too much emphasis on marriage as this special state that gets all these special rights and privileges other interpersonal relationships don't. Someone must be a spouse or a blood/adopted relative to have their relationship with you acknowledge by law. I'm in favor of marriage equality certainly, but in the long-term I'd rather society not put such an emphasis on marriage as the source of legitimacy or a sexual relationship as automatically the most important one in someone's life, in favor of acknowledging the importance of friends and families of choice in people's lives.

What's your view on nudity? On porn? On masturbation? On BDSM and kinks?

I don't have the strongest opinions of these subjects. I guess people can do what they want? Not of much interest to me. Most of what I know about porn videos is from arguments in the feminist community; I skim over about them. I do read and write explicit fanfiction sometimes, but I consider it more of a literary form than something that turns me on that often.

I have friends who are into BDSM or other kinks, but I'm not, so I have no opinion beyond "it's fine for them."

I don't believe in criticizing other people's clothing choices on principle, but I've usually been conservative in showing skin. Being asexual, I had an urge to avoid being seen as a potential sex partner by my peers. As I put it as a teenager, "as a sexually available female of the species," better to pre-emptively warn them off with my dress and mannerisms than go through the trouble of reacting to unwanted attention. In non-sexual situations where nudity is socially appropriate (ex. communal bathing facilities, helping each other into theater costumes), I'm totally indifferent to it.

Masturbation? Yeah, I do that once or twice a month when my sex drive remembers it exists. It's perfectly nice but not that interesting, as activities go.

How difficult is it for you to be asexual, in a sexualized world?

A metaphor I have to describe the experience: Imagine all your friends are really into table tennis. That's pretty strange, but okay. People keep urging you to play table tennis. You tried it a few times and it was fun, in the way moderate physical activity generally is, but you don't see what the big deal was and personally you found it less fun than a game of soccer. Yet, for some reason, the people around you have decided to base their lives around this. I need a table tennis partner. This movie needs to pause the actual plot so two characters who just met can play a game of table tennis. I have to put my table tennis partner first, above all my other friends and family. I'm going to be infatuated with some awful person because the table tennis game is so good. I'm going to move in with and raise children with my favorite person to play table tennis with. I'm going to base my political and voting decisions around regulating who can play professional table tennis together, even in leagues I'm not in. That's how other people's obsession with sex feels to me.

Can you tell me about a time when you have had to deal with intrusive questions or a difficult situation due to your asexuality, and what happened?

Hasn't really happened to me. I almost never talk about my asexuality and the few people who know have never asked questions about it. I've dated very few people, mostly for short periods of time, so things haven't gotten "difficult" with regard to sexual situations.

What are the positives about being asexual?

I like not wasting a lot of time thinking about sex, like other people seem to constantly. I'm glad I didn't spend my teens making bad decisions in a lust-driven haze. I've enjoyed some of the relationships I've been in, but I've never felt sad or incomplete on account of not being in one when I'm not, something I see my friends complain about. I'm at low risk of STIs and pregnancy from all that sex I'm nothaving.

I like falling into relationships with straight women where they can call me their boyfriend without worrying about things being "too gay" if we had sex, as a trans guy. I like not having to worry about seeking a partner who would both accept my gender and be sexually attracted to me and my genital configuration, from the straight or LGBT community.

If you could have one wish about being asexual, what would it be and why?

I would like asexuality to be something everyone had heard of and took for granted as something some people are.

If you were to look back at your life, what advice would you have given a younger version of yourself in regard to asexuality?

Love doesn't mean wanting to have sex with someone. Remember what's important.

What advice would you give to others who are just discovering about asexuality and considering whether they are or not?

There isn't a right or wrong way to be. Maybe you're asexual. Maybe you're kind of asexual with some twists. Maybe you're not. Labels are useful to communicate with others, but you should never change yourself to fit them. If you're not interested in having sex in general, or with a specific person, then never feel obligated to go further than you feel comfortable with, whether you end up deciding you're asexual or not. If you decide you do want to have sex with someone, do what makes you happy. If you still feel asexual afterwards, then you do. If you don't, then you can change the words you use. Either way you know more about yourself than you did before.

Do you have a story you would like to share or anything else you would like to say?

Thanks for doing this!

Extra Info

What name would you like to go under for this book? Full name, first name, or alias?

Ari.

What country do you live in?

United States.

What age are you specifically? Or what decade age range are you – 20, 30. 40s?

26.

What nationality and ethnicity are you?

Caucasian, Jewish.

Links to your website/social media.

http://a-lion-in-summer.tumblr.com/

32. Jen Mullen's Story

When did you first discover you are asexual?

2014. I was 19, almost 20.

How did you discover you are asexual?

I was watching porn and thought to myself, I hope I marry an asexual so I don't have to do any of that. It hit me about a week later.

How do you identify yourself asexually?

Aromantic Asexual.

Are you 'out' about being asexual? If not, why not? If you are out, whom to, and how did they react?

Mostly everyone. Haven't bothered with my co-workers because it hasn't ever come up. My friends are all cool with it, if occasionally confused. My parents steadfastly ignore it. My 13 year old sister said, "That's weird. You're like a toaster." And then ran away and I never did get an explanation.

What's your deepest fear, concern or worry, about being asexual?

I don't worry much about being ace. I guess in the back of my mind I know that corrective rape against asexuals is a thing but at this point in my life I'm not often in a place that could occur. Being aromantic, I worry that all of my friends will get significant others and leave me behind.

Why do you feel, in general, that society doesn't accept asexuality as a form of sexual orientation in its own right? And what can be done about this?

People are so obsessed with sex, especially LGBT people because so much of LGBT is about who you have sex with. I think some people put too much stock in their sex lives and when they see people who can be completely happy without that, they feel threatened because they think that their relationships have to have sex to be fulfilling. Maybe they worry that if their sexual prowess fades their lover will leave, while people who are in a relationship for romance don't have that worry as much.

What's your view on love? Have you been in love before?

I'm aromantic, so I don't think I've ever been "in love" as most people would put it. I have a very very close friend, also ace, and he knows that I'm aro/ace and I know he's panromantic and will probably get a significant other some day and we both know we are platonic friends and nothing more. But when we get the chance to be together (we live in different states), we cuddle and share a bed and hold hands and are generally affectionate.

Are you currently in a relationship, and if so, is it with another asexual (if yes, do they identify the same as you or how do they identify), or is it a sexual person? And how is either working out?

For a while the friend I previously mentioned and I were sort of in a queer-platonic relationship, but at this time he doesn't want to be in any sort of relationship because of an abusive ex. So for now we are just best friends and I'm ok with that because I respect him.

If you are not in a relationship, would you like to be in one and if so, why, and what type of relationship – romantic? Platonic? What would your ideal relationship look like? And would you be in a relationship with a sexual person or not, and reason why?

I would very much like to be in an official queer-platonic relationship with my best friend, but he's healing from an abusive relationship and the entire concept of relationships makes him uncomfortable right now. So right now I'm just hopeful for the future but I'm not going to push him.

What is your view about sex? Have you had sex before and if so, how did it make you feel? If you haven't, would you?

I'm sex repulsed. I've never had sex and never will. The entire concept grosses me out and if I can go my entire life without ever encountering a person's genitals in real life I will be very happy.

Do you believe if a sexual person had a relationship with an asexual, it can work? And what do you think about it being fair or not?

An allosexual and an asexual can have a relationship but it's best if they enter the relationship with the knowledge of whether or not they will be having sex. I knew an ace who realized he was ace while in a relationship and his girlfriend was rather unhappy and frequently tried to get him to do sexual stuff with her anyway. They ended up breaking up. As long as they both enter the relationship without conflicting expectations I think it's fair.

Asexuality is the lack of sexual attraction, as an asexual, what does this mean to you?

I've never looked at a person and thought that I wanted to have sex with them. The idea always grossed me out. I was honestly kind of shocked to realize that people can look at a total stranger and want to be sexual with them.

Do you believe sexual attraction and sexual desire are the same thing or different, please explain?

I think they're different. I think there are cases where asexuals who are sex positive or neutral and who have a partner who wants to have sex, may experience sexual desire. They might not be attracted to that person, but they could still desire to have sex with that partner.

Do you think sexual arousal and sexual attraction are the same or different, please explain?

I see sexual arousal as a physical occurrence, while attraction is mental. For example, a person with a penis might still get an erection, especially when it is stimulated, regardless of who may be nearby.

What's your view on living with someone?

I would be perfectly happy to live with my best friend my entire life, though I'm afraid it won't happen. He will probably end up married, but in truth I would be ok marrying him and living with him, not because of romance but because we care about each other a lot and being married might be more financially beneficial.

Would you like kids and if so how many? And how do you hope to conceive these? If you already have kids, did you know before you had them that you are asexual and how did that impact your life?

I've been saying my entire life I didn't want kids, and realizing that I'm asexual cemented that even further. I really don't like kids.

What's your view on marriage? And if you were to get married, would it need to be with another asexual?

Like I said before, if I get married, it will be for convenience, nothing more. That said, I'm not opposed to being married or single.

What's your view on nudity? On porn? On masturbation? On BDSM and kinks?

Nudity doesn't bother me unless it's directed at me and I've been fortunate enough to avoid that.

Porn just sort of confuses me.

Sometimes I masturbate because it helps me sleep, but it gets boring really quickly and I don't fantasize about anyone.

I'm not personally into BDSM or any kinky things but as long as the people who are doing that are consenting adults and not trying to involve me, I fully support them.

How difficult is it for you to be asexual, in a sexualized world?

It's annoying. I hate sex scenes in movies. It just seems really unnecessary, and especially in the theater I get kind of uncomfortable watching it next to people.

Can you tell me about a time when you have had to deal with intrusive questions or a difficult situation due to your asexuality, and what happened?

I've had friends get really confused because they really like sex. They weren't rude about it just super confused and it was hard to explain. I've had people complain about me saying that the A in LGBTQIA isn't for allies. It's caused a couple of arguments, but I still stand by it.

What are the positives about being asexual?

I never have to worry about STD's, no pregnancy scares, no concern of being in a relationship and one of us cheating because I wouldn't want to do that. Even if I did end up in a relationship it wouldn't be with someone that's so desperate for sex that they would cheat.

If you could have one wish about being asexual, what would it be and why?

I just want allies to stop trying to claim the A. The whole point of LGBT is that we aren't straight. Don't get me wrong, allies are great, I just want them to stop trying to pretend they're more important than an entire orientation. And technically the A can be for asexual, aromantic, agender and androgynous, so there's not really any more room to share. I feel that allies get enough attention, and it's time to put focus on actual LGBT+ people.

I think the A should stand for all the identities that are actually queer, asexual, aromantic, agender, androgynous. I guess one reason other than it feels wrong to include allies is that saying LGBT+ is a way of differentiating us from straight allies, so I would much rather say LGBT and allies rather than include them in the acronym itself

If you were to look back at your life, what advice would you have given a younger version of yourself in regard to asexuality?

I guess I wish I had come to understand the entirety of LGBT more. I was raised to be super homophobic and I wish I had changed sooner.

What advice would you give to others who are just discovering about asexuality and considering whether they are or not?

It's pretty common to think you might be demisexual before you land at asexual, don't stress on it. Identity and sexuality can be fluid; don't let anyone give you trouble because you said something before and realized you found something that fits better now.

Do you have a story you would like to share or anything else you would like to say?

I performed this poem at an event at my college last year. There are still a couple of people giving me trouble for it.

http://watcherofeternalflame.tumblr.com/post/ 113233124876/ dear-a-is-for-ally-let-me-tell-you-a-thing- because

Extra Info

What name would you like to go under for this book? Full name, first name, or alias?

Jenn Mullen. I don't think there's a spot for gender, but I'm genderqueer, they/them not she/her thanks!

What country do you live in?

USA.

What age are you specifically? Or what decade age range are you – 20, 30. 40s?

21.

What nationality and ethnicity are you?

American White.

Links to your website/social media.

http://jenn-mullen.tumblr.com/

http://www.jennmullen.com/

http://watcherofeternalflame.tumblr.com/

33. Stephen Smith's Story

When did you first discover you are asexual?

When I was 22, just before turning 23.

How did you discover you are asexual?

I was very depressed and suicidal after loosing my virginity.

How do you identify yourself asexually?

Asexual. I don't like kissing, hugging, or sex.

Are you 'out' about being asexual? If not, why not? If you are out, whom to, and how did they react?

I don't brag about it but when people start talking about their own sexual agenda I let them know and it's usually a big turn off.

What's your deepest fear, concern or worry, about being asexual?

Being alone.

Why do you feel, in general, that society doesn't accept asexuality as a form of sexual orientation in its own right? And what can be done about this?

Society is unsure without sex or feeling sexy.

What's your view on love? Have you been in love before?

Yes, I've been in love a few times but rejected very quickly for lack of sexual interest.

Are you currently in a relationship, and if so, is it with another asexual (if yes, do they identify the same as you or how do they identify), or is it a sexual person? And how is either working out?

Yes, it's a wonderful relationship. Very little kissing and even a little sex; I do what I have to do to keep the relationship.

If I enjoy being with her I do whatever it takes to make her happy but I try not to think about it.

What is your view about sex? Have you had sex before and if so, how did it make you feel? If you haven't, would you?

I just try to avoid it. I can feel attracted to someone's personality while avoiding contact.

Do you believe if a sexual person had a relationship with an asexual, it can work? And what do you think about it being fair or not?

Yes I believe it can work. But the other half does not believe it can work. Therefore I get dumped very quickly.

What's your view on living with someone?

Sharing a house is a wonderful thing.

Would you like kids and if so how many? And how do you hope to conceive these? If you already have kids, did you know before you had them that you are asexual and how did that impact your life?

I see no future for young people coming into this world; it gets worse every day. I do not want to bring up a child in this day and age.

What's your view on marriage? And if you were to get married, would it need to be with another asexual?

Marriage is great if you can find the right person; it's about sharing your life not about sex.

What's your view on nudity? On porn? On masturbation? On BDSM and kinks?

Nudity doesn't bother me. Porn is gross. Masturbation is equal to excrement.

How difficult is it for you to be asexual, in a sexualized world?

Used to be very difficult, but now I have a great relationship and life is much easier.

Can you tell me about a time when you have had to deal with intrusive questions or a difficult situation due to your asexuality, and what happened?

Yes, it was my first day on the job and a lesbian asked me are you straight or are you gay? I said, "Neither; I'm asexual." She answered "But you're not giving it a chance!!!" I felt I was shut out of everything the rest of the time I was at that job.

What are the positives about being asexual?

I never thought of anything positive or negative about it, it's just who I am.

If you could have one wish about being asexual, what would it be and why?

Wish it didn't exist.

If you were to look back at your life, what advice would you have given a younger version of yourself in regard to asexuality?

Don't try and fit in with the popular crowd, be who you are, not who you think you want to be.

What advice would you give to others who are just discovering about asexuality and considering whether they are or not?

The same advice, also isolate yourself in reading books and poetry.

Extra Info

What name would you like to go under for this book? Full name, first name, or alias?

Stephen Smith, nicknamed Smitty.

What age are you specifically? Or what decade age range are you – 20, 30. 40s?

I just turned 51.

I survived the 80's and 90's.

What nationality and ethnicity are you?

White.

34. Thylacine's Story

When did you first discover you are asexual?

About 15 years ago.

How did you discover you are asexual?

Asexuality was never discussed when I was a kid, so we pretty much never knew it existed. We just knew, growing up, that most people were 'like normal' and some people were 'like gay.' This was a long time ago when people didn't dare admit to being different. When I was around 12-13-14, I noticed other girls suddenly going crazy about boys, then all this sudden jealousy crap, friendships fell apart, all kinds of stuff going on... I didn't know what was wrong with people... time went on... girls "got in trouble," they had to get married, I went to college... I got jobs... people in the workplace all hooking up, having affairs, all sorts of nonsense... still acting jealous and competitive, acting like teenage kids while in their 30's... sheesh...! Anyway, I still could not figure out what was wrong with people. I thought everyone around me was crazy. Finally I read an article in the newspaper, (an actual newspaper, in print, this was before everyone is online 24/7), about asexuality... I said to myself, "Oh, that's it. That's what's wrong with everyone! They all have a sex drive and I don't!"

How do you identify yourself asexually?

Aromantic, just want to be friends with people, that's it.

Are you 'out' about being asexual? If not, why not? If you are out, whom to, and how did they react?

Not to very many people, really. A lot of people in my area are sort of "Archie Bunker" types; anything different is wrong, evil, and scary to them. I told my mother, and told my martial arts instructor because, well, funny story... I left one martial arts school because there was a lesbian who was angry with me for ignoring her, or actually, I just wanted to be friends, and I came to the new school and the Master got me alone and asked the real reason I left the old place... he was like, "Well, if you're not interested in other women, then why aren't you married, you're so pretty?" So I told him. He was so accepting about it. He never heard of it before. I respected him so much more for being open-minded about it. But I don't tell many people. I felt comfortable telling the martial arts instructor because he is of an ethnic background and he would understand the damages of bigotry in society.

What's your deepest fear, concern or worry, about being asexual?

People's prejudices about being different, I guess. It's sad. Some people think you're "sick," or worse, that you're just a loser who can't get a date. Hey, I've turned down marriage proposals, so I'm not someone who can't get a date.

Why do you feel, in general, that society doesn't accept asexuality as a form of sexual orientation in its own right? And what can be done about this?

Probably because the vast majority has this constant 'need' they have trouble managing that leads them into jealousy, adultery, and all that. If you look around you, you will see the effect it has on people's lives, they end up in divorce and all that. Very often, guys abandoned their pregnant girlfriends, because they had sex and then won't face their responsibilities. Sorry to sound old fashioned, but it makes a mess! It has such a hold on people, they see someone who doesn't have this problem, and they are like, 'Naw, that can't be real!'

What's your view on love? Have you been in love before?

We are capable of love, every kind of love, but myself, I have never "fallen in love." I love my family, I love my friends, I love my cats... romantic love is just something that's not in me I guess.

Are you currently in a relationship, and if so, is it with another asexual (if yes, do they identify the same as you or how do they identify), or is it a sexual person? And how is either working out?

I have friends who are asexual, but we're just friends. All my friends are just friends.

If you are not in a relationship, would you like to be in one and if so, why, and what type of relationship – romantic? Platonic? What would your ideal relationship look like? And would you be in a relationship with a sexual person or not, and reason why?

I'm not in a traditional romantic relationship. I tend to maintain good loyal friendships with people.

What is your view about sex? Have you had sex before and if so, how did it make you feel? If you haven't, would you?

It's never interested me, really. People have tried to 'make me,' but I've never been interested. No one attempted to force themselves on me physically, but there is always verbal harassment or emotional manipulation. I'm a quiet person, but no one realizes how damn stubborn I can be, and if I don't want to do something, I'm not going to do it. That's that.

Do you believe if a sexual person had a relationship with an asexual, it can work? And what do you think about it being fair or not?

I'm really not sure. I think the sexual person might feel frustrated, or unhappy. I'm not sure if it's fair or not. So, I'm not sure if I can answer that one.

Asexuality is the lack of sexual attraction, as an asexual, what does this mean to you?

Well, here is an example. I'm walking down the street with a friend. We see a guy walk down the other side of the street. My friend goes, "Oh my God, oh my God, isn't he hot?" "Nope." My friend will say, "Oh my God, what is wrong with you?"

Do you believe sexual attraction and sexual desire are the same thing or different?

I don't experience either, so... my guess would be they are the same thing.

Do you think sexual arousal and sexual attraction are the same or different?

Probably not, because some people experience arousal 'on their own,' or so they say.

What's your view on living with someone?

I'm old fashioned; I think people should be married first, but that's me. People will do what they want.

Would you like kids and if so how many? And how do you hope to conceive these? If you already have kids, did you know before you had them that you are asexual and how did that impact your life?

Maybe some day I would adopt. I hope I could be a good parent, even though I'm ace. The kids will ask me to explain the 'birds and the bees.' "Well, kids, you see, birds fly, and bees make honey! And that's the birds and the bees for you. Now go read your biology textbook that you got in school."

What's your view on marriage? And if you were to get married, would it need to be with another asexual?

I think that for marriage to work, people have to have a lot in common and have similar personality types and similar wants and needs. I'm not sure if "mixed marriages" can work. I'm glad

I didn't get married, really. I'm sure I'd end up divorced. I was asked to marry at age 19. I'm glad I turned him down.

What's your view on nudity? On porn? On masturbation? On BDSM and kinks?

I think it exploits women. I'm a feminist, but the old fashioned kind of feminist that does not agree with anything that exploits women or children. I'm not against people enjoying themselves, but to exploit others, some of it is sick, quite frankly.

How difficult is it for you to be asexual, in a sexualized world?

Just ignore the vulgar TV shows, read a book, live my own life; let other people do their own thing.

Can you tell me about a time when you have had to deal with intrusive questions or a difficult situation due to your asexuality, and what happened?

Well, I change the subject; say I'm not interested; I'm too busy, etc. Sometimes it's hard. Try to redirect a conversation.

What are the positives about being asexual?

I think we have more freedom, certainly. Other people are driven to pursue sex, then they are driven to reproduce, they are in this endless cycle, pursue, break-up, pursue, break-up, and then pay child support.

If you could have one wish about being asexual, what would it be and why?

I wish the world knew we existed; that we were more accepted.

If you were to look back at your life, what advice would you have given a younger version of yourself in regard to asexuality?

Don't listen to other people, let them make their mistakes; live your life, let them live their lives. If they get in trouble, it can't be helped. You can't save other people; they make their own lives.

What advice would you give to others who are just discovering about asexuality and considering whether they are or not?

Young people today are so much luckier than when I was growing up; back then you just couldn't be yourself, man! Now you see guys walking down the street wearing a dress. Yup. Kids today are lucky. We didn't have that kind of freedom. We didn't.

Do you have a story you would like to share or anything else you would like to say?

I'm glad that people are beginning to realize now that we exist. I look forward to a future when I can say the A word and not have to listen to disbelief or immature comments. And believe me, people can be very immature, even so called adults.

Extra Info

What name would you like to go under for this book? Full name, first name, or alias?

I use the name "Thylacine" while on Aven.

What country do you live in?

I live in the U. S. of A., in Massachusetts.

What age are you specifically? Or what decade age range are you – 20, 30. 40s?

I am slightly over 50. I look young for my age, probably because I don't have a husband or kids.

What nationality and ethnicity are you?

Mostly white, with some Native American.

35. Thomas's Story

When did you first discover you are asexual?

I discovered I was asexual around five years ago.

How did you discover you are asexual?

After changing my medication, I noticed that the idea of sex was no longer appealing to me. I began seeking more meaning in my relationships than just sex.

How do you identify yourself asexually?

I identify myself as a heteroromantic asexual.

Are you 'out' about being asexual? If not, why not? If you are out, whom to, and how did they react?

I am currently 'out' as an asexual. The first person I told was my ex-wife and brother-in-law. While they did not understand at first, they were ultimately very supportive.

What's your deepest fear, concern or worry, about being asexual?

My worst fear is that people will not understand what asexuality means, and say that I'm this way simply because I 'can't get laid' or that they'll think I'm just being snobbish.

Why do you feel, in general, that society doesn't accept asexuality as a form of sexual orientation in its own right? And what can be done about this?

On an academic level, I believe they don't accept asexuality as a sexual orientation because, by definition, asexuality is a lack of sexual preference. All that can be done to change this is to redefine what a sexual preference is and allow the word 'none' to be added to the definition.

What's your view on love? Have you been in love before?

If there is one thing I've always believed in, it is the power of love. Yes, I have been in love before, and have even been married. I just happen to find more happiness with a good friend than I would with a sexual partner.

Are you currently in a relationship, and if so, is it with another asexual (if yes, do they identify the same as you or how do they identify), or is it a sexual person? And how is either working out?

As of right now, I am single.

If you are not in a relationship, would you like to be in one and if so, why, and what type of relationship – romantic? Platonic? What would your ideal relationship look like? And would you be in a relationship with a sexual person or not, and reason why?

As of right now, I am not actively seeking a romantic relationship. I am working on building my 'social network' of friends and finding fulfillment that way. My ideal friend, however, would be someone that I could discuss various topics with that never doesn't understand what I'm talking about, and vice versa. I would never be in a relationship with a sexual person, as their goals and mine would be too vastly different.

What is your view about sex? Have you had sex before and if so, how did it make you feel? If you haven't, would you?

I believe sex serves its purpose in our modern society, without it there would never be reproduction and, eventually, our society as a whole, would disappear from the face of the earth. I've had sex before, when my ex-wife and I were trying to get pregnant, and it made me feel like I was performing an important service to my wife and our unborn child.

Do you believe if a sexual person had a relationship with an asexual, it can work? And what do you think about it being fair or not?

As long as there is a mutual respect between the two, then anyone can make a relationship work. It might not seem fair on the surface but, if there is more to the relationship than just sex, a compromise could be reached.

Asexuality is the lack of sexual attraction, as an asexual, what does this mean to you?

To me, the lack of sexual attraction means being unencumbered by the primal instincts that drive so many to bad partners, as sex eventually takes over their whole relationship. And, once that sexual attraction is gone, the relationship begins to suffer as well. A lack of sexual attraction means that, instead of going off on the primal 'urge to merge', an asexual can focus on the truly important aspects of the relationship.

Do you believe sexual attraction and sexual desire are the same thing or different?

I believe there is a major difference between sexual attraction and sexual desire. Attraction, in my opinion, is the simple act of finding someone "sexy", although there are no physical reactions to the person. Sexual desire, on the other hand, is the act of wanting to have sex with a particular person, in which a physical reaction is found.

Do you think sexual arousal and sexual attraction are the same or different?

Sexual arousal, while different from sexual attraction, does share characteristics with sexual desire. Both indicate a hormonal need to procreate, which most asexuals, either by choice or by biology, lack.

What's your view on living with someone?

I believe it is almost a necessity in our modern times. Even if there is not sexual attraction between the people living together, they still provide a strong companionship that is hard to find in most relationships.

Would you like kids and if so how many? And how do you hope to conceive these? If you already have kids, did you know before you had them that you are asexual and how did that impact your life?

At one time, I believed I wanted kids. After a failed attempt, I had learned of my asexuality and had 'given up the ghost' on the whole thing.

What's your view on marriage? And if you were to get married, would it need to be with another asexual?

I view marriage as a sacred institution that is not to be taken lightly. I've been married previously to a sexual person, and she and I remain great friends even after separation. I do not plan to get remarried, so it wouldn't matter if they were asexual or not.

What's your view on nudity? On porn? On masturbation? On BDSM and kinks?

I believe that, if you must use these things to market your product, your product must not be very good. I believe that there is more to life than simply the next 'physical high'.

How difficult is it for you to be asexual, in a sexualized world?

Extremely. Any time I mention to someone that I'm asexual, they give me a funny look as if they have no idea what I'm talking about. Then, when I explain it, they make rude comments about me being unable to 'get laid'.

Can you tell me about a time when you have had to deal with intrusive questions or a difficult situation due to your asexuality, and what happened?

Fortunately, I've yet to be put in any kind of difficult situation, as I view most 'questioning' as a chance to educate the public about my asexuality.

What are the positives about being asexual?

The positive to being asexual is that you can be friends with just about anyone, without being encumbered by carnal desires.

If you could have one wish about being asexual, what would it be and why?

I wish there were more role models out there for asexual people. Much like the homosexual movement, it would be nice if there were a public face for asexuality.

If you were to look back at your life, what advice would you have given a younger version of yourself in regard to asexuality?

I would tell myself to embrace it and not fight it. I would tell myself there is nothing wrong with not wanting sexual contact and that society is wrong in its view of sexuality.

What advice would you give to others who are just discovering about asexuality and considering whether they are or not?

I would tell them that they are in no hurry to come to a decision. Learn everything you can about asexuality, and see what makes sense to you. Don't listen to the people around you, for you know yourself better than they do.

Extra Info

What name would you like to go under for this book? Full name, first name, or alias?

Thomas.

What country do you live in?

United States.

What age are you specifically? Or what decade age range are you – 20, 30. 40s?

33.

What nationality and ethnicity are you?

I'm German Irish, and I am white.

36. Marnie's Story

When did you first discover you are asexual?

About a month ago.

How did you discover you are asexual?

My husband showed me a documentary about being asexual.

How do you identify yourself asexually?

I am a mid-aged romantic asexual.

Are you 'out' about being asexual? If not, why not? If you are out, whom to, and how did they react?

I am out to my family, but do not talk to others. They were just fine with it. Encouraged by my openness.

What's your deepest fear, concern or worry, about being asexual?

That I will never get my sex drive back and that it will cause more problems in my marriage because he loves sex and I couldn't care less.

Why do you feel, in general, that society doesn't accept asexuality as a form of sexual orientation in its own right? And what can be done about this?

Most people think you have to be of a certain sexual orientation in order to fit in. The majority is fearful of being accepted for who they are. We need to stop judging and be who we are and accept others for themselves.

What's your view on love? Have you been in love before?

I am in love. Love is a feeling, a bond. It is like gravity, you are drawn to someone you want to be with. Not just a sexual longing, but a longing in your soul. Someone who makes you feel valued, respected and cared for.

Are you currently in a relationship, and if so, is it with another asexual (if yes, do they identify the same as you or how do they identify), or is it a sexual person? And how is either working out?

I have been married for 25 years to a sexual person. I was a sexual being for years, but all of a sudden, it was gone. No reason, no explanation. Here one day, gone the next. It took a major toll on our relationship for years until I found out I was asexual. Now we communicate on a much deeper level. We are taking it day by day, but it is working. Since he is such a sexual manly man, I have agreed to participate once a week, but I do not want to. He understands it is only for him.

What is your view about sex? Have you had sex before and if so, how did it make you feel? If you haven't, would you?

My view on sex now: I can live without it and prefer to. It really has no place in my life. I can and do have sex, but watch the clock and want to get it over with so I can get on with my day. I become anxious beforehand and would rather not. I can climax if I focus, but still couldn't care less about it.

Do you believe if a sexual person had a relationship with an asexual, it can work? And what do you think about it being fair or not?

I believe a relationship can be had by both, because I am in one. He felt it wasn't fair, not having sex, until we found out why. Now we are free to be ourselves and things are wonderful. It can work if you want it to!!

Asexuality is the lack of sexual attraction, as an asexual, what does this mean to you?

I find it refreshing, because so many people have had a lack of sexual attraction for years and just never knew it was a real thing. Like me, I am no longer alone. It means freedom to be who I am without worry or fear.

Do you believe sexual attraction and sexual desire are the same thing or different?

I think they are one and the same. Without sexual desire, we wouldn't be sexually attracted.

Do you think sexual arousal and sexual attraction are the same or different?

Different. You can be aroused by thoughts, but sexual attraction is being sexually attracted to someone.

What's your view on living with someone?

I think you can just live with someone without the whole marriage thing. I think you could just live with a friend, it doesn't have to be all that.

Would you like kids and if so how many? And how do you hope to conceive these? If you already have kids, did you know before you had them that you are asexual and how did that impact your life?

I have three, one of my own from a previous marriage and two stepchildren. I did not know I was asexual at the time, but now that I know, they know. I am always open and honest with my kids. Being asexual and knowing what it is, I would have still have had children.

What's your view on marriage? And if you were to get married, would it need to be with another asexual?

I was married before I knew I was asexual. I love being married. He is not asexual but he knows I am, and so we just have to work a bit harder on the sexual part of our marriage.

What's your view on nudity? On porn? On masturbation? On BDSM and kinks?

Whatever floats your boat. I have no need for any of that. I can walk around the house naked now without fear of being groped or having sexual comments flying around.

How difficult is it for you to be asexual, in a sexualized world?

It was the hardest thing before I knew I was asexual. I felt broken, like something was physically or mentally wrong with me. Now I am free to be myself and I don't care what anyone thinks.

Can you tell me about a time when you have had to deal with intrusive questions or a difficult situation due to your asexuality, and what happened?

Before I knew about asexuality, just talking about sex with my husband was so difficult. #1: I didn't like talking about it because it made me feel uncomfortable. #2: We constantly had the same argument over and over again about sex. #3: I couldn't explain what I didn't understand myself. #4: My husband felt I was looking outside our marriage for sexual companionship since I didn't want to have sex with him. And he was extremely jealous of every other man in my life because of it. #5: It created a bad situation for us because we pushed family and friends away so they wouldn't feel the tension in our relationship.

What are the positives about being asexual?

Well now there are no worries of my husband being jealous of other men. He knows that no matter how hard they try; I will never be sexually attracted to them.

If you could have one wish about being asexual, what would it be and why?

To feel better about my lack of sexual desire/attraction, because my husband deserves to be loved; to feel attractive and desired as well.

If you were to look back at your life, what advice would you have given a younger version of yourself in regard to asexuality?

It is okay to be who you are, never let anyone else determine your value or sexual orientation. Don't lose sight of your true self. People will love you anyway.

What advice would you give to others who are just discovering about asexuality and considering whether they are or not?

No matter what: just be yourself. Those who love you, will love you no matter what and those who waiver, don't matter. Do not fear your true self. Staying true to you makes you happier and attracts more happiness.

Do you have a story you would like to share or anything else you would like to say?

Thank you for all you are doing!! I appreciate you!!

Extra Info

What name would you like to go under for this book? Full name, first name, or alias?

Marnie.

What country do you live in?

USA.

What age are you specifically? Or what decade age range are you – 20, 30. 40s?

47.

What nationality and ethnicity are you?

Caucasian.

37. Henry's Story

When did you first discover you are asexual?

When I was fourteen.

How did you discover you are asexual?

I first started questioning my sexuality once some of my friends started dating each other in Middle School. I had always distanced romance from myself, seeing it most prominently in fictitious works, where it's greatly exaggerated. But when the people around me started getting involved, it made me wonder, 'Why am I not interested in this? Like, at all?' Unlike most asexuals, I actually knew the terms 'asexual' and 'aromantic' through Tumblr, before I ever started wondering about my sexuality, so once I did start noticing I was different, it was pretty easy to latch onto the label. It fitted me, so I identified with it.

How do you identify yourself asexually?

Aromantic asexual. If I was inclined to, I could probably find a few more specific labels that fit me, but it's *so* much easier to explain without the more specific stuff. And while some other labels may fit me better, I'm perfectly content with just ace and aro.

Are you 'out' about being asexual? If not, why not? If you are out, whom to, and how did they react?

Yes. I came out to my parents first, and later starting mentioning it whenever it was appropriate, or when the subject came up, to my friends. So far, no one has reacted negatively. I've gotten a few "Isn't that like a plant?" statements, but once I (or someone else in the room) explains the definition, the person has been like, "Oh, ok, sorry. Cool." And then the subject is dropped. Although, I don't exactly expect that track record to keep up.

What's your deepest fear, concern or worry about being asexual?

I don't really have any. I mean, there's the obvious fear of rejection based on it, but I already know that the people I care about don't/won't mind, and those that do, I don't care about. My sexuality is a part of me, and I'm secure with it.

Why do you feel, in general, that society doesn't accept asexuality as a form of sexual orientation in its own right? And what can be done about this?

Xenophobia, mostly. People who aren't particularly bright, or were raised in a certain way, are afraid and wary of anything that isn't like them. Most of their thought process is just, "You don't like sex? But I like sex! You must be lying/broken/a demon!" The fact that the media is positively obsessed with sex doesn't help, either.

As for what can be done about it, the most prominent issue is visibility. Most people don't even know that asexuals *exist*. This lack of knowledge means that when they do hear about it, their opinion is much more likely to be wrong and harmful.

What's your view on love? Have you been in love before?

I'm aromantic. That means I don't feel romantic attraction; however, one of the most common misconceptions about aromantic people is that they don't feel love. Have I ever been in love before? Well, no, not in the way most people would assume. But when people assume that aromantic or asexual people "can't feel love", it's hurtful and wrong. I love my family. I love my friends. I love myself. Any of that love is just as real, just as important, and just as painful to lose as romantic love.

Are you currently in a relationship, and if so, is it with another asexual (if yes, do they identify the same as you or how do they identify), or is it a sexual person? And how is either working out?

I am not currently in a relationship.

If you are not in a relationship, would you like to be in one and if so, why, and what type of relationship – romantic? Platonic? What would your ideal relationship look like? And would you be in a relationship with a sexual person or not, and reason why?

I have no interest in a sexual or romantic relationship with anyone, nor a queerplatonic relationship as some asexuals find fulfilling. However, I thrive on platonic relationships. I couldn't do without my friends.

What is your view about sex? Have you had sex before and if so, how did it make you feel? If you haven't, would you?

I have not had sex and do not want to have sex. The idea of doing that with another person is frankly repulsive to me.

Do you believe if a sexual person had a relationship with an asexual, it can work? And what do you think about it being fair or not?

Yes, I believe that kind of relationship can work. I've heard many stories of them working. However, I do think it's harder to pull off; a lot of sexual people would not want to have a relationship with an asexual, and I can respect their reasoning. As for it being 'fair', in my view, I don't see how that would matter at all. Both parties would have agreed to whatever compromise they made, and so both are going into the relationship willingly and knowing the terms. Well, unless the asexual person didn't tell their partner, which I consider to be rude and underhanded, and will probably cause the relationship to fail.

Asexuality is the lack of sexual attraction. As an asexual, what does this mean to you?

The lack of a cognitive and conscious desire for sexual intercourse with other people.

Do you believe sexual attraction and sexual desire are the same thing or different?

They are closely linked. Sexual desire is wanting to have sex in *general*, and sexual attraction is a feeling towards a *specific person* you want to have sex with. The two go hand in hand. Sexual attraction doesn't really exist without sexual desire, but one can have a want for partnered sex without a specific partner in mind.

Do you think sexual arousal and sexual attraction are the same or different?

They are most definitely different. Sexual arousal is a bodily function, while attraction is more of a want. You can feel arousal without any intention to act on it. In terms of asexuals, some experience arousal, some don't, some experience less than sexual people, and some experience it only under certain circumstances. Whichever one it is, it has no effect on one's sexuality.

What's your view on living with someone?

It would need to be a person with a very, very specific personality for me to actually want to live with them. The only real scenario I can imagine in which I live with someone is if I need financial help paying for an apartment or something down the line.

Would you like kids and if so how many? And how do you hope to conceive these? If you already have kids, did you know before you had them that you are asexual and how did that impact your life?

I hate kids. I would never do that to myself. Nope. Not happening.

What's your view on marriage? And if you were to get married, would it need to be with another asexual?

I have no interest in marriage.

What's your view on nudity? On porn? On masturbation? On BDSM and kinks?

The only interest I've ever had on nudity is pure curiosity as to what female genitalia looked like. I've never had sexual reasons for wanting that.

I find porn abhorrent. I would not watch porn unless I was paid at least twenty dollars an hour for it.

I occasionally masturbate. Unfortunately, even though I'm asexual, I still have a libido (street term equivalent = I get horny), despite not liking sex. Masturbation is an effective way to get my body to shut up.

There are a few kinks that arouse me, but I'm only interested in the kink itself, not sex with the kink. I'm pretty sure that's unusual for asexuals though.

How difficult is it for you to be asexual, in a sexualized world?

So far, it hasn't been that difficult. I do me; you do you. If roughly 99% of the population enjoys sex, it only makes sense that media would be sexualized. I feel that if asexual people were acknowledged, and the media didn't say that EVERYBODY NEEDS SEX! YOU NEED SEX! I NEED SEX! SEX, SEX, SEX! Then I wouldn't have any problems with oversexualization. Even now, I just let it pass me by for the most part.

Can you tell me about a time when you have had to deal with intrusive questions or a difficult situation due to your asexuality, and what happened?

No, I can't. I have purposefully not come out to people that would ask stupid questions, because I hate dealing with that @#$%.

What are the positives about being asexual?

The biggest one I can think of is 'less drama', although that's more of an aromantic thing. In terms of asexuality, well, it's always one less thing I have to worry about.

If you could have one wish about being asexual, what would it be and why?

For asexual visibility to be more widespread and asexuality to be more accepted. We aren't the people who need to change; it's the people who think that who do.

If you were to look back at your life, what advice would you have given a younger version of yourself in regard to asexuality?

I don't think I have any advice to give; past me handled it pretty well. I didn't worry about it too much when I was questioning. I didn't ever think I was 'broken', and so far, I haven't told anyone I shouldn't have.

What advice would you give to others who are just discovering about asexuality and considering whether they are or not?

Don't be in a rush to find out your identity, it'll come to you in time. Also, no matter what you finally decide you are, it's important to know that you're great the way you are and to be happy with yourself.

Extra Info

What name would you like to go under for this book? Full name, first name, or alias?

Henry.

What country do you live in?

USA.

38. Jo's Story

When did you first discover you are asexual?

I lost all interest in sex about age 30-35. Prior to that, I had been sexual at what I would consider a normal level, but I usually lost interest after the first year of a relationship. I still wanted the companion aspects of relationships but felt it wasn't fair to imprison another person who had a normal sex drive in a sexless relationship.

How did you discover you are asexual?

After a particularly intense relationship (which started when I was 26 and lasted about 3 years) ended, I was so devastated I decided to just NOT date or even look for a while. I didn't realize at the time that it would become permanent. After a few years though, it became clear to me that it was no longer a conscious decision. I had truly lost all interest and even attraction, to others.

How do you identify yourself asexually?

I really don't know what all the terms mean. When I was a child, I always identified as male though I had a female body. (This was in the early 1960's.) There was no real discussion of any sexual variations back then. People were horrified by the word "gay", and "transgender/transsexual" wasn't even a term ever heard. Because I didn't seem to really fit anywhere, I lived as a lesbian for 30 years. (My family disowned me at age 17 because I said I was gay.) But truly I believe I am a male in a female body. I have no serious body hatred issues and no plans to "live as other" or have surgery. Maybe if I had seen the options when I was younger, but I've grown to accept myself with my strangeness. I do not like things about having this female body, but I deal with it. I would seriously like to get rid of the breast tissue though, even though it is nominal. At this stage in life, I do appreciate the human body as an art form (male or female), but I do not feel any sexual attraction or desire for it.

Are you 'out' about being asexual? If not, why not? If you are out, whom to, and how did they react?

If it comes up, I easily state that I have no interest in relationships. I don't care who the audience is. Most people just seem to think I'm a weirdo. The larger percentage is CERTAIN that I'm LYING! Lol. I don't know why it's so hard for them to imagine. In the past, I had sexual encounters with both females and males—females because I desired them, males because I got tired of hearing the begging. Lol. Never really got any pleasure from the males because I wasn't interested. But I've had enough experience to be sure of myself.

What's your deepest fear, concern or worry, about being asexual?

Living and dying alone with no one to handle my legal affairs at my death.

Why do you feel, in general, that society doesn't accept asexuality as a form of sexual orientation in its own right? And what can be done about this?

I wasn't aware that it was not really accepted. It seems to me people are more upset about people who ARE having sex and who they are having sex with. I don't see why anyone would care at all if people just aren't interested.

What's your view on love? Have you been in love before?

Sure, I have thought I was 'in love' a few times. You don't want to know my view on real LOVE though, too complicated and depressing. I'll try to make it short. My mother died of leukemia and was in/out of hospitals for four years. I watched my father give up his business and all his money to care for her. When she was gone, he literally had nothing left. I realized I do not have it in me to give ALL to ANYONE like that. And because I do not, I don't think I am really worthy of 'love'. Not that kind of committed love. Which is a large part of why I'm sure I don't want to look for it. Unfortunately, this coincided with the years of that last relationship that devastated me! And I am not really interested in any 'lesser' kind of 'love'. I know the real thing exists, and I am not willing to get involved in it.

Are you currently in a relationship, and if so, is it with another asexual (if yes, do they identify the same as you or how do they identify), or is it a sexual person? And how is either working out?

I am not and doubt I ever will be again. If I ever did have another relationship, it would have to be with an asexual. I miss having a reliable companion for adventures like camping, board games, dinners, etc. But at my age, it is difficult to find new friends who have available time.

If you are not in a relationship, would you like to be in one and if so, why, and what type of relationship – romantic? Platonic? What would your ideal relationship look like? And would you be in a relationship with a sexual person or not, and reason why?

I think I basically addressed this in the previous question. I think I would prefer a close friend or two. Not really a "relationship". As for 'romantic' — candlelit dinner, yes; slow dancing, yes. Kissing, etc. NO. I definitely would not get involved with a sexual person because that doesn't even make sense to me and wouldn't be fair to her.

What is your view about sex? Have you had sex before and if so, how did it make you feel? If you haven't, would you?

I think sex is a normal healthy part of most people's lives. Yes, I have had plenty, thanks; I'm done now. Lol. I greatly enjoyed it with the right partners when I was younger. I seriously doubt I will ever have interest in it again, but if I did, it wouldn't be a big deal.

Do you believe if a sexual person had a relationship with an asexual, it can work? And what do you think about it being fair or not?

I've already expressed that for ME, I would think it unfair of me. I can't speak for others; it may work for them.

Asexuality is the lack of sexual attraction, as an asexual, what does this mean to you?

I think architecture is gorgeous. I can stand and gaze at it and admire it for hours. But I do not want to have sex with it just because it is beautiful. Lol. Same thing with trees or dogs, etc. I find them amazingly beautiful in the sense of works of art, but that is not the same thing as having a "sexual" component to the attraction.

Do you think sexual arousal and sexual attraction are the same or different?

When I was a sexual being...if I SAW a hot woman; that was sexual attraction. If she and I started kissing, etc. and my BODY became "awake", that was sexual arousal. Just finding someone attractive does not mean I am aroused.

What's your view on living with someone?

I really prefer to live alone! It would be very rare to find a room-mate who never gets on your nerves—always washes the dishes, never has loud friends over, etc.

Would you like kids and if so how many? And how do you hope to conceive these? If you already have kids, did you know before you had them that you are asexual and how did that impact your life?

I don't like them; don't have them; don't want them.

What's your view on marriage? And if you were to get married, would it need to be with another asexual?

I think marriage is basically an archaic arrangement devised to protect property and to make one person the property of the other. I think domestic partnerships are more sensible for ALL people and that there should be no stigma attached to leaving a relationship as long as you fulfill whatever agreement you signed with the other person. I would not want to get married, but I would possibly enter a legal partnership to protect our mutual interests if it seemed necessary (such as health reasons).

What's your view on nudity? On porn? On masturbation? On BDSM and kinks?

Well, I can tell ya, I don't wanna see myself get out of the tub! LOL. Other than that, I don't think about these things. I guess I would say Americans seem too hung up about simple natural nudity though.

How difficult is it for you to be asexual, in a sexualized world?

It really doesn't seem to be an issue for me. I guess it might have been an issue if I had ALWAYS been like this and never had any sexual interests as a young person.

Can you tell me about a time when you have had to deal with intrusive questions or a difficult situation due to your asexuality, and what happened?

Not really. Mostly just annoying that people don't believe I can possibly not have any attraction. And some friends who ask about every 3 months again "Who are you dating now?" Even though

I've told them a MILLION times, "I don't freakin' date, jeez!" I guess they think maybe it's a phase or something. Actually, I guess I thought it was a phase too when I first began this life. Lol.

What are the positives about being asexual?

I guess I don't have to worry about disease. Or heartbreak if a partner cheats. Also, I believe that previously sexual energy can be better channelled into greater strengths.

If you could have one wish about being asexual, what would it be and why?

To find a compatible life mate with the same preferences and goals. Because life is easier and seems to have more meaning when it is shared with someone, even a close friend.

If you were to look back at your life, what advice would you have given a younger version of yourself in regard to asexuality?

Can't think of anything.

What advice would you give to others who are just discovering about asexuality and considering whether they are or not?

I would say there is no reason to really think about it. I mean if one day you're sexually attracted to someone then go for it. If not, why even think about it?

Do you have a story you would like to share or anything else you would like to say?

I think if you can't be happy alone, you won't be happy with anyone either. And you won't make anyone else happy.

Extra Info

What name would you like to go under for this book? Full name, first name, or alias?

Alias Jo.

What country do you live in?

USA.

What age are you specifically? Or what decade age range are you – 20, 30. 40s?

I am 55.

What nationality and ethnicity are you?

Caucasian.

39. Andy P's Story

When did you first discover you are asexual?

It really took me a long time to understand that aspect of myself. There's this tacit assumption that everyone experiences romantic and sexual attraction. I think the biggest thing that got in the way of understanding myself was that I developed a crush on a boy named Omar in elementary school. I thought because I had some kind of emotion towards him, I was like everyone else. Even then, there was/is so much in society saying that women can't be sexual beings. It wasn't until after college, so at 22, that I was able to get out of the studying fog. I saw all of my friends either pairing off or bemoaning their single status, that was when I started to really deeply recognize that I was a little different.

How did you discover you are asexual?

There's one moment that's always stuck with me. It really made me look at my life and how it differed from others. It's funny because I'm sure that for my friends it was such a throwaway moment. We were hanging out at our two-bedroom apartment, when one roommate comes in with a poster. She unrolls it excitedly and reveals a shirtless actor, sweat slicked and smoldering into the camera. She wants to put it up in her room and wants her direct roommate's approval. That approval is obvious when her roommate bites her lip and responds breathily with, "Mmm, I'd like to climb him like a tree". I felt incredibly betrayed in that moment; watching them happily run off to their room to put it up immediately. These were people that I'd never seen dating anyone ever. I think unconsciously I just gravitated to them because I thought that they were the same as me, and it was that moment that I could see that they weren't. It really made me think about all the other times that people had said these kinds of things. So it wasn't just a matter of some people not being as interested in sex as they were in intimacy, it was the fact that I never thought of myself in any sexual capacity and when it was pressed upon me I felt absolute rejection at the idea.

How do you identify yourself asexually?

I like telling people that I'm asexual and leaving it at that because it can get so complicated. But to really break it down... I'm Heteroromantic, in so far as I've never been romantically attracted to a woman in any way. I'd also like to say that I'm Gray (borderline aromantic), because while what I don't want is to have sex with another person or even myself, I do to a small extent still occasionally experience low grade arousal. This arousal is only experienced as a kind of empathy when I read a well-written explicit passage or see a really well drawn manga. However, I don't imagine myself in place of the characters. It's a kind of appreciation almost, with no real direction and no drive to do anything about it. The thought of aiming it towards anyone at all is repulsive.

As far as intimacy is concerned, it's a lot more complicated. I am easily repulsed by scent, skin texture, and temperature of skin. This is true even when I care deeply for the person and have known them for a long time. So if the person can properly meet all criteria, I'm fine with cuddling, any kind of platonic contact, and close-mouthed kissing. However, it should be noted that despite how I identify, I've been completely fulfilled by friendships to this point and would be willing to wait indefinitely for the right person with no real difficulty.

Are you 'out' about being asexual? If not, why not? If you are out, whom to, and how did they react?

I'd say I'm getting there. My siblings know I'm ace, and all of my closest friends. My parents don't know but they're incredibly traditional Roman Catholic Mexicans so to tell them would be another tick in the box of being mentally infirm. Based on other things I've said to them I know this to be true. Other than that, I'm only open when it comes up. I feel I don't really owe anyone an explanation about myself. Most of the people I came out to were generally positive even if they were almost all baffled by the very idea. My sister had trouble understanding I know, but eventually she accepted the sheer volume of evidence.

What's your deepest fear, concern or worry, about being asexual?

That I'm not my specific brand of asexual at all and I am actually just incapable of creating strong connections with other people. That there is something profoundly wrong with me that can never be adjusted enough to be an independent, essentially good, useful member of society. Sometimes it's hard to get out of that headspace and remind myself that none of those worries matter when I'm happy as I am.

Why do you feel, in general, that society doesn't accept asexuality as a form of sexual orientation in its own right? And what can be done about this?

I think it stems even from the name. Mathematically there was some difficulty accepting the concept of zero in the first place. Then to have a question of, "Where does your sexual attraction lie?" and to respond with "Nowhere", the question itself is already an implicit expectation. I'm not sure what it'll take for acceptance from such a sexually driven world, other than time and exposure.

What's your view on love? Have you been in love before?

I think love is really important. People feel very strongly about it. I haven't ever been in love though. I have a strong attachment to people and I can miss them and all that, but outside of occasionally wanting to be in a relationship, I haven't ever really felt anything like that for someone. As far as familial and platonic love, I've felt that. Not warm and fuzzy like others describe, just a bone deep determination to maintain their happiness if it's at all within my power. A kind of loyalty that once earned is difficult to lose: a feeling of contentment of being around them.

Are you currently in a relationship, and if so, is it with another asexual (if yes, do they identify the same as you or how do they identify), or is it a sexual person? And how is either working out?

I am not currently in a relationship.

If you are not in a relationship, would you like to be in one and if so, why, and what type of relationship – romantic? Platonic? What would your ideal relationship look like? And would you be in a relationship with a sexual person or not, and reason why?

My ideal relationship is a monogamous companionship with some form of exclusive tenderness and priority. It could be platonic, as long as their regard for me differs from that of others, and as long as they commit to creating something with me. I want to be challenged, and would prefer for them to have some kind of nerdy hobby. They also need to be okay with me playing videogames. Very important! As for being with a sexual person... I don't know. I don't want to feel like I'm not fulfilling them, but I also don't want to feel pressured into doing things I don't enjoy. So I'd say... maybe? As long as they accept that I would rarely do anything in that capacity.

What is your view about sex? Have you had sex before and if so, how did it make you feel? If you haven't, would you?

I'm okay with the thought of other people doing it, I just don't want to be involved. I've never had sex before except with myself, and I didn't like it any of the times I attempted it. I would not have sex unless maybe I was dating someone with sexual needs and maybe I really cared about them and didn't want to lose them? But not because I'd want to do it. I wouldn't enjoy it after all, and the very idea is just sad to me.

Do you believe if a sexual person had a relationship with an asexual, it can work? And what do you think about it being fair or not?

I definitely think it could work. Like with any other relationship, you'd just need to find someone compatible. I'm not saying it would be easy. It'd just involve finding someone that could accept your limits and be happy with that. A big part of that would be accepting that happiness and not handling everything fearfully. If you trust them to be with you, maybe trust them to tell you if it can't work for them after all.

Asexuality is the lack of sexual attraction, as an asexual, what does this mean to you?

Exactly what you just said: some kind of lack of attraction in a sexual capacity. I mean I don't expect every, or any, asexual to be exactly the subset I am.

Do you believe sexual attraction and sexual desire are the same thing or different?

I don't know? I guess I think of them as different in a kind of theoretic sense. Where sexual attraction might be aimed at someone and sexual desire would be the need to have sex? Honestly I couldn't care less about this, I feel removed from it.

Do you think sexual arousal and sexual attraction are the same or different?

In this case I do think these differ and kind of care about them. I think of sexual arousal being a bodily response while sexual attraction involves some kind of understanding of sexual compatibility with at least some interest involved. I think a prime example of the first is the way assault victims can oftentimes feel sexual arousal. Naturally, it's not their fault, but a bodily response that they have no real control over.

What's your view on living with someone?

I'd be happy to live with someone. I prize companionship, and I feel like living with someone is a good way to foster that.

Would you like kids and if so how many? And how do you hope to conceive these? If you already have kids, did you know before you had them that you are asexual and how did that impact your life?

I feel so so about kids. I do not want to create any of my own, and I never will. As far as adopting, I could see myself doing that. The biggest thing about this is I think if at all possible I'd like to adopt from Mexico. I don't mind whatever race the child is, but I sometimes worry that I'm going to be robbing them of their culture. I don't want to have to worry about that. This way, I can provide that culture for them while also binding us as family.

What's your view on marriage? And if you were to get married, would it need to be with another asexual?

I think marriage is fine. It's just a contract saying that you're together and making it easier for you to do things for each other. I'd prefer to create this kind of affirmation at the civil level first however, because of my views related to religion. As far as marrying someone: I won't do it unless I'm absolutely sure and have been with them for some time. If that's the case, their orientation is irrelevant when we already know that it can work between us.

What's your view on nudity? On porn? On masturbation? On BDSM and kinks?

I don't really like full on nudity, it's a little off putting to me. I don't mind partial nudity.

I think that porn is kind of awful. I've never understood how someone could watch that and feel desire.

I don't like masturbation at all. Still I think that a person can be asexual and masturbate.

I accept the concept of BDSM for others, but I reject it wholly for myself. The amount of trust that you are being given/giving is frankly terrifying to me. It impresses me that others can do it.

As for kinks... ah I guess I have some of my own, in a kind of non-sexual way. I like it when a guy is so tall that when he hugs me he can place his chin on the top of my head. It's nice. So given that I to some extent have my own, I wouldn't condemn someone for their own.

How difficult is it for you to be asexual, in a sexualized world?

I don't think it's that hard for me to *exist*... but it really isn't easy to enjoy media. Not only do you rarely see representation, but you end up seeing and reading the same tired heterosexual pairings even when they don't work. I just want the story or the friendship; I don't want to deal with the complete lack of chemistry between the male-female leads.

Can you tell me about a time when you have had to deal with intrusive questions or a difficult situation due to your asexuality, and what happened?

I was once hit on at a Starbucks by an older man. I felt really harassed because he kept pushing all these bad lines and hovering around my table when I had just come in to do some work. I tried to put him off by telling him essentially, "Ah, sorry but I'm ace". Not only did he not know what that meant, when I explained it he actually laughed! He said something like "Oh well that's just because you've never had sex with *me*". He followed it up by talking about my hair and body in romantic and explicit ways. I kept denying him over and over again as he asked questions about why I was asexual and then when he got it into his head to get something from his car, I packed up all my things and ran away. It was awful.

On a more common track, I have had some strongly Catholic people ask me intrusive questions. It just seems like to tell someone that you're asexual is to give them permission to ask questions about it that they'd never ask someone with a direct sexual orientation. Things about, what it is to be asexual, what might be wrong with me... or if I was abused at a young age. I even had my friend's dad tell me that I would never find someone that would willingly marry me knowing that. It's what made me maybe more leery at the idea of being completely out.

What are the positives about being asexual?

To be openly asexual you mean? I don't really see it as being positive or what have you, to just be asexual. I mean it's what I am. Although I think it's nice to identify because people at least understand that you don't have a sexual interest in them. It's kind of nice to know that you can make people feel safe with just that knowledge. What it says about the state of things? Maybe not so good.

If you could have one wish about being asexual, what would it be and why?

I don't really have any wishes. Other than the occasional fear, I'm really happy with who I am and how I'm living right now. Maybe that I could find someone that could tick all my annoyingly specific boxes and still want to be with me?

If you were to look back at your life, what advice would you have given a younger version of yourself in regard to asexuality?

That it's fine not to be interested. Even more than that, to not say all this dumb stuff to try to fit in! It's alright not to be interested. If you keep saying it to yourself, you're going to make yourself believe it to some extent. It just makes things difficult later on.

What advice would you give to others who are just discovering about asexuality and considering whether they are or not?

I guess... take your time. You don't have to know every aspect about it. It took me a few years to really know for sure how I felt about every single thing related to my orientation. You can shorthand your explanation to people. Or you can tell them nothing. You don't owe it to them to explain!

Do you have a story you would like to share or anything else you would like to say?

Good luck to all you peeps trying to figure yourselves out.

Extra Info

What name would you like to go under for this book? Full name, first name, or alias?

Andy P.

What country do you live in?

U.S.A.

What age are you specifically? Or what decade age range are you – 20, 30. 40s?

I'm currently 24, but I'm turning 25 very soon.

What nationality and ethnicity are you?

I am Latina. My nationality is U.S. Citizen but I'm working on Dual. Wish me luck!

40. Isadora's Story

When did you first discover you are asexual?

In 2003, I was 27 years old.

How did you discover you are asexual?

I was browsing posts on LiveJournal and came across a post about asexuality, with a link to the asexual LJ community. After looking up the definition and reading some of the members' posts I realized this was describing me.

How do you identify yourself asexually?

I'm an asexual aromantic. I'm sex-positive and actually pretty interested in sex as a human behavior, I just have no desire to have it myself.

Are you 'out' about being asexual? If not, why not? If you are out, whom to, and how did they react?

My husband knows and we've discussed the subject on several occasions. I'm also very out on social media. I don't socialize much offline though, so unless my offline friends follow me online, they don't know.

What's your deepest fear, concern or worry, about being asexual?

I think it would have to be being accused of lying about it, given my history of engaging in sex. Obviously that would come from someone not understanding the difference between attraction and behavior, but it bothers me that they would then be disinclined to listen to other asexuals they encounter. I don't want someone taking my experience and applying it to other asexuals, rather like how someone could tell a lesbian she's not really homosexual because she's had sex with men. I just really wish more people understood that what you do is very different from your attraction.

Why do you feel, in general, that society doesn't accept asexuality as a form of sexual orientation in its own right? And what can be done about this?

We've been told over and over that sex and romance – specifically hetero – is the be-all and end-all of human experience. That sex is the best thing people can do, and you should always be working towards making yourself sexually attractive, and that you should stay on the lookout for potential partners. Obviously boys get a different slant on this narrative than girls, but the basic story is the same. Sex is also sold as the only form of intimacy that is valuable, so if you are very deep and intimate friends with someone, you're 'just friends,' and sex is 'next level.' So if you haven't slept with someone, you 'obviously' don't know as much about them.

What's your view on love? Have you been in love before?

I'm aromantic, so I've never quite understood love in a romantic sense. I believe in love whole-heartedly (LOL) and I love my husband, my family, my friends, my cats, but I've never fallen in love and had romantic affairs. As a child I remember listening to songs about love on the radio (my parents both listened to country music) and thinking that love between adults sounded like hell on earth. I couldn't fathom why anyone would subject themselves to that. I still feel the same way, but now I understand that a lot of people enjoy the emotion and turmoil it can bring. I just feel relieved that I don't!

Are you currently in a relationship, and if so, is it with another asexual (if yes, do they identify the same as you or how do they identify), or is it a sexual person? And how is either working out?

My husband is allosexual, but he has asked me about asexuality and he understands, to a certain extent, how I feel. As I am sex-positive, we do negotiate times to have sex. He will let me know in advance that he's interested, and unless I'm really not feeling up to it, I'll have sex with him. It works out well for us, in that he gets to have the sex he wants, while my boundaries are respected.

What is your view about sex? Have you had sex before and if so, how did it make you feel? If you haven't, would you?

I have had sex before my current relationship, with both men and women. I find sex interesting as a human behavior, and all the trappings that have grown up around sex. Most of the time during sex I feel detached, like I'm watching someone else do it, and sometimes this makes me feel really embarrassed for myself.

Do you believe if a sexual person had a relationship with an asexual, it can work? And what do you think about it being fair or not?

That depends entirely on the people involved. If they can talk openly about what they want and don't want, and find a common ground, then they can definitely make it work. I also don't like the argument about an asexual being 'unfair.' If you want sex that badly go find another sexual person to have it with. It's not like you're being deprived of food or water. Not having sex won't kill you.

Asexuality is the lack of sexual attraction, as an asexual, what does this mean to you?

When I first read up on asexuality and it was framed as not having sexual attraction to anyone, it was a revelation. Early on I thought I was a lesbian because I wasn't attracted to boys. But then, I wasn't really attracted to girls either; it was just more comfortable for me to be around them. I put a lot of effort into trying to fake it until I made it and pretend to be sexually attracted, but I wasn't sure what to do to act the part and I came off as weird and probably creepy. It makes me cringe to think about some of the things I did to try to fit what I saw as the model of 'normal sexual attraction.'

Do you believe sexual attraction and sexual desire are the same thing or different?

To me they're different. Personally, I do feel sexual desire and fantasize about sex, but I'm not a part of my own fantasy, and neither are actual people I know. So I may fantasize about characters in a book I read, but if I see someone in public, their sexiness or desirability as a partner doesn't register with me. And even if the book character came to life, I wouldn't be interested in them.

Do you think sexual arousal and sexual attraction are the same or different?

I think attraction leads to arousal, but arousal doesn't lead to attraction. I may get sexually aroused because my hormones are acting up, but it doesn't lead me to want sex with someone.

What's your view on living with someone?

I feel that if that works for people, they should do it. Like any relationship they need to make sure the communication is there and be honest with each other.

Would you like kids and if so how many? And how do you hope to conceive these? If you already have kids, did you know before you had them that you are asexual and how did that impact your life?

I don't want children and haven't had any.

What's your view on marriage? And if you were to get married, would it need to be with another asexual?

Marriage: When you live with someone and the state gives you a tax break for it. All joking aside, marriage to me is a primarily religious bond, and should be handled by people's churches. The state shouldn't get to have a say in who is married and who is not.

What's your view on nudity? On porn? On masturbation? On BDSM and kinks?

All of these things are fine by me. I'm personally not very comfortable with showing off my body. It was just last week that I broke down and bought some shorts for the summer, and I live in Florida!

Political views aside, I don't generally have a problem with porn. Often, when I do see porn, the only thing I end up thinking about is whether the people in it, actually want to be doing what they're doing, and if they're being paid fairly for it.

Masturbation is just a normal, healthy thing. I do it, just not as often as other people, I'd guess. I wish it didn't still have so much stigma attached to it, because it doesn't hurt anyone and can even be good for you.

I also think it's entirely possible to be engaged in BDSM or a kink and not necessarily have it be sexual. Those things can be sexual for a lot of people, but I've talked to people with different kinds of kinks and things whose gratification is more emotional than sexual. They don't engage in, say, spanking, for erotic pleasure, but to satisfy an emotional need.

How difficult is it for you to be asexual, in a sexualized world?

As I am now, it's more of a nuisance than a problem. But I have what, to me, is an ideal situation. My husband isn't constantly pushing me for sex, and my mother never pushed me for grandchildren. I'm also very lucky in that my doctor understands asexuality and hasn't offered hormone treatments or stuff like that. I just feel annoyed that everything seems to be sexualized. Outside of my "bubble," there's nude women on everything, a constant stream of ads about how to look your sexiest, get your youth and vitality back, pick up women, lose weight so men will find you attractive, blah blah blah. Really? Is this the extent of our public discourse – naughty bits and boobies? It feels very junior high.

Can you tell me about a time when you have had to deal with intrusive questions or a difficult situation due to your asexuality, and what happened?

I haven't really had any problems like this. I tend to avoid discussing sexual relations unless I can do it in a distanced way, so I haven't had it come up in casual conversation.

What are the positives about being asexual?

I get to avoid all the fuss and bother people go through with sex. Instead of dealing with wanting a partner and dating and all that, I get to just shrug and go do something else. I often see the hoops people jump through for sex and I feel relieved that I'm not like that.

If you could have one wish about being asexual, what would it be and why?

That people would understand that lack of sexual attraction doesn't make you broken. And stop with the 'so you're a plant' joke, it's stupid.

If you were to look back at your life, what advice would you have given a younger version of yourself in regard to asexuality?

I would go back to that high school kid and simply tell her, 'Go look up asexuality. I guarantee it will take a huge load off your mind.'

What advice would you give to others who are just discovering about asexuality and considering whether they are or not?

Asexuality doesn't mean broken, it's just different. If one of the types of asexuality applies to you, then please don't worry when people suggest you're wrong, they don't know you like you do.

Extra Info

What name would you like to go under for this book? Full name, first name, or alias?

Isadora.

What country do you live in?

United States.

What age are you specifically? Or what decade age range are you – 20, 30. 40s?

30's.

Links to your website/social media.

https://www.facebook.com/jessie.raven.14

http://pshaw-raven.livejournal.com/

41. Eddie's Story

When did you first discover you are asexual?

Late 2015.

How did you discover you are asexual?

I pretty much stumbled upon the term 'Asexual' and thought that it described me fairly well.

How do you identify yourself asexually?

I guess I'm a heteroromantic asexual. I'm not huge on all the labels we see in the ace community right now; I think it just separates us.

Are you 'out' about being asexual? If not, why not? If you are out, whom to, and how did they react?

I've told a few friends and my mum. I don't place a huge emphasis on being out. It seems strange to me, to tell people you're *not* something. I don't drink, but I don't go around telling everyone about it, I don't think it's information people can do anything with, or that anyone would really be bothered about. I told my mum because she's the type to always ask me when I'm going to get a girlfriend, etc. But I haven't told my dad, for example, because we don't talk about that sort of thing it never comes up.

What's your deepest fear, concern or worry, about being asexual?

I don't really have any fears or concerns about my asexuality. It doesn't have the same stigma or hatred surrounding it as homosexuality. You don't hear about anyone getting in a blue over asexuality.

Why do you feel, in general, that society doesn't accept asexuality as a form of sexual orientation in its own right? And what can be done about this?

I live and breathe music. When someone says to me that they don't listen to music, or that they don't care about music, I have trouble understanding that. I think it's the same with sexuality. It's something that's at the core of a lot of people's lives, it's very important to them. When someone comes along and says that sexuality *isn't* important to them, they just can't understand it. It's much easier to accept something if you understand it.

It's even easier to accept something if you can see it in the world around you. People hear about asexuality, and they don't understand it, so they look for more examples of it. They see that asexuality isn't consistent with how most of the world is. People can look at the news, or celebrities who are openly, gay, bi, trans, etc., and they can accept that, because these are people they put on a pedestal. They can't do the same with asexuality right now. With time, that hopefully will change.

What's your view on love? Have you been in love before?

I can't really see the boundary between love and good friendship; I suppose it's a blurred line. I don't *think* I've been 'in love' as such.

Are you currently in a relationship, and if so, is it with another asexual (if yes, do they identify the same as you or how do they identify), or is it a sexual person? And how is either working out?

I'm not in a relationship, never have been. A cleft palate makes me a bit of a weird looking bloke, so I'm not going to pull a sexual any time soon, and I don't know any other Aces.

If you are not in a relationship, would you like to be in one and if so, why, and what type of relationship – romantic? Platonic? What would your ideal relationship look like? And would you be in a relationship with a sexual person or not, and reason why?

I wouldn't object to a relationship with a sexual person, the relationship couldn't be all about sex of course. If I were to limit myself to relationships with only aces, that's a very small amount of people, and I would be rejecting all of the awesome sexual people I will meet.

What is your view about sex? Have you had sex before and if so, how did it make you feel? If you haven't, would you?

I haven't had sex before. Given the right person, I would partake, because if I really liked her I would want to make her happy.

Do you believe if a sexual person had a relationship with an asexual, it can work? And what do you think about it being fair or not?

Of course it could work. There would have to be a bit of give and take on both sides, but that's no different to any other relationship.

Asexuality is the lack of sexual attraction, as an asexual, what does this mean to you?

It means looking at an attractive person the same as you would look at a nice sunset, or a good painting. Not as an object of desire, but just to appreciate the aesthetics of them. If I look at a nice car, I'm thinking, 'God I would love to drive that.' When a lot of people would be thinking, 'That looks nice'.

Do you believe sexual attraction and sexual desire are the same thing or different.

I think they are the same. Sexual attraction involves sexual desire toward someone. I'm probably the wrong person to ask, I don't experience either.

Do you think sexual arousal and sexual attraction are the same or different?

I think they are separate. I can have an erection without feeling any attraction to the person. I think arousal is a physical response to a physically attractive person. Sexual attraction, I think goes a little deeper than that.

What's your view on living with someone?

I'm very introverted, so I'm not crazy about the idea of living with someone. Although I'm sure that would be different if I was romantically attracted to the person.

Would you like kids and if so how many? And how do you hope to conceive these? If you already have kids, did you know before you had them that you are asexual and how did that impact your life?

I'm really not sure if I want kids. If I did I would only have 1. I'm not too excited about the conception process; I hear it involves some strange thing called sex.

What's your view on marriage? And if you were to get married, would it need to be with another asexual?

I really don't like the idea of marriage. To me, there must be a reason the majority of them end in divorce. Then the court proceedings; division of assets; child custody battle, on and on and on. You don't see that when girlfriend and boyfriend break up. It's much more simple. If a relationship ends, everyone goes their separate ways, job done. And, if we're honest, it doesn't change anything about the relationship. Two people get married, they go on a honeymoon, do some... things, then they come back home, and continue as they were. Why not skip all that, and avoid complicating the statistically inevitable break-up?

What's your view on nudity? On porn? On masturbation? On BDSM and kinks?

So long as everyone involved is consenting, each to their own. Being ace, I'm not into the whole BDSM, kink thing. I do, however, masturbate. This is one thing that sexuals don't get about aces. They see masturbation as a sexual release. I see it more for the dopamine hit you get out of it. It's like playing video games; you do it because it's fun.

How difficult is it for you to be asexual, in a sexualized world?

I think I've assimilated into the sexual world fairly well. I can make the sexual jokes; understand the innuendoes, etc. But I still get a bit uncomfortable when people start talking about sex, or about how attractive someone is, because I have none of my own opinions, none of my own stories. Anything I do say in those situations is a product of stuff I've heard elsewhere. I'll agree when someone says, "Scarlett Johansson is so hot!" But I wouldn't have noticed if I hadn't been told.

Can you tell me about a time when you have had to deal with intrusive questions or a difficult situation due to your asexuality, and what happened?

Generally, when coming out, people say things like:

"Oh you're jumping on the bandwagon are you?"

"How do you know, you haven't tried it?"

"Asexuality doesn't apply to humans."

When I came out to my mum, she said, "No you're not, you're heterosexual".

You end up having to explain it to people like they're 4 years old.

Then they get angry with you because you're treating them like they're stupid. Ask a stupid question; get a stupid answer.

What are the positives about being asexual?

- No unexpected pregnancy.

- No STIs.

- Free condoms can be used for their correct purpose, as water balloons.

- Everyday situations can remain un-corrupted by sexual innuendoes.

- Hard-drive space that would be filled with porn can be used for The Walking Dead.

- The plot of Game of Thrones is much clearer if you're not paying attention to all the hookers' errm…parts.

- Professional relationship with "hot girl" in the office is untarnished by creepiness.

- Less emphasis on physical appearance means I can dress comfortably.

If you could have one wish about being asexual, what would it be and why?

If people could not talk or ask me about sex that would be great.

If you were to look back at your life, what advice would you have given a younger version of yourself in regard to asexuality?

Google 'Asexuality' kiddo.

What advice would you give to others who are just discovering about asexuality and considering whether they are or not?

Give it time; really think about it. It's very easy to find a title and apply it to yourself, but it's important to make sure that's the right title. Read as much as you can, and be honest with yourself.

Extra Info

What name would you like to go under for this book? Full name, first name, or alias?

Eddie.

What country do you live in?

Australia.

What age are you specifically? Or what decade age range are you – 20, 30. 40s?

18.

What nationality and ethnicity are you?

Anglo-Australian.

42. Cassie's Story

When did you first discover you are asexual?

I suppose I started suspecting around the time I was 11, but actually realized I was asexual around the time I was 17, when I learnt that asexuality existed.

How did you discover you are asexual?

I noticed my peers' increasing interest in things that did not interest me, including but not limited to: getting crushes, finding strangers, classmates and celebrities 'hot'... I assumed that they were all faking these feelings in an attempt to seem more 'adult' (we all know that adults falling in love and experiencing sexual attraction is a big topic in most movies and books), but eventually I realized that to them, those feelings were real, and, since I never found anyone attractive in such a way, be they male or female appearing, I figured I was neither hetero- nor homo-sexual. Around that time I learnt of asexuality and realized that was the orientation I could comfortably apply to myself.

How do you identify yourself asexually?

I identify as an aromantic asexual.

Are you 'out' about being asexual? If not, why not? If you are out, whom to, and how did they react?

I am passively out to most people and have actively discussed this with the people closest to me.

My mother was, when I first told her at the age of 17, of the opinion that I just needed some more time, but has taken less than a year to fully accept it, and now, nearly 5 years later, she is completely okay with it and accepts it as a part of me, like me having brown hair. The rest of my family is vaguely aware of it.

Three of my friends were very understanding, two had actual knowledge of the terminology and helped me explain myself to the other one, all were, and are, okay with it.

Another one of my friends has suggested I go to see a doctor or a psychiatrist, but ultimately accepted everything. We are still good friends and there's no problems regarding my asexuality.

There are some other people who know, have found out, or I have mentioned it to in passing, but I never cared for their reactions so I do not recall them. None were particularly negative. The most negative ones would be disbelief or denial of the orientation's existence. (And comments along the lines of, "You just haven't met the right person yet!")

What's your deepest fear, concern or worry, about being asexual?

I have no real fears or concerns about it. It is an aspect of me I am fully comfortable with and I do not concern myself with the opinions of strangers much, so those do not worry me either. My friends and family seem to accept me as I am, which eliminates the potential worry of them rejecting me for it. I was worried about them negating this part of me before telling them, but since 'coming out' that worry has obviously gone away.

Why do you feel, in general, that society doesn't accept asexuality as a form of sexual orientation in its own right? And what can be done about this?

Most likely because people tend to shy away from what they do not know or understand and not feeling sexual attraction is something completely unimaginable by most, especially considering most of the things in the world are somewhat based on sexuality. So, they don't accept it, because they refuse to believe in it, because it seems so different from themselves and there's no visible proof of it. The only thing that I believe can be done about this, is to make asexuality visible. To talk about it, to have books about it, to have asexual characters in books, movies, TV-shows...

What's your view on love? Have you been in love before?

I believe there are many different kinds, or facets, of love. I firmly believe in parental love and the love children feel for their parents, the love between friends and, in a way, romantic love. I do however think that people too often mistake infatuation for love. I believe love to be a feeling you work on, one that exists in addition to you, without making you completely blind to another's faults. I have never been in love.

Are you currently in a relationship, and if so, is it with another asexual (if yes, do they identify the same as you or how do they identify), or is it a sexual person? And how is either working out?

I am currently not in a relationship, nor am I actively seeking one.

If you are not in a relationship, would you like to be in one and if so, why, and what type of relationship – romantic? Platonic? What would your ideal relationship look like? And would you be in a relationship with a sexual person or not, and reason why?

I do not particularly wish to be in a relationship, if I did, it would be for convenience reasons mostly (splitting of living costs etc.). I feel complete as I am, and thus feel no need to find someone to complete me. If I were to be in a relationship, I would prefer it to be with someone I find aesthetically and intellectually attractive, like most people want to be with someone who they find sexually and romantically attractive (to my understanding). I suppose ideally it would be between a romantic and a platonic relationship of a monogamous kind. I would be willing to be in a relationship with a sexual person, but only as long as they were able to accept my decisions about my own body, and were faithful to me. I would not accept them going behind my back to have sex with someone else. If they felt unfulfilled, I would like them to talk to me so we could find a solution we were both comfortable with together.

What is your view about sex? Have you had sex before and if so, how did it make you feel? If you haven't, would you?

I see sex as something that has been given way too much importance in today's society. A relationship is said to not be valid if it doesn't involve sex, sex is what every person should strive for and sex is what is used to sell most products. I do not agree with that and that mentality often annoys me a lot. Aside from that, I see it as just another activity, like volleyball. Some people like it, some people love it, some people cannot imagine life without it, and some people find it a waste of time. I, myself, am not fond of it, but see no problem in other people enjoying it as long as they do not try to force me to join.

I have had sex before, before I knew asexuality existed, when I thought that maybe having sex would make me find people sexually attractive. Needles to say, it didn't work that way. I didn't particularly mind sex, but neither did I particularly enjoy it. I found it relatively boring, despite there being no lack of activity, and my mind kept wandering. I suppose the experiences could have been better if I really focused on it and tried to mentally anchor myself in the moment and the sensations, but, as far as I'm concerned, that's too much effort for something I'm more than comfortable without. It certainly didn't make me feel like a whole different person and like it changed my life forever.

Do you believe if a sexual person had a relationship with an asexual, it can work? And what do you think about it being fair or not?

I believe it can work, if both partners are open and honest with each other and work on finding solutions that appeal to them both as problems arise. I think that the fairness of it depends largely on both partners' ability and willingness to communicate. What works for some would not necessarily work for others.

Asexuality is the lack of sexual attraction, as an asexual, what does this mean to you?

It doesn't really mean anything to me, since I can't fully comprehend what sexual attraction would be. So, in a way, it helps, because my lack of understanding of sexual attraction makes me realize that I do not, and have never, experienced it.

Do you believe sexual attraction and sexual desire are the same thing or different, please explain?

I do not feel familiar enough with either to answer this question well. I suppose they may be different with attraction being on a more primal level and desire on a more conscious one.

Do you think sexual arousal and sexual attraction are the same or different, please explain?

I believe they are different. As I understand it, sexual attraction is focused on something outside oneself, most often another person. Meanwhile sexual arousal is a sensation of one's body with no need for an external anchor. So, sexual arousal is focused inside the body, while attraction holds its focus outside it.

What's your view on living with someone?

It largely depends on the person, I could put up with living with someone, but I would most prefer to live alone.

Would you like kids and if so how many? And how do you hope to conceive these? If you already have kids, did you know before you had them that you are asexual and how did that impact your life?

I would not like to have any children, though I believe that to be connected to my personality, rather than my asexuality.

What's your view on marriage? And if you were to get married, would it need to be with another asexual?

I have no particular views on marriage, other than that marriage vows are too often made only to later be broken (I do not believe you should promise something, like fidelity, only to go back on your word later) and that it can be a financial advantage.

If I were to get married, it would not particularly matter to me if my partner were asexual or sexual, as long as we were capable of honest communication with each other and had mutual respect.

What's your view on nudity? On porn? On masturbation? On BDSM and kinks?

I don't mind nudity, however I do have something against it being so sexualized.

I don't mind porn in the way I don't mind mindless action films. I don't enjoy them, so I do not watch them, but I don't mind people enjoying or watching either, as long as they don't expect all of reality to reflect what they see on the screen.

I believe there is nothing wrong with masturbation, it is just you doing something you enjoy to your body without involving anyone else and I can't see how there can be anything questionable about that.

Some people like strawberry ice cream, some people like pistachio. People are different and have different tastes. BDSM and kinks are just certain preferences, as far as I'm concerned. As long as everything is consensual and everyone involved is on the same page, I see nothing wrong.

How difficult is it for you to be asexual, in a sexualized world?

It was highly confusing when I was growing up and I thought that the sexual attraction and desires that made people act crazy in books and movies were there just to make the stories more interesting, like dragons and talking animals and moving forests. Now, it's mainly annoying. I find it ridiculous that a commercial for hamburgers would include a woman in a bikini sensually licking the food and that the majority of jokes in popular shows include some sort of a sexual meaning. Everything is so focused around sexuality, like it's the most important thing in life. There's pills, treatments, toys, dolls... being researched and made to make you desire more sex, to make you last longer, to make you go at it multiple times, to beat the lowering libido that can come with age or stress... Like having less sex is the worst thing that can happen to a person.

Can you tell me about a time when you have had to deal with intrusive questions or a difficult situation due to your asexuality, and what happened?

There have been times when acquaintances would question my being single and dismiss my asexuality saying I just need to lower my standards already, that it'll all change once I meet the right person, that I'm just in denial because I want to be special, that I should just go out and live a little, have fun with different guys et cetera. Not really difficult but highly uncomfortable especially since they refuse to listen.

As far as intrusive questions go, sometimes acquaintances learn of my asexuality and take it upon themselves to question me on whether I've ever dated/had sex (and upon learning that the answers are yes, claimed that my partners just didn't do a good job, so I should try someone else); whether or not I ever masturbate (as if it's any of their business what I do or don't do with my body, and as if that has any connection with me finding anyone sexually attractive or not); what my parents did when they found out (like they were supposed to DO something), and whether or not I've been to the doctor/psychiatrist/had myself checked out... All of these are both intrusive and highly annoying. As well as the implication that if I don't find anyone sexually attractive, I must be ill one way or another.

What are the positives about being asexual?

I can only speak as an aromantic asexual, things may be vastly different for romantic asexuals. As I see it, you are free to be yourself without the added pressure about whether someone will find you desirable or not. You avoid the apparent emotional turmoil people go through when they are attracted to someone but that someone doesn't find them attractive in turn. You can keep a clear head most of the time, for your brain does not get clouded by infatuation, which means you can be more reasonable. You don't feel unfulfilled just because you're not sharing yourself with another person and you feel complete as you are. I actually think that most of the things regarding being asexual are positive. The only negatives I can think of are the reactions of others and being bombarded by over-sexualization of nearly everything in this society, so mostly things tied with the outside world, rather than being asexual in itself.

If you could have one wish about being asexual, what would it be and why?

I suppose it would be just the ability to be able to *understand* what exactly it is sexual people feel that makes everything work the way it does, because I hate not understanding things and sexual attraction seems to be a very important building block upon which most of our society rests.

If you were to look back at your life, what advice would you have given a younger version of yourself in regard to asexuality?

Don't doubt yourself in favor of others, you just don't work in the same way, and that's okay. It doesn't mean there's anything fundamentally wrong with them (or you), just accept the differences and move on.

What advice would you give to others who are just discovering about asexuality and considering whether they are or not?

My advice would be to listen to yourself most of all, don't give into peer pressure, feel free to experiment and try different things if that appeals to you, but feel just as free to say no to something, talk to someone if you want to, and don't try to force yourself to be something you're not. There's nothing wrong about being asexual just as there's nothing wrong with being sexual, be it hetero, homo, bi, pan, or whatever.

Do you have a story you would like to share or anything else you would like to say?

If anyone's struggling and would like someone to talk to, I am more than willing to offer a listening ear and they can write to me on cassie.sparrow.ace@gmail.com. Other than that, just stay true to yourselves.

Extra Info

What name would you like to go under for this book? Full name, first name, or alias?

Cassie.

What country do you live in?

Slovenia.

What age are you specifically? Or what decade age range are you – 20, 30. 40s?

I am to be 22 in the year of writing the answers.

What nationality and ethnicity are you?

I am a white Slovenian.

43. Ann's Story

When did you first discover you are asexual?

It was a fairly recent discovery, about six months ago. I had been familiar with the term before, but had always rejected it out of hand because I had had crushes on other people before.

How did you discover you are asexual?

I had gotten out of a relationship that was unhealthy and controlling, maybe even emotionally abusive in some respects. While I previously acknowledged that when I started dating I would be required to do sexual acts with my partner at some point, I ended up with someone who had certain expectations to be met. He asked and pushed for far more than I wanted to give, and I eventually gave in because I grew tired of fighting over it. A couple of months after the relationship ended, I was reading an author blog about tropes in romantic fiction, and one of the commentators mentioned the common trope of the heroine of the story not being sexually attracted to anyone but the hero. This was how I learned of the term 'demisexual.'

How do you identify yourself asexually?

I would consider myself a panromantic demisexual, as the sex of the person has very little to do with whether I consider them in a sexual manner. In fact, thus far in my life, the only person I have ever desired in a sexual manner is my boyfriend. Perhaps I tend to be a sapiosexual as well.

Are you 'out' about being asexual? If not, why not? If you are out, whom to, and how did they react?

The moment I realized I could be demisexual, I immediately told my boyfriend, who accepts who I am in any case. Since then, my brother, who I am close to, has some knowledge of the matter (though undoubtedly thinks of it as some stage of mine), as well as a couple of close friends (one of whom is demisexual himself). For the most part, however, I would not disclose my demisexuality if I didn't need to.

What's your deepest fear, concern or worry, about being asexual?

When I first found out about my demisexuality, I immediately discussed the implications with my boyfriend, fretting over whether he would still want me around over someone more... well, typically heteroromantic heterosexual. He made clear that he wouldn't be happier with anyone else. Once that was established, I easily accepted the lot, and it made a lot of my memories make a great deal more sense in retrospect.

Why do you feel, in general, that society doesn't accept asexuality as a form of sexual orientation in its own right? And what can be done about this?

I think many people have trouble seeing outside of their own experiences. Only a few are really successful at imagining things they've never dealt with before, whether through empathy or extensive studying. Sort of like explaining to a deaf person what a symphony sounds like, which could be described as a bunch of musical instruments playing a series of different tones in harmony (or not at times, once you get to the modern period...). Imagine what it'd be like to explain to someone with sexual urges that you can physically look at someone without ever feeling the remotest urge to have sex with him / her, regardless of how sexy / hot she / he supposedly is.

What's your view on love? Have you been in love before?

For myself, I spent a great deal of time wondering if I was bisexual, although I hadn't felt any physical drive to have sex with anyone, male or female. In my last relationship, I believed that I had a future with that man, so while there was an element of curiosity at first with performing sexual acts, I eventually got tired, then bored, and eventually began to dread going over his house for overnight stays altogether. When I eventually came to date the man I am with now, it was so completely different than with anyone I had been with before. I could talk with him for hours about anything and in a blink of an eye, our time together would be up. I never understood when my ex-boyfriend had told me how much he missed me because it had only been a few days since we last saw each other. With my current boyfriend, I understand that now. I think it's because we unconditionally accept one another. It was perplexing to me when I actually began to sexually desire him as well. As for me, I can't really picture being outside of a long-term, committed monogamous relationship. Especially now that I know just having sex does nothing for me. If other people choose other things for themselves and can handle it and are happy with that, I don't have any issue with their choices. It's just something I wouldn't want for myself.

Are you currently in a relationship, and if so, is it with another asexual (if yes, do they identify the same as you or how do they identify), or is it a sexual person? And how is either working out?

Yes, I am currently with my boyfriend, who I can truthfully say is the only person I have loved in such a way. I don't believe he's asexual, although he does have a certain level of discomfort, perhaps aversion, to discussing sex sometimes, especially with anyone who he's not with. I would say he's a heteroromantic heterosexual. But I don't think he's ever been with someone he fully trusted or even felt completely comfortable around. He was the first to admit that he didn't think he had ever been in love before, the same conclusion I eventually came to when trying to figure out why this relationship with him was so different than the ones I had before.

If you are not in a relationship, would you like to be in one and if so, why, and what type of relationship – romantic? Platonic? What would your ideal relationship look like? And would you be in a relationship with a sexual person or not, and reason why?

The idea of being sexually attracted to someone is still very new to me. I very much desire the relationship I am in now, and wouldn't change it out for another one. I don't know if an asexual person and I could work theoretically, but just because one is a particular sexual orientation doesn't mean we would automatically be incompatible. Each orientation on its own seems to have a very diversified group of persons. I value my sparse number of friends and a few of the ones in my family unit. And as I've learned from my experience with my last boyfriend, I personally find the idea of getting in an open relationship abhorrent.

What is your view about sex? Have you had sex before and if so, how did it make you feel? If you haven't, would you?

My view of sex has been complicated by the fact that I was sexually assaulted as a teenager by an EMT (Emergency Medical Technician), while being transported to a hospital. When the case against him was dismissed on lack of evidence, he and his wife sued me; the police department; and the county government that prosecuted the case, which dragged out in a five-year legal battle. For a very long time, I felt a great deal of reluctance to even think about sex.

When I dated my ex-boyfriend, he pushed for sexual acts, and though I never had vaginal intercourse with him, he took far more from me than I wanted to give by putting pressure on me, and crying and arguing with me when I wanted to stop sexual activities. When I started the relationship with the man I am dating now, if we physically touch each other, it seems to be a natural progression of things, rather than something I give up just to make him stop badgering me.

I was raised a Protestant, and my boyfriend is a Catholic. I hope that we don't have sex until our wedding night, though it can get difficult waiting...

Do you believe if a sexual person had a relationship with an asexual, it can work? And what do you think about it being fair or not?

It may be able to, though I don't doubt those relationships can be challenging as any other. Fairness is a difficult thing to gauge; if both mutually agree to have sex or not with each other, and are able to openly communicate what they want or need, it may be able to work. Then again, if the word 'unfair' comes to play, as if the relationship has some sort to tallying sheet for who gets the most concessions out of it, then it wouldn't augur well for the future.

Asexuality is the lack of sexual attraction, as an asexual, what does this mean to you?

Since I identify as a demisexual, I suppose I'm not completely lacking in sexual desire, though I seem to have only have felt it towards the person I'm with now. So I view it as being on the asexuality spectrum, sort of like how Asperger's syndrome is considered to be on the autistic spectrum.

Do you believe sexual attraction and sexual desire are the same thing or different?

I can see the two being somewhat different, as I view desire as a stronger form of attraction. Both concepts seem to be somewhat nebulous to me in any case.

Do you think sexual arousal and sexual attraction are the same or different?

I think of arousal as somewhat different from attraction in that arousal has a greater physiological presence, while sexual attraction tends to be subtler in terms of its effect on human behavior.

What's your view on living with someone?

Preferably married if it was someone I was in a relationship with. I would hope to get enough time on my own before deciding to try to make it work with living with someone I intend to share the rest of my life with.

Would you like kids and if so how many? And how do you hope to conceive these? If you already have kids, did you know before you had them that you are asexual and how did that impact your life?

In my early twenties, I viewed the entire prospect of motherhood with apprehension. I even called it being a man's incubator at one point. When the man I was with before desired kids, I demurred, pointing out the many kids that needed to be adopted, he insisted on his own. Facing the prospect of being forced to bear this man's children was part of why I'm no longer with him; I felt an immediate revulsion at the idea.

As for my boyfriend, we would like one, maybe two, once we're financially more stable and married. I'm not sure what exactly happened here; maybe I trust him to be a good father and provider, and to love me and any of our children unconditionally. Of course, I'm already in my early thirties, so time may very well run out for me to have children. I would like to adopt, but apparently the process is exceptionally difficult and expensive.

What's your view on marriage? And if you were to get married, would it need to be with another asexual?

I suppose I view it as a formal declaration in the eyes of the public and God that you are formally together. From an emotional standpoint, it's a covenant of love and faithfulness to one person, through the good and the bad.

I'm aware that some people seem to make the open marriage work and are satisfied with that arrangement. I'd prefer just being with one person. I may have even called myself a one-man dog at some point. I don't think it would have to be with another asexual at all. I seem to be happy with or without.

What's your view on nudity? On porn? On masturbation? On BDSM and kinks?

Nudity is aesthetically pleasing in art, and since I was raised by immigrant parents of Chinese descent, it doesn't seem as taboo to me as it is with some Westerners. I'm not offended with women breastfeeding in public.

As for porn, it seems to be an effective stimulant for some, and if people don't abuse or become addicted, I'm pretty indifferent.

Masturbation is a funny thing for me, because while I do occasionally indulge, prior to starting my relationship with my current boyfriend, I was completely unable to fantasize about other people. Part of what cemented what went wrong in my last relationship, was that I realized I had to shut my eyes and tune out the voice of the man touching me to get anywhere.

BDSM and kinks? I guess whatever floats one's boat! I can't really condone necrophilia, bestiality, incest, and rape. Maybe rape fantasy if that's their thing...

How difficult is it for you to be asexual, in a sexualized world?

I seem to be pretty oblivious to my surroundings. I've felt a great deal of discomfort because I wasn't viewing things sexually as much as other people did, but didn't put the pieces together. I remember talking with a classmate about the Maslow hierarchy of needs, like the human need for food and shelter and fulfillment, and someone brought up needing sex. That made me openly scoff, and I got a few funny looks from it.

Overall, I've always been socially inept for various reasons, and this just offers yet another explanation on why that is. Since I have plenty of oddball qualities already, it's not a huge deal.

Can you tell me about a time when you have had to deal with intrusive questions or a difficult situation due to your asexuality, and what happened?

Well, being exceptionally fond of some of my female friends in my life got awkward, although having sex with them wasn't even a consideration. I've had a lot of people gossip about me at points in my life that connected to various bullying/hazing incidents.

When a male acquaintance found out about my virginity, he immediately proposed having sex with him to solve the issue. When I showed a complete lack of enthusiasm for the idea, I was immediately branded as frigid and uptight and treated with scorn by him from that point on.

What are the positives about being asexual?

I guess it's nice not to look at someone and get sexually aroused, that alone sounds like a boon to me. Do I think sexuality can cloud judgment? Most definitely. It's why the physically attractive are generally more successful than someone who isn't. It's probably better that I don't have to deal with that because I can be awful at judging character to start with. I really like the idea of being with someone not because of the way they look, because people get older and change, but because of the person they are and working to become.

If you could have one wish about being asexual, what would it be and why?

The idea of people accepting asexuals and those on the spectrum as a genuine, legitimate category, sounds like a good place to begin. I like the idea of people understanding each other better.

If you were to look back at your life, what advice would you have given a younger version of yourself in regard to asexuality?

"If you don't want someone to touch you in a way that's uncomfortable to you, you don't have to just accept it. You're allowed to refuse and say no. If that person insists on it, she/he is the one at fault, not you."

What advice would you give to others who are just discovering about asexuality and considering whether they are or not?

Keep an open mind as you learn. Just because you don't seem to 'fit' anywhere doesn't mean there's something wrong with you. It's an identity that may work for the time being but not at another point in your life. It's a way of trying to understand yourself, but it shouldn't be a straitjacket.

Do you have a story you would like to share or anything else you would like to say?

Thank you to those who are working towards raising awareness about asexuality. Without that understanding of myself, I think it would have been a detriment to my own life and those who I wish to be a part of it. I hope that others who are confused about their feelings may be able to get clarification about themselves or otherwise benefit from knowing about asexuality.

Extra Info

What name would you like to go under for this book? Full name, first name, or alias?

Alias: Ann.

What country do you live in?

United States.

What age are you specifically? Or what decade age range are you – 20, 30. 40s?

Early thirties.

What nationality and ethnicity are you?

I was born in the mainland United States, but I am of Chinese descent.

44. 5mart2n's Story

When did you first discover you are asexual?

I found out I am asexual on 15th of January 2015, when I was 21 years old. However, I somewhat knew (and found it a little funny actually), that I wasn't as interested in sex growing up while others at least made themselves out to be.

How did you discover you are asexual?

I don't actually remember what threw me in the direction of asexuality (discovering it), but I remember doing a good amount of research on it and thinking about it on the way home from college that day, before deciding that I am (at least currently), asexual.

How do you identify yourself asexually?

Currently, I identify as an aromantic asexual. However, I'm sort of on the edge of aromantic and heteroromantic.

Are you 'out' about being asexual? If not, why not? If you are out, whom to, and how did they react?

Never found the courage to do so, plus I know someone who doesn't even believe in bisexuality. My cousin knows but found out about it through my YouTube video rather than me telling him. And my uncle (my cousin's dad) may know about it, but he doesn't seem bothered about it (in a good way; he doesn't talk about it, which is fine with me).

What's your deepest fear, concern or worry, about being asexual?

More stress, too many changes in life at once (if I were to come out, that is), and not being taken seriously about it.

Why do you feel, in general, that society doesn't accept asexuality as a form of sexual orientation in its own right? And what can be done about this?

Because a lot of people in the world are sexual, and not enough word is being spread about asexuality for those who are asexual but not as confident, to feel confident about being open about their asexuality. (This is just my opinion.)

What's your view on love? Have you been in love before?

I think it's a possibility, and while I have been in love before, I doubt it'll happen again for me personally (in terms of a relationship), which is fine with me.

Are you currently in a relationship, and if so, is it with another asexual (if yes, do they identify the same as you or how do they identify), or is it a sexual person? And how is either working out?

Nope. No current relationship.

If you are not in a relationship, would you like to be in one and if so, why, and what type of relationship – romantic? Platonic? What would your ideal relationship look like? And would you be in a relationship with a sexual person or not, and reason why?

I wouldn't mind being in a relationship (depends on the person though, of course), but overall it doesn't bother me if I were to not find one. An ideal relationship would be me and a girl in a non-sexual relationship, preferably with another asexual, since I wouldn't want anyone to feel like they've lost out, and would likely find another asexual more interesting (that's my assumption though).

What is your view about sex? Have you had sex before and if so, how did it make you feel? If you haven't, would you?

Sex, to me, overall disgusts me, and while I can talk about it, the actual act of it and such, puts me off a conversation (or anything really), therefore I wouldn't want to hear about it. I haven't had sex before, but it's one of those things I almost know I wouldn't want (like a cactus shoved up my backside).

Do you believe if a sexual person had a relationship with an asexual, it can work? And what do you think about it being fair or not?

I think it could work, as not every sexual person needs sex to feel comfort, therefore could live without it, and not every asexual person doesn't want sex, therefore that could work out as well. However, in a scenario where the sexual person wants sex and the asexual person doesn't, I believe an agreement should be set for the sexual person to be able to have sex with someone on the side, as long as the asexual person gets something in return (as part of the agreement); it's a very tricky area to discuss.

407

Asexuality is the lack of sexual attraction, as an asexual, what does this mean to you?

Having and desiring sex with another person or being.

Do you believe sexual attraction and sexual desire are the same thing or different?

Different. I believe that sexual attraction is to find someone sexually attractive in some form and want to do a sex game of sorts with them, which can lead to sex (due to arousal), or can just mean sex (as in the person would actually just want the sex). As for sexual desire, I believe it is the desire to have sex within one's sexual preferences (male, female, etc.) and limitations (what they'll do in the bedroom with another person).

Do you think sexual arousal and sexual attraction are the same or different?

Different, (at least slightly). I believe that sexual arousal is being aroused in some form or shape, such as thinking of a scene a person would like, seeing someone they like, etc., whereas I believe sexual attraction is to find someone sexually attractive, to think about a sexual scene with just them.

What's your view on living with someone?

For myself, I think it would be possible to live with someone, regardless of their sexual orientation, as long as we consider each other's feelings and such on sex.

Would you like kids and if so how many? And how do you hope to conceive these? If you already have kids, did you know before you had them that you are asexual and how did that impact your life?

Not really. Having children of my own isn't something I really want to do...at all, really.

What's your view on marriage? And if you were to get married, would it need to be with another asexual?

Like with children, getting married isn't something I want to do, even if I did get together with someone.

What's your view on nudity? On porn? On masturbation? On BDSM and kinks?

As long as it doesn't concern me in any way, I don't mind it in other people. I wouldn't generally involve myself in any of these things with other people.

How difficult is it for you to be asexual, in a sexualized world?

Not difficult at all. Nothing bad has happened from finding out I was asexual, many positives actually (despite coming across one piece of acephobia during my life, but it's only been 14 months since I discovered it, so I doubt it's stopped for good for me).

Can you tell me about a time when you have had to deal with intrusive questions or a difficult situation due to your asexuality, and what happened?

Like I said, I've only come across one piece of acephobia during my time as an asexual, and it actually caught me off guard, so I unfortunately didn't deal with it (I wish I did), but if I were to come across more acephobia in such scenarios, I'm almost sure I'd be able to deal with it better (since I'm more knowledgeable now).

What are the positives about being asexual?

Learnt a lot more about sexuality (and romantic orientation) in general, and have been somewhat less confused about myself since I found out.

If you could have one wish about being asexual, what would it be and why?

That people were more understanding of the sexual orientation (including homosexuality and bisexuality, but mainly asexual since it's talked about less).

If you were to look back at your life, what advice would you have given a younger version of yourself in regard to asexuality?

Going back to when I started secondary school, the advice that I'd give would be that I am actually asexual, and to look up the orientation, but maybe not to be open about it since I wasn't as confident back then as I am now. This way, I'd be less confused about myself and more confident about whom I actually am.

What advice would you give to others who are just discovering about asexuality and considering whether they are or not?

To research the topic before making any assumptions; I've seen so many comments (particularly on videos), where people are asking about asexuality that I've even pointed it out as 'them being allergic to research/Google' or 'missing the Google Search Bar' and commenting it on a conveniently placed video.

Extra Info

What name would you like to go under for this book? Full name, first name, or alias?

Alias: 5mart2n.

What country do you live in?

England.

What age are you specifically? Or what decade age range are you – 20, 30. 40s?

Aged 22.

Links to your website/social media.

YouTube Account: https://www.youtube.com/user/5mart2n

Twitter Account: https://twitter.com/5mart2n

DeviantArt Account: http://5mart2n.deviantart.com/

AVEN Account: 5mart2n.

45. Claire Evelyn's Story

When did you first discover you are asexual?

I would really call it a discovery. I was always different for as long as I can remember. I was about 14.

How did you discover you are asexual?

When I was 14 the people in my peer group dated and discussed boys that they were interested in. Sex became an inside joke that I didn't get, I went along with everything, making it up as I went – thinking that eventually I would understand. I knew that I simply wasn't interested in men. Just wasn't interested was the best way to describe it, it was only later did I discover others that felt similar and that there was a word for what I was experiencing.

How do you identify yourself asexually?

I don't really go for labels. I don't know if I am following my own personal don't ask and don't tell policy, but over the years it has become one.

Are you 'out' about being asexual? If not, why not? If you are out, whom to, and how did they react?

Nope I am not really out, I guess that people know I am not interested in marrying and dating, but out as an asexual – no. I suppose I am just very private. I did tell someone but he dismissed the idea as stupid, kind of like everybody feels like that sometimes but *did*, then they meet someone and it goes away.

What's your deepest fear, concern or worry, about being asexual?

I fear that I will be alone. I have long ago come to a point where all my friends are married with children or paired off. And although they didn't want to, I guess I was pushed out of their lives.

Why do you feel, in general, that society doesn't accept asexuality as a form of sexual orientation in its own right? And what can be done about this?

I think that the world is so sexualized that anyone thinking different is a radical idea. The only thing that can be done is to educate.

What's your view on love? Have you been in love before?

I believe love is chemical and although that sounds scientific I still believe it is magical. I have sort of being in love, with a friend. But it did not end well.

Are you currently in a relationship, and if so, is it with another asexual (if yes, do they identify the same as you or how do they identify), or is it a sexual person? And how is either working out?

No I am not in a relationship.

If you are not in a relationship, would you like to be in one and if so, why, and what type of relationship – romantic? Platonic? What would your ideal relationship look like? And would you be in a relationship with a sexual person or not, and reason why?

I would like to be in a relationship. I miss that strong human interaction and intimacy that comes with that relationship, regardless of sex. It would be a connection of minds rather than bodies. I wouldn't mind a relationship with a sexual person but it will take a lot of compromise.

What is your view about sex? Have you had sex before and if so, how did it make you feel? If you haven't, would you?

I think of sex as something other people do, like shark fishing or climbing Everest. I haven't had sex; I would like to, just to try it out, and yes I kind of think of it like trying sushi.

Do you believe if a sexual person had a relationship with an asexual, it can work? And what do you think about it being fair or not?

I think a sexual person can have a relationship with an asexual but it will be a lot of compromise and really depends on how sexual the person is. There are so many things going on in the relationship that it would just be another discussion point, but it will really depend on the people if they are willing to make it work.

Asexuality is the lack of sexual attraction, as an asexual, what does this mean to you?

I would rather describe it as a lack of sexual interest.

Do you believe sexual attraction and sexual desire are the same thing or different?

No – I sometimes feel attracted to good looking or charismatic people in the same way sexual people are, but I don't feel any desire for them. I simply would like to be part of their world and to be near them.

Do you think sexual arousal and sexual attraction are the same or different?

No they are not the same. I feel sexual arousal is a biological reaction of the sex organs; it is simply the body doing what it is made to do. The brain however, is what matters.

What's your view on living with someone?

I have no problems living with anybody as long as I can maintain my personal space.

Would you like kids and if so how many? And how do you hope to conceive these? If you already have kids, did you know before you had them that you are asexual and how did that impact your life?

I have considered having children either through adoption or IVF treatment.

What's your view on marriage? And if you were to get married, would it need to be with another asexual?

I don't really like the concept of marriage. I like traditions but I feel many marriages today are done as an extension of people's egos and whims. I would get married to an asexual or sexual, but I wouldn't do a wedding.

What's your view on nudity? On porn? On masturbation? On BDSM and kinks?

I have no problems with nudity; the human body is beautiful.

I don't get porn; I do not understand the appeal. I understand that some people are aroused by it. The same applies to masturbation. It's their body and why not. I find the only thing it does for me is help me to sleep.

BDSM and sexual kinks I find funny, I simply don't understand how people are aroused by them.

How difficult is it for you to be asexual, in a sexualized world?

It is very difficult as you are immediately an outsider. You don't get the jokes, you miss the sexual innuendo and sexual cues.

Can you tell me about a time when you have had to deal with intrusive questions or a difficult situation due to your asexuality, and what happened?

Getting strange looks from doctors and nurses when you tell them that pregnancy tests are not required when you are feeling ill. Having everyone feel sorry for you when you tell them you are single at your age. When people assume you haven't got a life when you don't have a husband and children.

What are the positives about being asexual?

I don't think there are any positives.

If you could have one wish about being asexual, what would it be and why?

That it was more prevalent.

If you were to look back at your life, what advice would you have given a younger version of yourself in regard to asexuality?

That it is okay to follow your own path and not follow the masses.

What advice would you give to others who are just discovering about asexuality and considering whether they are or not?

That nobody fits in a clearly defined labeled box, everybody whether they admit it or not.

Do you have a story you would like to share or anything else you would like to say?

It is very difficult to be asexual in South Africa and indeed it is very difficult to be homosexual in South Africa, especially for the black communities in the rural areas. Many South Africans would rather live a lie for their whole lives than break with custom, tradition, and their family. Indeed, admitting who they are is physically dangerous. I admire asexuals in the world who are out and proud, but our situations are not the same. I hope for the day when African asexuals can share that too.

Extra Info

What name would you like to go under for this book? Full name, first name, or alias?

Claire Evelyn.

What country do you live in?

South Africa.

What age are you specifically? Or what decade age range are you – 20, 30. 40s?

30's.

What nationality and ethnicity are you?

South African.

46. Waywalker's Story

When did you first discover you are asexual?

I was 36 years old and in the middle of a sexual relationship. I was also at university at the time getting my undergraduate degree (Bachelor of Arts).

How did you discover you are asexual?

In the middle of 'things' I realized I had never liked this activity. I did it to shut people up, endured it so I wouldn't be shamed for not giving my man what he needed, etc. But yeah, ZERO interest. Body works properly and all. No pain, but no desire to be doing it. When I reflected, I mostly used 'sexy times' to mentally organize my next art or writing project, figure out my priority items for the next day's office work, that sort of thing.

How do you identify yourself asexually?

Demiromantic (I think? – this is hard to nail down), sex-repulsed, agender, and asexual. I am 100% sex positive for everyone else (just please, for the sake of all that is HOLY don't tell me anything about it!).

Are you 'out' about being asexual? If not, why not? If you are out, whom to, and how did they react?

Yes. I'm out to my parents: they forgot about it within 3 days of discussing it. I used to come out to them every few days; I spent a year doing that. Remember – you can come out all you like – and with some people the only good that will come of it, is the fact that you know you were truthful and they have no legitimate excuse for marginalizing your reality. I'm also out to: my online friends – who are incredibly supportive and loving. Some of them are also asexuals!

What's your deepest fear, concern or worry, about being asexual?

"No, thank you, I'm asexual," is interpreted as a challenge instead of as an acceptable response to sexual advances. With 36 rapes under my belt as of now, and all but 2 of those being motivated by the 'generous' desire to 'fix' my orientation – yeah, I tend to not leave the house anymore on my own.

Why do you feel, in general, that society doesn't accept asexuality as a form of sexual orientation in its own right? And what can be done about this?

When the most common attitude to simply not pairing up, or pairing up platonically, is either to forcibly match make, or to make relentless inquiries as to the quality of the sex, it seems to me that anything except asexuality is accepted socially.

I don't know if anything can be done. The majority of creatures of all species are inclined to reproduce. While we are not unnatural, and with the population of our species at an all-time high, it is quite logical that more of us would be born, our utter lack (or predominant lack) of inclination is not something that the majority will ever really fully comprehend. And that's not their fault. We can minimize the stigma of not wanting nookie simply by being bold and speaking out on how wonderful our lives are (when they are wonderful), and celebrating their joys with them. In my experience, when they learn from interacting with us that we love, have joy with them when they have reason to be joyful (even if they know we are not into the happy 'sexy time' thing), they can begin to understand that we're not all that different from themselves. We just have different sources of joy.

What's your view on love? Have you been in love before?

I have studied this since I was a child. I have been guided from a young age by the concepts used by the ancient Greeks. There are six kinds of love. Eros (sexual, physical love, the kind of love you lose control of yourself when in), Philia (deep friendship, exemplified by the camaraderie forged between members of a military force when in combat), Storge (which is similar to this, but in the context of parent and child), Ludus (playful love, as between children or young lovers), Agape (love for all beings, or all humanity), Pragma (the deep bond between a long-established pair or love bonded group), and Philautia (self-love or self-compassion – we call it self-esteem and often misunderstand it's nature).

I tend to experience Philia as my primary love-bond, and usually a platonic Ludus type love starts it out. As most of the world of human beings wants Eros and shuns the others, I'm not overly hopeful for a life partner to stroll into my world anytime soon. It would be nice if one did. I would love to experience Pragma.

Are you currently in a relationship, and if so, is it with another asexual (if yes, do they identify the same as you or how do they identify), or is it a sexual person? And how is either working out?

Not in a relationship at all.

If you are not in a relationship, would you like to be in one and if so, why, and what type of relationship – romantic? Platonic? What would your ideal relationship look like? And would you be in a relationship with a sexual person or not, and reason why?

Maybe a relationship would be good. I don't particularly have a drive to be paired up. It would be nice, but isn't necessary at all. If I were to seek one out, it would be platonic, based on mutual interests and things we enjoy doing together – exploring the common roots of world faith traditions, studying world cultures to see what the oldest stories say, doing ancestral type skill building, that sort of thing. No sports at all, unless you count archery and such. Going to punk shows and playing video games.

I will never get into a relationship with a sexual person again. I was married three times; all three were sexuals. That type of mixed relationship can work, or so I've been told. But in my experience, it only injures both parties and is massively unfair to both parties. In my case, allowing sex basically had the exact same effect as if I had been raped, but topped with the massive guilt of knowing, 'I let this violation happen to me.' I know what the effects of rape are, as I have been on the receiving end of corrective rape 34 times and also the regular no-real-motivator-but-the-assertion-of-animal-dominance rape twice. So I know what I'm saying here. Conversely, my ex-husbands felt I denied them their marital rights when I chose not to. And the last boyfriend I had actually broke up with me because I was honest with him about not wanting sex any more. I suspect that he cheated on me the last several months of the relationship, but had the good taste to be less than obvious about it. He pretended to care about my heart, and up until the last moment told me we had a future together and that my nature was wonderful and acceptable and we could make it. The break-up was unexpected and hurt more than the three previous divorces, mostly because of the lies.

What is your view about sex? Have you had sex before and if so, how did it make you feel? If you haven't, would you?

I am sex and touch averse for the most part. I was before the sexual abuse started, and I was while it was going on, and I remain so today. Childhood sexual trauma was a major part of my life from about 2 years of age until I was 10 years old. I could not, for the life of me, understand the fascination the abusers had with what they appeared to obsess over. I have never had much sensation (although I'm told everything reacts naturally, so I know it's not low hormones – which so many people, including medical professionals (I will never forget the expression on my gynaecologist's face – I was spot on for normal), seem to enjoy telling us we have going on), so I often reflected that they must not have much in the way of feeling either, so their choice of abuse method was baffling.

Many within the ace community would prefer I not talk about the trauma, as they seem to believe that being direct and honest about the experiences many of us endure (like the 34 corrective rapes in my life, all aimed at FIXING my asexuality), somehow invalidate the orientation. That is not biologically possible, not even a little bit. Trauma does not instil or change anyone's orientation, never has, never will. It might prompt deep introspection, or the discovery of something previously unrecognized, but the orientation is not a result of the trauma, it was always there. Silencing those who have endured trauma only damages the community and further marginalizes those who have already endured hell and social isolation. So I speak up.

At best, sex is boring for me. At worst, it feels like a violation. Even kissing and hugging feel violating to me. If I love a person deeply, I will endure the worst things to make my beloved happy, or I used to. I now know that anyone who would want me to do that knowing how I feel about it, is not worth my time. They're not a real lover of ME as I am, and they don't respect my needs at all. And as I don't like disrespecting or minimizing other people's needs (which most of the time includes sexual activity), I don't date. And have no intention of ever dating again.

Do you believe if a sexual person had a relationship with an asexual, it can work? And what do you think about it being fair or not?

There are folks who believe this. Having been married three times and in a long-term dating relationship after those – I laugh at the starry-eyed naivety. There may well be that magical person who has sexual desire and loves you enough to not have sex. I hope you find them. Lord knows, I surely never have. I've heard of mixed couples who work out – mostly what I hear is that the ace is in a polyamorous (the description given by the people I knew who were involved) relationship, and their primary relationship is platonic with one person, but the other person has sex with other people. That is a valid situation. I cannot do that. I'm fiercely monogamous. So anybody with me needs to not ever need sex and be there for the long haul. Anything less will destroy us both.

'Mixed relationships' inherent fairness or unfairness is irrelevant on the larger scale. The assumptions implied by the question of whether being ace in a sexual partnership or sexual in an ace partnership are rooted (to my mind) in sexual-normative assumptions. The only people who can legitimately answer are the people in the mixed sexual/asexual relationship, and each one of those answers would be different, because each relationship is unique. For me, behaving in a sexual manner was so unfair to me that it damaged me. I allowed myself to behave sexually when doing so destroyed my heart and soul, and eventually, even my sanity to a degree. For someone else, it might be a delightful self-giving opportunity. Everyone is different.

Asexuality is the lack of sexual attraction, as an asexual, what does this mean to you?

This means I look at the world and do not see anyone or anything that inspires a desire for physical interaction of genital bits. There is nothing that ever inspires a longing for genital interaction in my life. My friends of the sexual persuasion tend to frequently comment about the 'doability' of this or that stranger, and have described to me that this sort of thing is a constant subtext for their lives. If this is the case, I do NOT have sexual attraction. At all.

Do you believe sexual attraction and sexual desire are the same thing or different?

Attraction is not the same thing as Desire, For example, I have been married 3x. I wanted (DESIRED) to please my former spouses, so I WANTED to have sex with them. It was not due to any innate URGE to do so, but entirely because I wanted them to be happy, as they DID have that innate URGE.

Do you think sexual arousal and sexual attraction are the same or different?

Arousal is not the same as ATTRACTION. Arousal can be measured physically in a lab. Human bodies tend to like to ensure the continuation of their genetics -- so AROUSAL *can* happen whether or not the human in possession of the body wills it. Any victim of sexual assault or abuse, male or female, can tell you that this is true, the body can be aroused even while the soul and mind and core being is in abject terror and rejecting all things relating to the situation. Since Arousal is a PHYSICAL EFFECT of TOUCH, it CANNOT be the same thing as Attraction, which does not require TOUCH to exist.

What's your view on living with someone?

I have no problem living with a person who is not in my bed, and enjoys silence. I had a great roommate once, I do love her dearly, but neither romantically, nor sexually – she remains one of my dearest friends today and she is one of two people who hear my troubles. We lived together for three years. Best years of my life, so far!

Would you like kids and if so how many? And how do you hope to conceive these? If you already have kids, did you know before you had them that you are asexual and how did that impact your life?

NO. I conceived twice in my life. Both times, the children were murdered in utero by their father, after I had told him they existed. He beat me until I miscarried. Twice. I don't want more. I miss them terribly and even so, I don't want more.

What's your view on marriage? And if you were to get married, would it need to be with another asexual?

Tried it three times. Failed three times due to asexuality and being too keen an observer of reality. Never again, I don't care what the orientation of the other person is.

What's your view on nudity? On porn? On masturbation? On BDSM and kinks?

I'm sex positive for EVERYONE ELSE. Nudity is for when no one can see me and even then, it's rare.

Porn is most frequently a vehicle for exploiters of the weak and enslaved, so I hate it. If you are a free person and enjoy such work – GO FOR IT! But I have personally known too many young women who were trafficked and forced into that work, so I have a ban on that in my home. I don't touch my body other than to clean up, and I don't want to know if anyone else does.

BDSM is not a bad thing. You can explore your physical limitations in that context safely – for me it was about finding out my body's limits, not pleasure or power/control paradigms. Once I found out the information I needed, I've not gone back. Like all sex, way too boring for me. I now live a very dull life (from the perspective of sexuals who are fairly obsessed, I think), which I really enjoy, trying to figure out how to start a business and what that business should be. So much more exciting.

How difficult is it for you to be asexual, in a sexualized world?

It's not. Perhaps a better question is, how marginalized do you feel you are, given every single human interaction seems sexualized? Not sure, though. For me, others are fine being them; I'm fine being me. I don't have to watch the TV or the adverts if I don't like the content. And if I want stuff I LIKE, I can create it myself. Which I'm working toward with a novel series.

Can you tell me about a time when you have had to deal with intrusive questions or a difficult situation due to your asexuality, and what happened?

Not clearly. Thirty-four of my experiences like that ended in corrective rape. As a result, there's a great deal of dissociation associated with this question for me. It is not that I don't want to answer, it's that the flashbacks from the history associated are quite distressing.

What are the positives about being asexual?

Sounds stereotypical, I know, but I have more time to do fun things, work on projects, read books, write books, do art, and generally enjoy life while everyone else is rutting or trying to find someone with whom to rut. I feel that being ace is the most freeing thing a person can be. We're not tied to convention unless we want to be. (I'm also agender, and I don't have a gender I identify with. Pronouns and titles are what my dear ones think of me as, and I'm so fine with that.) I will forever be eccentric aunt or uncle so and so and that's awesome by me.

Please note, I feel that those for whom sex and touch are as delightful to them as all my various projects are to me – they are to be celebrated and their joys honored as much as any I have. I only ask not to be ignored, excluded, or forgotten because my delights don't involve getting naked in pudding (or whatever the sexual folk are into!).

If you could have one wish about being asexual, what would it be and why?

More mainstream media representation. Nobody should have to grow up thinking they're weird, ugly, broken, and all the many other lies that get hurled at us. By the way, the film Zootopia's primary pair of protagonists fully represented my preferred primary relationship style. YAY! First time in my whole life I could say, "WOW! That's me and..." And not have it be sort of right, or right until the end when the film studios usually force the pair up to make audiences happy.

If you were to look back at your life, what advice would you have given a younger version of yourself in regard to asexuality?

"You know that vision of normality everyone is holding up for you? That's not for you. Remember Cousin Barb? THAT is what you're going for, AIM HIGH! Be the art you need to see in the world!"

What advice would you give to others who are just discovering about asexuality and considering whether they are or not?

Be you. If a label helps you get comfy in your skin, sweetheart, use the heck out of it. If none of them fit, that's ok, too. Just trust your gut, and never allow yourself to be violated. Especially not because, "that's your primary relationship, you're really being unfair and not putting out is abuse!" That line is a big fat lie! Don't buy it.

Do you have a story you would like to share or anything else you would like to say?

I spent 5 very intensely formative years in South Korea. My whole way of handling the world is a mixture of my grandfather's First Nations culture and my time in South Korea. THIRD CULTURE FOLK/GLOBAL NOMADS REPRESENT!

Extra Info

What name would you like to go under for this book? Full name, first name, or alias?

Alias: Waywalker. Believe it or not, my family would feel humiliated if I were public. Sigh.

What country do you live in?

I live in the United States of America, Washington State (west coast).

What age are you specifically? Or what decade age range are you – 20, 30. 40s?

43.

What nationality and ethnicity are you?

National affiliation – United States citizen.

Bodily ethnicity – some Irish, some German, some Cherokee.

Cultural matrix – a mix of Ani Yunwiya (white folk call us Cherokee), South Korean, and Irish.

You can get to me through Sandra (@Asexualise on Twitter) if you have further questions.

47. Darcy's Story

When did you first discover you are asexual?

I have always known something was a little different when it came to sex with me. As a little kid, I had so many crushes, like most kids do, but as I matured, I was always stuck in 'crush' mode. I liked some people, but I never really thought things past kissing. Sexuality has never offended me, but I was always uncomfortable when it came to including my own body. I didn't realize until I was about 25 that there was a name for it and it was just normal.

How did you discover you are asexual?

I dated a fair amount as a teen, and less as an adult. I tried sex but it never felt like anything to me. I never felt any emotional attachment really, but more than that, it just never felt much physically to me. I can feel things, but I also feel sort of detached. I joined *tumblr.com* back in 2013, and that's how I was exposed to the term asexual and the information there. That's when I started identifying as asexual.

How do you identify yourself asexually?

I identify right now as a pan-romantic a-(grey a-)sexual.

Are you 'out' about being asexual? If you are out, whom to, and how did they react?

I am out to people I am close with. It's not really something I try to hide, but I also don't shout it down the hallways. I have told some people in my family. My family was somewhat disappointed, in a way. My mother mostly chooses to ignore it. She sarcastically asked me if I wanted a "cake or something" when I told her. I had to laugh, given the asexual predilection towards cake. I've had friends (and potential romantic partners), tell me that I was just a lesbian, or I just needed more sexual experience, or I just 'wasn't doing it right'. I've even had family members ask me if I was sexually abused as a child. I wasn't.

What's your deepest fear, concern or worry, about being asexual?

My deepest fear used to be that there was something wrong with me, that I was damaged somehow. Then I worried that no one would ever want to be with me without the guarantee of sex as part of a relationship. I worried that I would be pressured to have children. I worried that my high libido would be mistaken for interest in sex. I mostly worried that no one would accept me.

Why do you feel, in general, that society doesn't accept asexuality as a form of sexual orientation in its own right? And what can be done about this?

I feel like being asexual is sort of being a black hole in sexual space. We are there, but we are kind of a negative, in that we are just not sexual in a way that is understandable. People generally see it as an excuse to get out of sleeping with someone, like we are faking it. Or it's just such an abstract concept to most people that they just can't grasp it, especially in a heteronormative society. But even in the queer community it can be a struggle: we are basically fighting for the right to be ignored, in their eyes.

The only thing to do is to try to speak about it. Tell more people. That's the only great way to teach some things – exposure. It's kind of like how some (straight) people don't understand gay people. Then they meet one and go, "Oh, that wasn't so weird after all. They're just people!" That's kind of how I see it.

What's your view on love? Have you been in love before?

I used to sort of mock love. When I was a teen I thought I might be in love (a few times), but on reflection that was just nonsense. I have always been wary of love, as it's a tough topic in my family. But I feel like now I can truly say that I am in love. It's only been in the last couple of years that I have felt like I would really do anything or give anything for someone else. But more importantly, I feel like I get that back in return.

Are you currently in a relationship, and if so, is it with another asexual (if yes, do they identify the same as you or how do they identify), or is it a sexual person? And how is either working out?

I am currently in a long-term relationship with a (bi)sexual person. It's working out wonderfully because this person understands asexuality (they even researched it when I told them), and they were of the opinion that they could do without sex to be with me. Meaning that they respect me and care enough that it wasn't even an issue.

What is your view about sex? Have you had sex before and if so, how did it make you feel? If you haven't, would you?

Sex doesn't bother me, but it makes me very uncomfortable when my own body is sexualized or when I feel expected to have sex. I have had sex, but it didn't really feel like anything. If anything, I would describe it as boring. I feel mentally disconnected from my genitals.

Do you believe if a sexual person had a relationship with an asexual, it can work? And what do you think about it being fair or not?

I do, as long as both (or all) parties are considerate and accepting. Any pressure to conform to another's standards is not a way for it to work. I feel like honest communication is vital. I feel like it can be fair, as long as no one feels like they are missing something and no one feels like they are expected to do more than they want.

Asexuality is the lack of sexual attraction, as an asexual, what does this mean to you?

For me, it just feels like an indescribable disconnection. My 'sexuality' is purely mental. Physical touch is almost just a waste of time, but a strong mental and emotional connection feel to me much more intimate and attract me.

Do you believe sexual attraction and sexual desire are the same thing or different?

This one is difficult. I have heard sexual friends make sexual comments about individuals known or unknown, whom they find sexually attractive, and I just don't understand it. I don't know that I sexually desire someone really. I may find someone I want to be close with, but it doesn't mean I want to be sexually close with them. So it's difficult for me to separate the two ideas in my head.

Do you think sexual arousal and sexual attraction are the same or different?

These I feel are different. In my case, I have an active libido, so I do know sexual arousal. It actually annoys me most of the time. It's more like something I have to take care of, as part of my body's normal functions. But I am not really aroused so much when it comes to other people; that really doesn't factor into it.

What's your view on living with someone?

I used to be against it, but that was before I met my current partner. I still have some adjusting to do, but that comes more from my personality type than from my sexual preference.

Would you like kids and if so how many? And how do you hope to conceive these? If you already have kids, did you know before you had them that you are asexual and how did that impact your life?

I have never really been one to see children in my future. My partner has kids, so in a way I now have kids, but I never had to think about conception for them. I have thought about artificial conception for another couple to adopt a child, as a sort of donor, but other than that I have really never thought about it.

What's your view on marriage? And if you were to get married, would it need to be with another asexual?

I have never been one to dream about my wedding, even as a child. I am actually engaged to be married to a sexual person. Marriage is a serious commitment to me, and I have high standards for the person I am marrying. Meaning that I do not want to feel like I am settling at all, which I don't.

What's your view on nudity? On porn? On masturbation? On BDSM and kinks?

Nudity has never bothered me, either on a screen or in person. I feel like the human body is normal and natural and as a machine it fascinates me.

Porn doesn't offend me. I sometimes find it quite amusing.

Masturbation for me has been a necessity more than something "fun".

And BDSM and kinks don't offend me; I just am not interested in participating.

How difficult is it to be asexual in a sexualized world?

Not particularly, since I am not repelled by sex. It's just part of life. Sometimes I don't understand some of the decisions sexual people make, because I feel sometimes like I am more rational, but I just tend to go about my business in this world.

Can you tell me about a time when you have had to deal with intrusive questions or a difficult situation due to your asexuality, and what happened?

Some people ask me really personal questions, but I have always been one for learning and also one for educating when I feel I have something to add, so I just answer them as best as I can. I don't really get offended easily.

What are the positives about being asexual?

I feel like I am a good sounding board for friends when they are having sex/relationship problems. I offer a different outlook usually that helps them make decisions most of the time. It sounds very arrogant, but I say this because friends have told me directly. I have one friend that calls me when she needs to be "rational".

If you could have one wish about being asexual, what would it be and why?

I think I would wish for asexuality to be better understood and better known in the world. So I wouldn't have had to spend years questioning if there was something wrong with me, and people wouldn't act so strange when I tell them I am ace.

If you were to look back at your life, what advice would you have given a younger version of yourself in regard to asexuality?

I would tell myself not to try so hard; that everything would be okay; that I would find my place in the world and I would be accepted eventually.

What advice would you give to others who are just discovering about asexuality and considering whether they are or not?

I guess the same as my previous answer. Also, sexuality is fluid, so don't try to pigeonhole yourself, especially not as a young person.

Extra Info

What name would you like to go under for this book? Full name, first name, or alias?

Darcy.

What country do you live in?

I live in the USA.

What age are you specifically? Or what decade age range are you – 20, 30. 40s?

I am 28 years old.

What nationality and ethnicity are you?

I am white.

Links to your website/social media.

Social media: *queermidas.tumblr.com*

48. South American Anonymous's Story

When did you first discover you are asexual?

When I was around 13-16, I used to think being genderless, asexual and androgyne, were the same thing.

How did you discover you are asexual?

I never felt any sexual desires towards any crush or icon I ever had, but I never really questioned it. I started questioning my gender and I found out I was not only asexual but repulsed by sex. I always found sex gross; I always found genitals disgusting. I find my genitals disgusting, and I always felt awkward when people talked about sex near me or tried to seduce me in that way.

How do you identify yourself asexually?

Well, so I'm an apothisexual (sex repulsed) asexual, that's my sexual orientation. For my romantic orientation, I'm ANDROGY-NEhyporomantic (I have an very low romantic drive and I hardly feel romantic desires, that explains HYPOromantic), the 'androgyne' part also sometimes called 'androgyno' or 'ambi' is related to 'what' I feel attracted to, in that case, masculine, feminine and androgynous persons, however it has nothing to do with genders or sexes, I'm attracted to masculinity, femininity and androgyny in a hyporomantic way. Sometimes I call myself ANDROGYNEalterous because alterous is like an umbrella term for hyporomantic. Alterous means I'm open to friendships with benefits and romantic relationships, but I have a low romantic drive, anyway I want an emotional bond, just that.

Are you 'out' about being asexual? If not, why not? If you are out, whom to, and how did they react?

I came out to my mom and to a few friends. My mom was so shocked, like I told her I would never have sex and I would totally end up in a no-heterosexual relationship, I say that because people read me as both a gay and a lesbian, cos of my gender. My gender also shocked my mom a lot, she stills doesn't understand how my biological sex hurts me. About my friends, they were more supportive and didn't criticize me and I found that awesome. I also found out one of my best friends was pansexual; she was very supportive and helped me come out to my mom somehow. I haven't come out for my dad or other family members yet because they're disgustingly queer-phobics and machos. This kinda hurts me because I feel unhappy when I'm near them, specially around my dad, sometimes also around my mom, she's very sexist and queer-phobic as well, she accepts me but she doesn't accept other people like me and this pisses me off. She says all she wants is to see me happy, but most of the times she forgets those words.

What's your deepest fear, concern or worry, about being asexual?

Well, my biggest fear is to end up alone with like 50 cats. I also hate when people say asexuality doesn't exist, I already heard that from psychologists, sexologists and doctors, both have different explanations for why asexuality isn't a thing and most of the time they imply we are broken or traumatized.

Why do you feel, in general, that society doesn't accept asexuality as a form of sexual orientation in its own right? And what can be done about this?

Because there's no concerns or awareness about asexuality enough to make a difference, nor is there a group standing for us. I think through explaining it in the media, throughout articles, books, interviews, etc., would mean a lot. Also we need meet-ups, and we totally need to prove therapists and doctors that there's nothing wrong with being asexual and that's a thing, not a problem, we are humans too.

What's your view on love? Have you been in love before?

Sex should be the least important thing in love. Love is about forming a bond with someone and spending your lives together. Love has its ups and downs but lovers should always be able to count on one another.

I already had crushes before, the worst I ever had was for a girl older than me, she was perfect, there was nothing I wouldn't do just to stay near her, we were the best of friends but oh well, things just didn't work out because she was heterosexual and wanted a man, a real man, and I'm just an asexual androgyne and she had dreams only a man could make happen.

Are you currently in a relationship, and if so, is it with another asexual (if yes, do they identify the same as you or how do they identify), or is it a sexual person? And how is either working out?

I'm single.

If you are not in a relationship, would you like to be in one and if so, why, and what type of relationship – romantic? Platonic? What would your ideal relationship look like? And would you be in a relationship with a sexual person or not, and reason why?

I would like to be in any kind of relationship except a sexual one; I just don't want to be alone. I want someone to stay by my side till the end like the best of friends even if we are lovers or not. I want somebody to take care of and share experiences with and I want them to take care of me, I just want company and, maybe romance, and I just want to have fun as well.

Well, I would date a sexual person if they could keep their sexual desires for themselves; I wouldn't have sex with them. I think the hardest part would be me feeling bad because I would be letting them 'starve'. I would like to do sensual things also, I just can't stand sexual acts; I can't stand masturbation as well; I just don't mind it if my partner did it without letting me know. I wouldn't date hypersexual persons though; this would never work out. I'm fine with kissing (I just don't like mouth kisses); hugging, cuddling, going on dates, sleeping in the same bed maybe, marrying, having kids maybe and living together.

What is your view about sex? Have you had sex before and if so, how did it make you feel? If you haven't, would you?

Sex is disgusting. I don't see it as wrong but it is disgusting. I wouldn't ever have sex, it disgusts me to a point I even feel nauseas.

Do you believe if a sexual person had a relationship with an asexual, it can work? And what do you think about it being fair or not?

Yeah, it can totally work out, love is stronger than sex. I think if people respect each other it can work, well if they love each other enough. The sexual person can try holding their desires or the asexual person can try having sex, to please their partners, for example.

Asexuality is the lack of sexual attraction, as an asexual, what does this mean to you?

I see my crush and I can't ever imagine us having sex, all I can imagine is romantic fluff or sensual acts at the very least. I can even find them sexy, but I wouldn't have sex with my lover.

Do you believe sexual attraction and sexual desire are the same thing or different?

Well it's the same thing, unless you are talking about the desire for sex because the desire for sex is different than getting attracted to someone sexually, like you only would have sex with that person. The desire for sex is like you are open for just having sex with anyone. Sexual desire and sexual attraction are synonymous though.

Do you think sexual arousal and sexual attraction are the same or different?

No because some things like porn are sexually arousing while only the person you want sex with is sexually attractive.

What's your view on living with someone?

I don't know, it's like having a friend living with you, however you can do things friends don't. It's like having a pal the closest as possible next to you.

Would you like kids and if so how many? And how do you hope to conceive these? If you already have kids, did you know before you had them that you are asexual and how did that impact your life?

Well for me, kids aren't important, it depends on my partner and how much they may want, we would have to share a lot of chores and responsibilities. If we don't have kids, I prefer having pets, I love cats, I would be sad if my partner disliked the idea, anyway we would 100% adopt, I like toddlers, I wouldn't adopt babies, too much work.

What's your view on marriage? And if you were to get married, would it need to be with another asexual?

Marriage is just a status; it wouldn't matter if I didn't marry my partner, I would like dating asexual persons more, to be honest.

What's your view on nudity? On porn? On masturbation? On BDSM and kinks?

Oh well all those things disgust me except nudity, it's a natural human thing, like they disgust me to a point I have nausea.

How difficult is it for you to be asexual, in a sexualized world?

Well, I feel awkward, sometimes I feel like I'm too weird or too eccentric, I feel like it's hard to find the love I want in such a world and I usually feel disgusted. I live in a very sexualized country though.

Can you tell me about a time when you have had to deal with intrusive questions or a difficult situation due to your asexuality, and what happened?

Well, people always ask me if I'm a homosexual or they ask me out, I don't know if they are serious or not, but both males and females do, so then I tell them I'm asexual and they won't be happy with me, or I simply tell them I don't date. I also feel awkward when people ask me if I'm heterosexual or not, usually people understand I'm not available for their desires but they find me odd.

What are the positives about being asexual?

You get to experience a more pure love, but it's not better than any other orientation or worst.

If you could have one wish about being asexual, what would it be and why?

Well I wish I find an understanding partner, because it's hard to find people who don't want to have sex or can keep their desires. It's hard to find love as an asexual.

If you were to look back at your life, what advice would you have given a younger version of yourself in regard to asexuality?

Seriously, I would explain to myself everything I know about orientations and genders right now and I would emphasize that we are not broken, and there's nothing wrong with being who we are, and what other people say doesn't matter and we should have more courage to face what's up ahead.

What advice would you give to others who are just discovering about asexuality and considering whether they are or not?

Well asexuality is simple, you either are or not, and there's nothing wrong with you and you'll have to face bad opinions from other people with no shame. Also love does not equal sex.

Do you have a story you would like to share or anything else you would like to say?

I just find it awkward with the reactions people have when they discover I'm not typical. They get disappointed.

Extra Info

What name would you like to go under for this book? Full name, first name, or alias?

South American Anonymous.

What age are you specifically? Or what decade age range are you – 20, 30. 40s?

I'm 17 years old.

What nationality and ethnicity are you?

Brazilian and European descendant.

451

49. Samantha G's Story

When did you first discover you are asexual?

I discovered I am asexual when I was 18 years old.

How did you discover you are asexual?

I always knew asexuality (as a sexual orientation) existed, but I never knew what it actually was until one day I got curious as to what asexuality is and I Googled it. Needless to say I was shocked that it actually fit me.

How do you identify yourself asexually?

I identify as an aromantic, bigender asexual person.

Are you 'out' about being asexual? If not, why not? If you are out, whom to, and how did they react?

I am not open about my asexuality, but I have come out to two different people. One of them is my best friend and he was sensible about it and played it cool. The second person I came out to was a classmate in high school. I only came out to him because he said asexual people don't exist, but I proved him wrong, and he just shut his mouth. (I wasn't mad at him, and he wasn't intentionally being insensitive. I could tell he really had no idea asexual people existed.)

What's your deepest fear, concern or worry, about being asexual?

My biggest fear about asexuality is that if I come out to someone as asexual they might think I don't have the capacity to love, or want to get loved emotionally and/or physically (sans sex), but I do want to be loved, and I do want to share my love with close friends and family.

Why do you feel, in general, that society doesn't accept asexuality as a form of sexual orientation in its own right? And what can be done about this?

People don't accept asexuality for one or two reasons:

1. They don't think asexuality is real.

2. The asexual population is so low that they feel like they will never meet an asexual.

One thing that can be done to help people accept asexuality is spreading awareness. If you or someone you know is asexual and you hear bigotry against asexuality then just talk to that person. It is their decision to believe you or not.

What's your view on love? Have you been in love before?

Love is spending time with people you enjoy being around any day of the week just to be around them. I have been in love before, with people outside my family, and I would take each relationship back. Each time I was in love my heart got broken.

Are you currently in a relationship, and if so, is it with another asexual (if yes, do they identify the same as you or how do they identify), or is it a sexual person? And how is either working out?

I am not in a relationship.

If you are not in a relationship, would you like to be in one and if so, why, and what type of relationship – romantic? Platonic? What would your ideal relationship look like? And would you be in a relationship with a sexual person or not, and reason why?

I would only want to be in a completely platonic relationship, but I would have to know that person for several months or years to even consider dating them, and yes they could be a sexual person, I would just wish for them to give up sex forever to be with me. If they go off to have sex with someone that isn't me then I feel like they don't love me, or I am not giving them everything they need in life.

What is your view about sex? Have you had sex before and if so, how did it make you feel? If you haven't, would you?

I think sex is pointless. I have never, and will never, have sex with another living being. Every time I imagine myself having sex with someone I instantly get sick to my stomach and want to vomit.

Do you believe if a sexual person had a relationship with an asexual, it can work? And what do you think about it being fair or not?

I think relationships between asexuals and sexuals could work as long as one person gives up something sexually, i.e. the asexual having sex, or the sexual never having sex again. I don't think those relationships are fair based on what I said previously.

Asexuality is the lack of sexual attraction, as an asexual, what does this mean to you?

Lack of sexual attraction means that I don't want to have sex ever.

Do you believe sexual attraction and sexual desire are the same thing or different?

I think sexual attraction and sexual desire are different things. Sexual attraction to someone is when you want to have sex with them. Sexual desire is just a want to have sex.

Do you think sexual arousal and sexual attraction are the same or different?

No, sexual arousal and sexual attraction are different things. Sexual arousal is when you are feeling pleased sexually, and sexual attraction is when you want to have sex with someone or something.

What's your view on living with someone?

I want to live with people, but I would prefer them to be friends as opposed to a romantic or sexual partner.

Would you like kids and if so how many? And how do you hope to conceive these? If you already have kids, did you know before you had them that you are asexual and how did that impact your life?

I want no kids at all.

What's your view on marriage? And if you were to get married, would it need to be with another asexual?

I do not believe in marriage, but if I were to get married I would only ever marry an asexual who also doesn't want children.

What's your view on nudity? On porn? On masturbation? On BDSM and kinks?

Nudity: Fine.

Porn: Enjoy at your own risk.

Masturbation: Fine.

BDSM and kinks: They gross me out, but if you enjoy it, more power to ya.

How difficult is it for you to be asexual, in a sexualized world?

It is not difficult at all. I don't pay attention to people making sexual jokes, or comments, and I don't pay attention to the hyper-sexualized media.

Can you tell me about a time when you have had to deal with intrusive questions or a difficult situation due to your asexuality, and what happened?

Whenever a *Victoria's Secret* commercial (a commercial for women's lingerie), comes on television while I am watching it with my dad, he always gawks at the women and eventually ends up asking if I was gawking at them too, and I used to say I was, but now I just pretend I didn't hear him.

What are the positives about being asexual?

A. More free time to do whatever I want without having to worry about finding a partner.

B. More chances to see someone as an actual person instead of an object for sex.

C. A better chance to understand what it is like to be a minority in today's hypersexual society.

If you could have one wish about being asexual, what would it be and why?

People would instantly understand it on a conceptual level, and never bring up sex around me again.

If you were to look back at your life, what advice would you have given a younger version of yourself in regard to asexuality?

You are not gay, you are not straight, you are asexual. You don't want to ever have sex again, but that is totally alright. P.S. All your crushes are and were, purely aesthetic.

What advice would you give to others who are just discovering about asexuality and considering whether they are or not?

Don't let anyone tell you who you can or can't be. You are you through and through. You don't have to please anyone but yourself because you are only going to spend 100% of your life with you. P.S. Sexual preferences can change over time, so it is alright if you are asexual today and homosexual tomorrow.

Extra Info

What name would you like to go under for this book? Full name, first name, or alias?

Samantha G.

What country do you live in?

I live in the United States of America.

50. Wanita Redman's Story

When did you first discover you are asexual?

I think I have only just discovered it now, I have always not hugely been into sex, even within long-term stable relationships, I just thought that maybe I wasn't in love with my partner enough. I have been single over the last year, and on trying to re-enter the dating scene I have realized that other single people view sex with excitement, and I view it as a threat and with vulnerability and fear, and one day I thought maybe I'm asexual, maybe sex is just not my thing, maybe I should go and join the monastery or go and meditate with the monks!

How did you discover you are asexual?

Well as soon as I started to feel I was healed enough from my last break-up, I started talking to friends and other singles, and I was shocked at how keen the other singles and all the people I know, talk so excitedly about the thought of having sex, I wouldn't say I am repulsed by it, but I certainly think it's a bit animalistic with someone I don't know, and I think I carry a lot of shame around the idea of having sex. Anyway, through my shock at how much the entire world is so into sex and I am not, I thought, 'shit, I must be different somehow, and maybe it's not a bad thing, maybe it's just who I am!', so I Googled 'asexual' just to see if I fitted the description, and low and behold there is an entire online community in existence of people who aren't really into sex either, and it just felt like a breath of fresh air.

How do you identify yourself asexually?

I am definitely a romantic, historically I have been gay so I guess I am a homoromantic, and I think demisexual sounds the closest to what I think I am, but I am still reading and learning about all the terms.

Are you 'out' about being asexual? If not, why not? If you are out, whom to, and how did they react?

Funny, I am out about being gay, and that has never been an issue, but the idea of telling people I am asexual just makes me feel full of shame and embarrassment, only because the entire world is sex obsessed and I just feel overwhelmed by the idea of telling people just yet, until I really come to terms with this. I have told a few close friends and they are fine, one said, "Yeah well, I think that's the way the world's going", another said, "You're fine, you're just healing from the last relationship", another said "You might find out a lot about yourself" (she was referring to me trying online dating in the asexual world) and another kind of bypassed my comment, either not knowing what to say or not believing it.

What's your deepest fear, concern or worry, about being asexual?

My biggest concern is that I desperately want a relationship and a life companion and to my previous knowledge of the gay girl scene, no one is going to want a long-term relationship with someone who wants sex rarely.

Why do you feel, in general, that society doesn't accept asexuality as a form of sexual orientation in its own right? And what can be done about this?

I think the world is and has been overly sexualised; definitely since the sexual revolution (the 60's) and I think the majority of people are in disbelief that there are those whom really are just not that interested. I think more awareness in general, like there were a few articles online of asexual people in relationships talking about their relationship and that made it all feel normal and okay.

What's your view on love? Have you been in love before?

I am very much a romantic, I like the idea of people meeting and going for walks to get to know each other and holding hands to create intimacy. I have said before that I feel I was born in the wrong era; I feel overwhelmed being in this era where people see someone they like in a bar, get drunk and fuck. I am very much a slow burn type of girl, which is why I think I identify with the demisexual label. Yes I have definitely been in love before, I have had a few long-term relationships and in the space in-between I always developed feelings for people in an unrequited way. I think for a long time, because I never really wanted to do the sex thing, I have had feelings for someone and wouldn't tell them or have a pash and then flatline in the bedroom, and it would always really freak me out because I was so in love with them but could never get to the sex part (well not like the rest of the planet).

Are you currently in a relationship, and if so, is it with another asexual (if yes, do they identify the same as you or how do they identify), or is it a sexual person? And how is either working out?

Not currently in a relationship, have been single for a year. Am looking to have another relationship and feel I might have better luck in the asexual community and could even go straight within the asexual community just to be with someone who understands.

If you are not in a relationship, would you like to be in one and if so, why, and what type of relationship – romantic? Platonic? What would your ideal relationship look like? And would you be in a relationship with a sexual person or not, and reason why?

My ideal relationship would be with someone who is also demisexual, that I meet and have a slow get to know situation, and then settle down, have the house, the kids, the lot. Sex wise I would be happy to be with someone who enjoys sex only within the relationship and maybe with someone who is more comfortable with their sexuality than I am and maybe could inspire me to want it a little bit more than I do now, but that they totally understand that I don't really have a drive for it myself and certainly doesn't complain that I don't initiate (which has happened to me in past relationships).

What is your view about sex? Have you had sex before and if so, how did it make you feel? If you haven't, would you?

Sex is beautiful when one is in love, but sex is really confronting with a stranger or with someone I don't yet feel an emotional connection with and feel 'safe' with, in those situations I feel completely overwhelmed that I almost, or usually, shut down (as I call it, I flatline). But at times in the past, within a really happy loving relationship, sex has been fun and silly and kind. But I haven't felt that for maybe 15 years as my heart has not felt safe for quite a long time.

Do you believe if a sexual person had a relationship with an asexual, it can work? And what do you think about it being fair or not?

I really don't know, I have read some articles where they have said yes that is possible, but personally I think people should get together with people who have the same appetite as themselves, unless they are happy for their partner to get their appetite met somewhere else (as in, outside the relationship). I did consider there for a second that I would be happy to have a companionship with someone and they get their sexual needs met outside the relationship, but I haven't found that person yet, and realistically I don't know if I would cope.

Asexuality is the lack of sexual attraction, as an asexual, what does this mean to you?

Most of the time I am attracted to everyone on the same level, which is that I recognise beauty and loving people and their senses of humor and characters but I don't necessarily want to have sex with them. This has led me to question if I am really gay! Because I find men as attractive as women on this generic level, but I don't want to actually have sex with anyone, the idea of it freaks me out...but in saying that, when I really get to know someone on an intimate level, then I think about becoming more intimate and fantasise about kissing, but still I get blocked at the idea of actually having sex, I might think about sex or even watch porn, but flatline when it goes beyond kissing, but if I love them I will go beyond the kissing but really only to keep them happy, not really for myself.

Do you believe sexual attraction and sexual desire are the same thing or different?

Attraction is a very complex thing, attraction can be so many things, such as being attracted to someone because you spark off each other's sense of humour or heightened energetic conversations, it's not sexual in nature but then I would consider flirting, which is a prelude to sexual contact.

Whereas sexual desire is more about the body than personality, someone walking into a room and seeing someone that you find pleasing to the eye, most of the world would call that sexual desire if their mind went to 'god I'd love to have sex with that', but of course that's not us aces.

I think sexual attraction (especially for the demisexual people), comes before sexual desire, I think you can be attracted to a person but not have the active desire to do anything about it, and then something shifts and suddenly the desire to do something about it occurs.

Do you think sexual arousal and sexual attraction are the same or different?

No, attraction again is an energetic thing, not a physical thing, and sexual arousal is very physical, you can have an energetic attraction that then inspires physical arousal. Again, attraction happens prior to arousal.

What's your view on living with someone?

I like the idea of living with someone, but I really like the idea of having separate bedrooms. My mum has a separate bedroom from her boyfriend and they seem to be happy so why not me. I read somewhere for people who are highly sensitive, which is me, I think I am somewhere on the highly functioning spectrum of autism/asperger's, I find the social sphere overwhelming and certainly the intimate sphere. I think I would function the best in a close relationship if I had lots of personal space and I choose when someone can enter that space.

Would you like kids and if so how many? And how do you hope to conceive these? If you already have kids, did you know before you had them that you are asexual and how did that impact your life?

I would love children, and I have thought about this before, the concept in certain religions is that sex is only a function for pro-creating, I think the concept was born of an asexual person, because I completely dig that idea, do it to get the kids and then leave me alone.

What's your view on marriage? And if you were to get married, would it need to be with another asexual?

Again, I think marriage is about companionship, family and community. Personally I would love to get married to a demisexual who has a low sex drive like me but can walk through life as my life partner creating a wonderful life together.

What's your view on nudity? On porn? On masturbation? On BDSM and kinks?

I am easy with nudity. I could be a nudist but not good for city living as you'd get too many people videoing you and posting you on YouTube, but yes, I think nudity has nothing to do with sexuality, that has only been thrown at us by our over-sexualized society.

Porn I think is very male centered and most of it is degrading to women. In saying that, I have watched porn in my time, I usually use it to masturbate to, and I'm usually done in about 4 minutes, and once I have climaxed the visuals just look disgusting and sometimes I have felt embarrassed and shameful that I've watch it.

How difficult is it for you to be asexual, in a sexualized world?

I find it quite confronting that I realise I'm not as interested as I should be (as in, what the world is telling me). I have been a bit of a chameleon in my life; with a history of being great at theatre and drama I have this talent to match the energy of who is around me, so in my life I have been very overt, especially when out drinking in clubs and bars. I have a few drinks and the music comes on and off I go, I throw my sexuality out there on the dance floor and of course every sex addict in the place comes at me like a moth to the flame, and if someone does get lucky and takes me home, my sexuality that I have shown on the dance floor does not translate to the bedroom. This has been my biggest problem with being an asexual in a sexualized world, that just being me can be interpreted as a come on or that I'm being flirty; and I'm just playing with energy, I don't actually want to get my gear off. My sexuality really consists of dancing and kissing; that is enough for me.

Can you tell me about a time when you have had to deal with intrusive questions or a difficult situation due to your asexuality, and what happened?

Once some girl in an open relationship wanted to kiss me and I said 'I don't believe in kissing unless you're in love' and she looked at me with shock and said, 'well that's a waste of your youth'.

Really, because this is so new to me, I haven't really had the questions, but I'm sure they will come if I attempt the dating scene.

What are the positives about being asexual?

Well if there's no random sex happening, less drama, less sexually transmitted diseases and no accidental pregnancy.

If you could have one wish about being asexual, what would it be and why?

That there would be more demisexual people in the world who realise sex is not the most important thing in the world. That kindness, platonic love, compassion and love that is patient, is more common than 'wham bam thank you mam'.

If you were to look back at your life, what advice would you have given a younger version of yourself in regard to asexuality?

I would have gone to university instead of getting into a relationship and going to Mardi Gras and Sleaze Ball thinking that was the avenue to 'my people' (being the gay community), they are not my people and it's only taken me about 20 years to figure that out! Nerdy university science types are my people.

What advice would you give to others who are just discovering about asexuality and considering whether they are or not?

I would say take it slow, there is no rush to have sex or even get into a relationship, this is not the 16th century anymore where marriage saved you from poverty, there is no need to get married anymore to connect with a family who owns land or resources, we have the state that looks after us when we are old, women can work. You can live your whole life never having sex and you will be fine. Go and enjoy your hobbies and your passions, there are other ways that we can get companionship and community so that you don't feel alone. That is why the asexual community is so good, it's a way that we as a species can find and create alternative ways to being with each other that is not based on sex and marriage (or religion).

Extra Info

What name would you like to go under for this book? Full name, first name, or alias?

Alias name: Wanita.

What country do you live in?

Born in London, UK, and currently live in Sydney, Australia.

What age are you specifically? Or what decade age range are you – 20, 30. 40s?

I am 41.

What nationality and ethnicity are you?

English/Australian – Caucasian, not religious.

Part III

Introducing *Pride Matters'* Darren Marples

51. Interview With *Pride Matters'* Founder

Although I personally don't actively take part in the LGBT online community, because I am not LGBT and I am asexual, rather than sexual, which I see as two separate things, I do have Gay and Lesbian friends. I also know Homoromantics, Bi-romantics and a Trans asexual, as well as many other variations within the ace community and some outside of it. I think it is great to support each other as much as possible. One person who does this very well is Darren Marples, who is gay and writes a blog called www.pridematters.com where he interviews people from all sexualities, including asexuals. I interviewed Darren about why he supports asexuality and what he believes should be done about getting asexuality recognised as a sexual orientation in its own right.

How did you discover asexuality?

I saw an interview with David Jay, the founder of Aven in the USA and I was aware that A was added in the extended LGBT+ for Asexuality but wasn't aware of much more.

Why are you interested in asexuality?

I'm interested in all sexualities, not just asexuality or gay (as I identify as a gay man). I think it's important to understand others in order to accept others and ultimately yourself. There seems to be a lot of intolerance towards other sexualities other than one's own. Everyone is aware of heterosexuals often showing signs of homophobia but often I have seen it too with the minorities towards each other. I noticed it recently with a gay man saying he couldn't understand bisexuality, yet he would be appalled if he heard it about his own sexuality. I began to blog about the LGBT family in order to show others the diversity of the family and help others understand each other better. Of course asexuality is a part of this.

What do you think about asexuality as a form of sexual orientation in its own right; that is the lack of sexual attraction?

It makes sense to me, asexuality doesn't mean you haven't got a sexuality at all, after all there are varied parts of the sexuality, demi gray, aromantic, heteroromantic and so on.

What do you understand a 'lack of sexual attraction' to mean?

Exactly that, you are not interested in someone sexually, but this could vary too from none to little.

What do you think about someone not experiencing sexual attraction?

I don't view them as any different to anyone else, the sexual spectrum is colourful and they are just as valuable in understanding sexuality as the next. We all are nature's creations; people need to accept that. Many years ago people used to say 'oh I have just got a low sex drive' now we are identifying things better, so we can understand ourselves better than ever.

Do you know anyone personally who is asexual?

I didn't, but recently I mentioned about asexuality to someone I know and she was like "wow that's me, tell me more...". I also talk to a lot of people online, if that counts too. Talking to the right people helps. There is still a lack of understanding out there, this is why projects like this helps.

How long have you been a supporter of asexuality?

Since mid 2015, I say this because that's when I began my research. I have a blog of history on sexualities and I decided to mix in parts of asexuality. There was a lack of information on history and so I posted recent history, mixed in with a few facts.

Why do you choose to be a supporter of asexuality?

It's more like I support all sexualities rather than just the one, and I try and be more aware of everyone. Everyone has their own needs and all need better understanding. I'm no sexual expert and there is more I need to be aware of. I am just a guy who had it tough getting himself understood what being gay is all about, if I can just help someone else to be accepted more or feel accepted, then I have done my job, but will continue.

Can you tell me in what ways you have shown your support for asexuality?

I have wrote an awareness article for a blog, placed a topic on my Tumblr account that I reblog often and I do interviews for different genders and sexualities in order to raise awareness. I always bring asexuality up because I feel someone could be listening in and not be aware of it, then they start to expand their knowledge and help themselves.

Why do you think some people are prejudice against asexuality?

Prejudice is born out of the lack of knowledge. There are statistics that suggest that asexuality accounts for 1% of the population, then they go on to say, but because of the lack of knowledge some people may not be aware they are Asexual. So how do they know the stats are right? They don't.

It's hard to understand anyone's sexuality other than your own, there isn't enough awareness in general, remember asexuality lacked any form of awareness only 14 years ago, even though Alfred Kinsey spoke about it in the 1950s, not many people took him serious enough in any of his findings.

What do you think is the biggest challenge asexuals face, and how can they overcome it?

Awareness, and like other minorities that's coming together. It's difficult for any minority because of the lack of numbers, that's why the best groups to teach about asexuality is the LGBT+ family and then fight the same issue together. Break the majority of that group and you will be stronger as more of a universal group of varied sexualities, then together you pick up allies internally and externally on the way.

What more can be done to get asexuality recognized as a form of sexual orientation in it's own right, that is a lack of sexual attraction?

Campaigning I guess, to do online petitions, rally up numbers for gay pride events, probably most of all a figurehead celebrity would help; radio, TV, film. Talk to soap writers and ask for story-lines. Talk to schools and ask them what campaigning they do on behalf of asexuality within the schools. There are a lot of projects out there that may or may not be making people aware of asexuality. The more people they receive emails from on the matter, the more likely people will understand.

Extra Info

What name would you like to go under for this book? Full name, first name, or alias?

Darren Marples.

What country do you live in?

UK.

What age are you specifically? Or what decade age range are you – 20, 30. 40s?

48.

What nationality and ethnicity are you?

English.

Links to your website/social media.

pridematters.wordpress.com

Twitter: @mattersofpride

Tumblr: darren-marples.tumblr.com

Email: pridematters1@gmail.com

Part IV

Introducing *Asexual Perspectives*' Author Sandra Bellamy

52. Interview with *Asexual Perspectives*' Author

You have read my story and that of the many different asexual per-spectives across the globe; with a diverse range of identifications and experiences, now this is the part where you get to ask me the exact same questions that I asked all of my interviewees. Yep, up close and personal, with no holding back about my perspective! Revealing exclusive and personal details to help you in your own asexual journey. Here I go...

When did you first discover you are asexual?

If you have read the beginning of this book, you will already know my story and how I came to discover asexuality and that I am asexual; it was March 2014.

How did you discover you are asexual?

I was seeing a counsellor about the problem that I wanted to have a relationship with a guy without sex but I still loved kissing. Af-ter she told me I would have to have sex in a relationship to keep a good guy and that she was worried about me, I thought 'this can't be right, why should I have to do something I don't want to do, to keep a good guy?' So I went home and Googled I love kissing but not sex and then I came across asexuality and Aven (asexuality.org – the biggest online community for asexuals) and I read some of their forum threads and related to what they were saying. After more research I thought I am asexual. And if you have read the beginning of this book, you will know the rest of my story.

However, I need to be honest and say that a blogging friend who often wrote about sex – but not in a bad way, in a good way; informative and educational way, suggested I was asexual and I think that was a couple of years before my discovery. I dismissed the idea at that time, and because the concept sounded so alien to me, I immediately retorted in a comment that, "I don't think so, I just don't associate sex with love, that's all, (and I never have done) and I still love kissing". Some time after discovering my asexuality I admitted in a private message on Facebook that he had been right back then after all and I thanked him.

How do you identify yourself asexually?

I identify as a Heteroromantic, Hyper-romantic, Grey A, Asexual (younger) Cougar, who doesn't like sex, just kissing. I never call myself a Grey Sexual, because I am definitely asexual. And these days I never call myself a Grey Asexual, because I am definitely asexual and that implies there is some sort of questioning over my asexuality. However, I do take on the 'Grey A', but unlike most other Grey A Asexuals, I do *not* rarely experience sexual attraction or under specific circumstances, or experience it but not enough to want to act on it, which is often the definition of a Grey A. When I began to learn about asexuality I used to think maybe I experienced sexual attraction but not enough to want to act on it, but that was due to my high levels of arousal and hyper-romanticism that I mistook for sexual attraction, because when

I am passionately kissing a guy my body experiences high levels of arousal but my mind does not want sex with that person. Even though my body may be hurting for the person arousing me and in that way my arousal is aimed at them in that moment, I have never actually *thought* I *want* sex with that person. Since exploring my asexuality, I have learnt I can easily get aroused just from talking or thinking about kissing a guy, or just by nothing but feeling and thinking in my mind about being aroused and not related to any person whatsoever. But when kissing a guy my body sometimes wants to have a mind of its own and feels differently to how my mind thinks.

As I mentioned at the beginning of this book, at one point it stated on Aven Wiki that Grey A is actually a 'catch all term' for those who do not fit directly into the asexual box, although this seems to have been removed and it is often teamed up with the other two terms, Grey Sexual and Grey Asexual, but again the terms have been changed slightly on Aven Wiki at the time of publication of this book.

Aside from that, I don't mind *re-defining Grey A*, and saying it applies to me, as I have Grey Areas (that is what I mean by Grey A – Grey Areas). I believe that is what specifically 'Grey A' should mean. It certainly helps with the asexual dating scene. So for example, because I experience high levels of arousal and like to feel naturally excited through passionate kissing with the tongue, but with my clothes on, for some asexual guys that is too sexual for them – but I am not sexual enough to be with a heterosexual as I don't like, need or want sex. So if I had an asexual boyfriend for example, which I currently don't, and I loved him and trusted him, I would like to be on top of a bed with him, and kissing him passionately with my body pressing tight against his, with legs intertwined with clothes on. Clothes start to come off and I get bored, and as I am nudity repulsed I don't like it anyway. A guy looks far better with his clothes on – I am guessing you would call that 'clothes attraction?' Well I would anyway. Which could be part of my aesthetic attraction, although that is predominantly for his face. I also like to sit on a guy's lap (my boyfriend's if I had one), but with my clothes on.

I am *asexy* and don't mind being called sexy or seen as sexy, so long as a guy does not expect me to actually have sex with him, and I like to do 'dirty dancing' (grinding) with a foreign asexual guy if I had one, but again, this is all with clothes on and no desire to have intercourse whatsoever and I will let him know where he can and can't touch. I once did this in a nightclub with a heterosexual foreign guy on a date and the DJ's eyes were popping out and that quite amused me – I kinda like to shock people sometimes, as in surprise people about what I can do and be a bit controversial. I hated being stereotyped into a certain box while at school, I like to be free to do my thing and to sometimes do the unexpected!! This heterosexual guy ended up in my bed with clothes on, and I enjoyed the kissing and only wanted the kissing which he found frustrating, but did he get sex out of me, no way. I never wanted sex with him; I can be sexy in behavior without wanting sex. I say foreign, because I don't get attracted to British guys that much and mostly not enough to want to kiss them and be physically close to them. I can sometimes think a guy is 'hot' or 'sexy', foreign guys I am talking about; are particularly 'hot', as I think they are so stunningly gorgeous and I want to be close to them as in hug them and snog their face off – not have sex with them. I never make that connection with sex, it does not compute in my head and I only want one guy to be my boyfriend – not guys, I may get aesthetically attracted to a lot of foreign guys but I am not a polyamorous person.

Are you 'out' about being asexual? If not, why not? If you are out, whom to, and how did they react?

This is a funny question for me, not funny as in I don't want to be taken seriously, but funny as in I am very much out to the world. I am all over social media. I have my asexualise.com site with products, resources and services for asexuals and my 'Asexualise My Asexual Life' YouTube channel – just Google it, and my aim with that channel is to empower and enhance the lives of asexuals and educate others. My main aim is to get asexuality recognised as a sexual orientation in its own right throughout the globe, that is the lack of sexual attraction, so that no asexual ever has to live in fear of ridicule ever again. That is why I created my 'Asexualise' brand. I am connected to a lot of entrepreneurs from around the globe on Facebook, and these are often seen as thought leaders in their industry. I believe if we can get asexuality recognised on a more global scale with thought leaders and those with a lot of influence and impact, then we can start to change the world's view of asexuality. I really want to make a difference to other's lives in this way.

I also have a Facebook page – just look up 'Asexualise' spelt Acexualise with a C for the web address, and you can find me on Twitter @asexualise. I also sell 'Asexualise' T-Shirts on Amazon.com – just type in 'Asexualise' in the search bar and all the T-Shirts that say 'by Asexualise' are mine and I also sell them on Redbubble under Asexualise, and you will see that it's not just T-Shirts I sell there, but hoodies, vest tops, skirts, duvet covers, phone and laptops cases and much more for asexuals. I design all of them myself, so you should never find an identical design – because that would be breach of my copyright. I used to create the designs and then get a designer to do the artwork for me but I learned Photoshop so I can design them and do the artwork myself. I actually love creating my own designs as I am by nature a very creative person and when I have a sale my eyes light up because someone is buying my artwork and they are obviously helping to spread awareness too, even if it is very subtle in some instances and you would not know the designs were specifically for asexuals if you did not know for example, what 'ace' meant – the slang term for asexual.

Oh, I am guessing you want to know about family and friends. If you have read the beginning of this book, you will already know that my mum and dad have been awesome about it and very supportive, I just told them in a matter-of-fact way, on the phone, and by the next phone call they said, "It sounds like you", so they must have looked up the term using Google. I didn't even know back then that it was called 'coming out' and I had no fear about telling my parents. As I am an only child I don't have to worry about the opinions of siblings. My friends all know and at work I think most know. I work in a large retail department store (for my day job as I like to call it), and am very vocal in the staff canteen and locker room about being asexual and what asexuality stuff I am up to and I also talk about how the asexual dating scene is going for me as I am on two asexual dating sites, one being Asexualitic.com, the other being ace-book.net. I also hold small asexual meet-ups in Exeter, in the UK. Anyone who is genuinely asexual is welcome to join us, you don't have to live in Exeter and there are B&Bs and hotels if you need to stay overnight. I hope attendee numbers increase over time.

What's your deepest fear, concern or worry, about being asexual?

That I have an Indian asexual romantic soulmate somewhere in the world and I may not find or meet him in this lifetime, but I am always hopeful I will. I can feel him and miss him, even though he is not with me and I haven't met him yet. I even know roughly what he looks like and what job or major interest he has. I guess in the law of attraction I need to act as if he is already with me and stop hoping and start being with him but I also enjoy my single life and I don't want to ever feel I 'need' a guy. In fact, I reprogrammed my mind in 2012 to be happy being single, forever if need be, so it's kinda hard to be happy being single while missing my soulmate and wishing he was with me, and therefore acting as if he is with me can be too painful at times. And I guess this is why the universe gets confused. Sometimes I feel I am too young to settle down or that I have too much to do in my businesses, but I know I would make time for him, because he is always in my thoughts anyway, and I have been preparing for him by taking time out to speak to others and thinking I could then make time for him. As love is a major distraction for me and finding him is too – it would actually be very beneficial for me to be with him right now, as then I could know I have that to take care of, as well as getting on with the rest of my life.

The amount of Indian guys that are actually gay or homoromantics, that want a marriage of convenience with an asexual female, or in the case of gay guys they would also be with a lesbian; to please their parents and cover up their real sexual identity, is absurd in numbers and until there is a cultural shift I fear this makes it even harder to find a suitable asexual Indian guy because even the heteroromantics want a marriage of convenience at the very least to please their parents, even if they themselves are not that bothered about marriage.

My other concern is for asexuals and asexuality in general. I really want all asexuals to not have to live in fear that they cannot say they are asexual because they will get ridiculed, pushed away, disowned, or worse; physically hurt in some countries or circumstances.

Why do you feel, in general, that society doesn't accept asexuality as a form of sexual orientation in its own right? And what can be done about this?

Many people don't realise asexuality exists.

I think a lot of people talk with uncertainty in their tone of voice when they speak about asexuality to others, instead of being self-assured. You need to say it as a matter-of-fact that you are asexual and be strong about it – I was guilty of talking with uncertainty with the first friend I ever told, never again; I learnt my lesson with that one.

A lot of people have been brought up to believe that heterosexuality is the only normal sexuality and that all other sexualities are wrong, when they are not. Those that are open-minded can accept there are other sexualties whether they agree with them or not. Most of us get conditioned in our thinking from a very early age by our parents or guardians; we tend to either agree with their thinking or we don't and rebel against it. Those that agree with it will take this conditioned thinking well into adulthood and often to the end of their life, because they are stubborn in their ways or their thinking, and their conditioning has been ground into them and they accept it without question. Those who are brought up to question things, to speak for themselves, or who don't agree with or believe in that conditioning, can be open to new ways of thinking, (open-minded, rather than closed-minded) and open to new ways of being and new possibilities. And they can either accept those possibilities as is, or they can recondition their mind to believe in them.

490

In order to attempt to change this narrow-minded thinking, asexuality needs to be broadcast across the globe, on TV, in newspapers, on the Internet, in magazines, comics, movies, books, every day, multiple times a day. For some people, like any new concept, they need exposing to it multiple times before there will be any likelihood of acceptance. There will still be people who do not accept it, as some people are homophobic for example and are sticking to the fact that they believe it is not acceptable. It may be a fact that they don't *believe* it is acceptable, but it is also a fact that it exists whether they like it or not. But society is burying its head in the sand if they are denying people the right to be who they are and live how they want to live regardless of what others may think. So they would rather people lie to the world and their families, their friends, whoever, or live in secret with who they really are, just because they can't deal with it! This is very sad. This is dictating, not accepting. No one has the right to tell anyone they are not something if they believe they are and they don't have any right to tell them how to live their life. If you had a global campaign – say for at least a year, people would be being reconditioned in their thinking, even if it was on a more subconscious level. But for any kind of permanent change it needs to be a forever campaign. Just imagine if the tables were turned and say there was a ban on sex; sexualisation; nudity; scantily clad women and men; porn etc., in magazines, on TV, in movies, in books, on the Internet and such, and in its place was asexuality and how to love without sex, how to live without sex, how to create more happiness and fulfilment without sex – through hobbies and interests and human connections of a non-sexual type, of loving people for their personality and choosing the right life partner based on mutual interests, similar or complementary personalities, based on them, not their procreational advantages; based on pure deep love, even if thousands of miles apart. Just imagine if the world became pro-asexual and everyone lived more of an asexual rather than sexual existence, what would be the outcome?? Imagine if that went on for years, generation after generation, wouldn't that become the new normal, wouldn't that be the way everyone should be? Of course, you would then have the reverse effect and sexuals would feel lonely and lost and like they don't fit in and they would have to keep their sexual desires a secret for fear of ridicule, and of feeling it is not normal to get those urges. In some foreign countries sexuals can feel repressed in this way – especially if they come from a religious or family background where sex is forbidden until marriage.

My parents do not agree with sex before marriage – this is how I was brought up. I have had sex and I have never been married but I would always recommend if you want a sexual relationship with your partner after marriage, to try sex out with them before you get married. If you are not sexually compatible physically, let alone mentally and emotionally, you will start your married life with a major problem and you don't want that. I talk with experience when I say; if for example you are a heteroromantic female and you have sex, and your partner's penis is the wrong size for you, it could hurt a lot if it's too fat, or if it's too small then what's the point! Compatible 'bits' are important, so is being in tune with what each other does and doesn't like physically.

I have never had sex outside of a relationship and never would, and as I am now personally sex repulsed, it is something I never wish to have again in my life. Just in case you were wondering, I have no problem with others enjoying sex and I have no problem talking about sex in a certain amount of detail. Ironically a lot of my friends are highly sexual and that includes females, who often seem to have a high sexual appetite and the problem is getting the right guy to satisfy them. One of my friends in work is gay and has sex as a hobby – he was actually opposed to me being asexual for about a year, but now we are so cool, I talk about my asexual life and he talks about his sexual one, including shaving his bum crack – yeah, I know gross, but I can still make sexual jokes and innuendo because it doesn't affect me or my life. I get a lot of asexuals ask me for relationship advice usually in private messages and I also get a few sexual people asking for my advice too. From the age of 15 to 2011, so for half of my life, I was always in relationships with heterosexuals, but again, ironically, it is only since discovering I am asexual that I have ever openly talked personally about sex, pushing through my fears and shyness about the topic, to really open up to others.

I wish for every child to be educated about all sexualities, including asexuality, in school and from a young age. Some kids are having underage sex or starting to know about it very young; it is important that all young kids are made aware they can have love without sex and be in a relationship without sex, forever, if they want to. Maybe then there would be less peer pressure to do sexual acts that are not right for the individual.

What's your view on love? Have you been in love before?

I have been in love many times before of varying degrees. Sometimes it hasn't always been a healthy love for me and now I am waiting for the right person and happy to be single forever until I meet the right guy. Sometimes I feel a little sad for myself, in a self-love way, that I have not met the right person who is worthy of my love, someone who wants to be my very bestest ever friend, my soulmate, and love of my life, who is faithful and kind and expects nothing more from me than love, friendship and support, not based on money or housework, or shared household stuff. I have always wanted someone to like my looks but my personality more than anything. I know until I find a guy compatible with my personality or who adores me for it, that I will stay single for my own good. I love my life and I like my personality and never get bored of being with me, I am a best friend to myself and have learnt to love myself so much. I am far too quirky and different to be normal and boring and I love being that way.

One of the things I find extremely difficult is being a hyper-romantic and not experiencing platonic attraction. This means I often automatically skip the platonic friendship stage and can fall in love at the drop of a hat very easily, to the point of annoyance, because it distracts me and takes my focus off my work and what I am doing. So I can fall in love or get love feelings over a few text or Facebook messages or from a few messages and a Skype session, I am not saying it is full blown deep love, as the more you know someone, the more you can fall in love with them because the stronger the emotional connection and bond you form, I am just saying the love is very real and hardly anyone in the world seems to understand this concept or accepts it. I have been training my brain to not fall *in love* at the drop of a hat and sometimes I do better with this than at other times depending on who I am talking to, but because I can still develop feelings *of love* or something very close to it at the drop of a hat, it's tough. I agree it seems absurd but put it this way, when it happens, it is like having my heart ripped out of me time and time again, this is how very real it is for me. I cry, feel pain, and then I have to realise this will pass, although it feels like it won't and it can go on for months. And I know to an outsider this may seem stupid or unbelievable but nevertheless, this is very real for me.

These days I am able to connect with many people very easily and when talking to some guys for the first time, it feels like I have been talking to them for ages. Some of these people claim to not be able to talk very easily to many people, then that makes me think I must a have a special bond with them and it often begins to feel more like romantic love. I reiterate this is mostly with foreign guys, I don't usually get that much attracted to British guys, despite living it Britain. I can still develop some feelings for them if they are in their early 20s, but it is not as strong to actually want to be in a relationship with them or kiss them – the thought of kissing a British guy nowadays mostly grosses me out – unless they look a bit foreign or have some foreign blood in them, but even still, I cannot picture it. When I am with foreign guys – I have foreign guy friends and my top aesthetic attraction is for Indian guys, then Bangladesh and then Middle Eastern and then some others – I feel at home and really comfortable. It's like I was always meant to be with a foreign guy all of my life. It's like I am at home when I am with them. I have no desire, want or need to have sex ever again in my life but if I had of had it; it would have been with a foreign guy. All the guys I dated since from around October 2012 – July 2014; a few months after I found out I am asexual, were all foreign guys 21-27 years and unfortunately all were sexual but not one of them got sex out of me, or came close to it, even though most tried. Now, I cannot date sexuals because they cannot live without sex their whole life and I cannot be in a relationship with someone who would want to do that with anyone else. Just because I am asexual does not mean to say I do not deserve the same monogamous relationship that heterosexuals can enjoy, minus the sex. I am not poly and most heterosexuals would never stay in a relationship with an unfaithful partner – so why should asexuals be expected to? It's ridiculous. One of the guys I dated suggested this. After one date he wanted me to be his girlfriend – he was 21 and the best kiss I ever had to date. It was a good experience as I realised I could be in a relationship with a guy who was even younger than I first thought I could. But it was a bad experience because he wanted sex and to sleep with other girls – what a not a very nice joke!!! I only wish he had of been joking, but he was very serious. Disgusting behavior.

Another problem I have; because I don't experience platonic attraction I can experience multiple attractions for multiple guys, usually up to three guys at once but I don't want to be in a relationship with more than one guy. So within my multiple attraction umbrella; I experience romantic attraction; aesthetic attraction; clothes attraction on a guy – I love the street look the most, you know, from Street Dance movies, for example, I love the clothes the guys wear and it makes me attracted to them. Or the clean-shaven biker look from Grease the musical for example – so the leather jacket, black or white T-Shirt and black trousers – yum! I also experience intelligence attraction; creative attraction; emotional attraction and connection; and spiritual/soul attraction and connection. So I can be romantically attracted to one guy, aesthetically attracted to another, and intelligently attracted to another. If I love a person I would usually feel many of those types of attraction for that one person and at least romantic and aesthetic attraction. But all of these attractions to multiple guys, distract my focus and attention because they often accompany or bring out my hyper-romanticism and it's like here we go again and believe me, I try to work hard on stopping this and sometimes it works to a degree – but not enough, and it does my head in. It is like a constant emotional rollercoaster than I could do without. Add that to the fact I am a bit of a kissing addict but I have no one to kiss and well – you can imagine the nightmare I have. It can get to the stage where I feel physically sick because it has been so long since I last kissed someone and I feel very kissing frustrated. And I cannot just kiss anyone either, it has to be someone I am highly aesthetically attracted to, and preferably in a relationship with. I thought about getting a kissing buddy as I am fairly self-sufficient and don't 'need' a guy much, apart from the kissing would be good as there is only so much you can kiss yourself – ha! But as I would no doubt fall in love with him, there is not much point as that would cause me a much bigger problem, better to wait for the right guy unless I can train myself to not fall in love but then I would want to fall in love with the right guy.

And because I don't experience platonic attraction, I also end up having some attraction for most of my asexual friends and some sexual ones sometimes – particularly if they are foreign, almost immediately. And then this can take up to 8 months for it to turn into just liking them, or thinking of them as my friend. This is backwards. Most people feel friendship first, and then later develop feelings that may or may not lead to love. I develop love feelings or romantic feelings, or intelligence feelings or soul connection feelings, or emotional feelings, almost instantly, and then I have to work hard on trying to stop it or live with the pain of it – as it is almost always unreciprocated if it is an asexual person. And heterosexuals are no good for me as I cannot be in a relationship with one and this is quite heartbreaking at times. I think if only they could love me and be with me without sex forever as I am sure I would be good for them in other ways and would truly give them that deep soul connection love from my heart that some of them so badly want and need. And they think if only she was sexual and wanted sex, marriage and kids, then I would marry her – I have declined this offer before with heterosexual Indian guys.

Are you currently in a relationship, and if so, is it with another asexual.

No, I am currently single and have been single since November 5th 2011, apart from one three week relationship with a Bangladesh guy in 2013, if you can call that a relationship. We split up because he wanted sex with me and I would not do that with him and he started seeing another girl while I was still with him – now you know why I am adamant when I say I will not date another sexual guy – because they cannot live forever without sex and be happy and content as much as if they were having it. Not in my experience or to my knowledge and I would always want my partner to be the happiest he could ever be with me, while maintaining my individuality and quirky teenager lifestyle without doing housework for him.

My mum actually laughed at the fact I did not want sex with the Bangladesh guy or any guy who would be my boyfriend. I told her this on the phone and my dad was laughing in the background too, they said, "You just want a platonic friend, that's all you want." This was extremely insulting to me as I told them "I do not want to kiss my 'only friends'. I like kissing; I just don't like sex." They did not seem to get it at all. As they don't agree with sex before marriage, I was quite shocked by their laughing. Now they know I am asexual, their attitude is completely different and their understanding of me is much, much better. In fact, my mum can now spot a younger foreign guy that I would be attracted to aesthetically and tell me so. They also understand I need a younger guy and my mum tells me she cannot see me with an older guy and will tell me if a particular guy looks too old for me, or is too old for me in terms of their hobbies and interests. It's so funny in a good way and great to be supported this much, I feel very blessed.

If you are not in a relationship, would you like to be in one and if so, why, and what type of relationship – romantic? Platonic? What would your ideal relationship look like? And would you be in a relationship with a sexual person or not, and reason why?

I would only ever want to be in a relationship with an asexual romantic guy, never a sexual guy, because in my experience they all need sex as part of a relationship to be completely happy and fulfilled and they cannot fulfil my need of lots of kissing without sex, so we are not compatible. I think it is counterproductive to start a relationship with problems like this and trying to make it work – the world is huge and asexuals are thousands in numbers, 1% of the population is still huge. Why limit yourself to being with someone who you are not compatible with from the offset in this way? Having said that my heart does go out to each and every asexual that struggles to find a compatible match. I understand this better than a lot of people with my hyper-romanticism and multiple attractions that are not reciprocated, but as a friend once said to me, finding my soulmate is not meant to be easy but it will be rewarding when I find them. I have known since 10 that I have a soulmate – I did not know he was foreign or Indian until after I discovered I am asexual.

Asexuals struggle to get a match because if sex is never involved that means we have to focus much more on other things in a relationship, such as the compatibility of likes, dislikes, interests and hobbies, and the varying degrees of physical affection one likes to give or receive – or not, as the case may be. This can be hard because although we have asexuality as the common link we can be so very different in these areas.

But this is where some heterosexuals will fail. Because they are so focused on the passion of the relationship and sometimes the

499

sexual addiction, they will let other incompatibilities go unde-tected and when there are harder times ahead and/or they can't have sex as much for some reason, these incompatibilities show through and there is often less communication because they are both feeling sexually neglected or rejected. Talking was probably not as important as it should have been made in the beginning of the relationship and because they are not as used to talking about such things; the gap between them widens.

Open communication and the ability to talk about anything and everything with ease with your partner and wanting to do that, can make or break a relationship and this is what a lot of people don't realise and it can lead to divorce or splitting up. A lot of people have emotional needs that aren't met either and the way those are communicated should also be through talking. I have learnt that if a guy is not willing or wanting to talk with me openly or honestly and enjoy doing that, then it is no go, however much I like him, as it won't work. Or at least it would not work for me. I have met people who say they are interested in me or others and they don't like talking that much, but believe me, when they have found 'the one', their behaviour changes, then they want to talk to them and message them lots, it's natural for them. So if it's not natural for them with me, then I am not the one for them, sadly or fortunately, depending on which way you look at it.

So, my ideal relationship would be with an Indian asexual het-eroromantic or demi-romantic guy, who loved me implicitly and who couldn't get enough of me and my quirky personality. I would like him to want to talk to me for hours about anything and everything and he would love snogging my face off just as much as I loved snogging his face off, knowing it will never lead to sex. I would like him to be nudity repulsed like me or in the very least, not be attracted to it or want to look at it – particularly in movies or at the cinema, as that is the one thing that makes me angry in a relationship if I have a boyfriend and he is looking at that. I am a bit old fashioned in that one way, because although I have no desire to be naked with anyone, including my boyfriend if I had one, I do believe he should only have eyes for me in that regard, because he is in a relationship with me. I hardly ever watch TV and am selective about the movies I watch – trying to avoid nudity, which most of the time with the films I like, I can do. If there was nudity on TV and I happen to have it on once in a blue moon, I would turn it off, or turn it over, or look the other way. In the cinema if nudity happened to be on, I would usually look down at the floor or up at the ceiling. Or if watching movies at home, I would fast forward it if it had sex in it, but usually I don't have films with that in it. I hate nudity as you might have guessed; apart from I am okay with looking at myself naked in the mirror every day after I shower.

I would want the Indian asexual romantic guy to have a quirky teenager style relationship with me, without sex, without marriage and most certainly without kids. And for it to be a Living Apart Together Relationship, where he would move to live very near me in the UK but not with me as I enjoy living on my own and as I said before, I would not want the responsibility of joint housework and bills. I would want him to look after himself and his place and me to look after myself and my place. Then we would meet up once or twice a week and spend ages looking into each other eyes and talking intelligently to one another. I can picture me and him sat on top of my bed opposite each other and holding each other's hands, feeling warmth, love and sincerity and both smiling so much. He has beautiful dark chestnut brown hair, is clean shaven, and thin, with maybe slightly toned muscles and he works in IT, probably as a website designer or developer, as I build my own websites without code, I find this talk very intellectually asexy and it would be very stimulating for me. And/or he would be into business or be an entrepreneur – although this is not essential so long as I am interested in the same type of work things as him so we can talk about it and/or creative hobbies, such as writing. 21-27 is my ideal age range. 24 would be good or even 28 would be fine if he looked his age or younger, after 32 though, it really is getting way too old for me and at 32, he would need to look like he was in his 20s or I could not kiss him and I need kissing and lots of it – which is another point. I would need specific kissing time too and he would have to enjoy cuddling and holding hands in public and some kissing in public. I don't like to be hidden away like some dirty little secret, so unless a foreign guy is prepared to show his love publically for me, again, it is no go. I broke up with a sexual foreign boyfriend who did a lot worse stuff than that years ago, but it was because of him not wanting to hold my had in public that I could never stay as his girlfriend. If I had a boyfriend, he would have to be able to put on his Facebook status that he is in a relationship with me and want to do that. I know there are many foreign guys who don't seem to want to do this, they will publically 'love their brother' but when it comes to their partner it would appear they are single. If you are proud of the woman you are with, and you are not looking for another, you should show it. Anyone should be proud to be with me, just as I should be proud to be with them and therefore they would not have to care about the age difference but be very happy with an older girl and not worry what parents, friends or relatives think – this is why I need an individualist like me – someone who does not follow the crowd and could not care less what others think. I love the Bollywood look, the guys who are in Bollywood movies who are clean-shaven, handsome, and with dark hair, but sometimes they look too old and I like a boy next-door look best. The guy in the film the 'Life of Pi' is cute but I am guessing he is not asexual and he may have been too young for me when the film was made! He is 23 now! I would like my asexual guy to love going out to the cinema with me as it is one of my favourite things to do, and go to theme parks (the ones with rollercoasters), zoos, aquariums, and out for meals.

I believe a relationship should empower and enhance your life, not take anything away from it and that works both ways. So for example, I love romance and being loved-up 24/7 as this is the way I feel about my life pretty much every day, by myself. I would want a guy to love me the way I am and be attracted to my quirks and love me for them and want the same teenager magical lifestyle and relationship that I so dearly already love with myself. And I would want him to never try to change me in any way. I live like a 15 year old, with cuddly toys, a fiber optic lamp, Iron Man alarm clock, coloured boxes, sparkly things and Disney stuff around my bedroom. I love living like a teenager and I intend to live to be at least 100 and always want to live this way forever, as I am the happiest I have ever been in my life. I do not do normal and conventional – I would hate to be normal, so if you never call me normal then that is great. I do not want to live with magnolia walls and neutral carpets, and I like cosy not minimalistic. My lifestyle mindset age is 23 so I often end up being the younger person in the relationship and the guy the older one, if say they are 24 or older. In fact some younger guys are just too old for me in their lifestyle. I am not into nature, or history, and I also don't like to travel apart from to London for business or pleasure or to Disneyland Paris by Eurostar. I am not a scenic sightseer or sunbather type of person, I like doing young, fun, 'kids' stuff. So one of my favourite attractions to go to is Shrek Adventureland in London, it's so magical there and unless I have an equally enthusiastic person accompanying me, I prefer to go on my own. I self-date a lot and love it. My birth certificate age

I don't usually reveal to anyone unless they want to date me, because it is irrelevant, it is not me or who I am, age is a state of mind. When I was younger in birth certificate age, I was older, now I am older in birth certificate age, I am younger, and that is the way it is staying forever. I am stronger in my mind like this and I love it and it is my life at the end of the day. So I think I can do anything a 23 year old can do if I want to. I don't have many inhibitions so I can pretty much do what I like, if I want to. I love going clubbing, for dancing. I don't drink alcohol or smoke; I just get high on orange juice and life itself. Most of my friends think they are too old for clubbing now or they don't like it, that's up to them, I am still young as far as I am concerned and I love club music to energise myself daily or similar 'natural high' music. I love the 'Trolls' CD at the moment – music is from the Trolls movie, if you haven't seen the movie yet, it is acesome, so make sure you do. I also love the theme tune from frozen – 'Let it go' – great uplifting track, so my guy must like my music or not mind it. I would love for my guy to also enjoy watching superhero movies and Action/Thrillers and Disney/Pixar movies, as these are my favourites. Some Sci-fi, Drama and Family movies are okay too. I hate Horror or Supernatural films.

I think asexuality is not abnormal but uncommon, but I do enjoy being not normal since 2012, when my life began again after overcoming depression that I had for years. I overcame it using my own 'Embrace Your Quirky' philosophy that is all about being your true authentic self, regardless of what anyone else says, thinks or does, and this underpins everything I do across my World Of Quirky brands. And I did not have meds while being depressed for years as I believe medication does not solve the root cause of the problem and I don't like taking pills anyway as I believe you end up needing another pill to counteract the effects of the other. My aunty was a manic-depressive and could not live without her medication and the medication damaged her liver and in the end she ended up taking her own life. People do not seem to realise what the prolonged effects of some drug use, even medicinal, can do to your body. If they believe they need it then they do, and no, I am not giving medical advice or telling anyone to stop taking meds, I am just saying my opinion and experience as I am not a qualified doctor or medical practitioner and you should always consult one of those for advice in this regard before taking any action. I was actually offered meds by the hospital, as taken by some people suffering depression, after my diagnosis for my unseen fibromyalgia disability that I rarely talk about because I manage it well and use the power of my mind to block out a lot of the pain. I turned the medication down and do not take any medication for it. I cannot die from Fibromyalgia, but I have it forever. I would need someone who is gentle with me because of this and who would be able to look after himself like I said before. All my energy is focused on blocking out pain and enjoying life to the max and I need this to continue for my quality of life. I have been blessed through my disability to know now, that I will not compromise my young teenage lifestyle, my happiness, my energy, for the sake of conventional conformity and relationship expectations and I would rather be single forever than end up on crutches or in a wheelchair because my mind was made old by some guy who says he loves me, but clearly wants a housewife and cleaner upper. I want to be a quirky girl, not a mother to any guy or living a boring conventional life. I want to stay young forever in my mind. Of course in business I am super intelligent and experienced and I don't mind being referred to as business woman or business girl – but the rest of the time is girl, thank you.

What is your view about sex? Have you had sex before and if so, how did it make you feel? If you haven't, would you?

I have had sex with a total of 5 guys in my life, 2 foreign and 3 British. I never need, want or wish to, ever have sex again my life, it hurts and I personally I don't like. I am fine with it for everyone else who wants it and likes to have it. Since discovering asexuality I now know I can have love without the sex, and that is amazing. And because I hardly ever get attracted enough to British guys to want to kiss them these days, there is no way I would ever want sex with one – gross!

As I mentioned in the beginning of this book when I was talking to the counsellor, my long-term British ex's best asset was sex. He was good at it and at his most gentlest and kindest when doing that, despite being abusive the rest of the time in most other ways. It got to the stage where I became frightened to say anything and of course it is always your fault, never theirs, and you are the bad one – NOT! When he was having sex, he was different, he would make me as comfy and in least pain as possible and like I said before, he was extremely good with his finger, but I always preferred his finger to his penis and just wanted that and to kiss him, not the sex. I hate washing up, but when I was washing up in my home and he came up behind me and tried to touch my breasts and instigate sex, I didn't like it and preferred to continue doing the washing up and listen to music if I had it playing. One time he bought me a female Santa outfit and yeah, it was nice for the girl in me to wear it and I looked attractive in it, but he wanted me to sit on his lap and have sex with him with it on and I would have preferred not to. I didn't like wearing it because of this. I can't remember ever looking at him and actually thinking I *want* sex with him or at all. Occasionally I used to prefer to be a bit more dominant and take a lead so I felt more in control of the situation, but that was just for that reason, not because I desperately wanted to have sex or at all. All sex was consensual with him and I worked out the most times a year for me that I would have wanted to have sex with him, was 4 times a year, for his benefit rather than mine and that would have been enough.

Prior to asexuality I would never have revealed this stuff and it's kinda still hard to talk about as I really don't need to be reminded of my ex but I am doing this to help show you that it does not matter how much in love you may be, if you are asexual like me, you just don't experience sexual attraction and I understand you. And yes, I felt everything as I should, I was not emotionless as some people say, and as far as I was concerned it was a normal sexual relationship, just we did not have sex for one or two months and then I would do it sometimes like three times in a row to satisfy him more while I had the chance and get it out of the way. I figured if I can do it a few times, then each time should be less painful and as I was risking pregnancy anyway (I was taking the pill but nothing is 100% safe), then I may as well do a proper job of sex. There was a lot of experimentation on his part rather than mine, I just liked the normal position but I was almost kicking myself for buying him a pocket book that had drawings of a variety of Karma Sutra positions because I never really thought he would want to try every one out with me!!! I never even thought about sex with him when buying that book. That's how innocent my mind thinks. I just thought, oh he likes sex and to try various positions and this is a book he will like to read and as it did not show real people and I think he had previously picked up a book with real people in it, I thought, 'great, he can look at and read this'. I had no thought he will want to use this on me!! Why did I not think that??? OMG!! So obvious, but my head did not think that way. I was more concerned with giving him something that did not have nude pictures in it, as I so hated nudity back then as much as I do now. And he used to ask me if I was a lesbian when I said I hated seeing naked women, I could not stand it – why would I be a lesbian, if I don't like naked women's body's? No doubt it was to detract from the fact he loved looking at other women's naked bodies. He also accused me of this when I sometimes did not like to be touched in certain places, at certain times or under certain circumstances – no doubt because I wasn't interested in having sex. I have never fancied a woman in my life and I can't stand seeing a woman naked in a communal changing room, it often makes me feel sick. I don't want to see their bits, why would I? I am female; there is no logic to that for me.

Apart from the release of fluids, I cannot see a point to having sex and you can do that without the intercourse, which would be my preference.

Do you believe if a sexual person had a relationship with an asexual, it can work? And what do you think about it being fair or not?

No. I personally don't think it can work. I do not believe it is fair if a sexual person says they can be in a forever relationship with an asexual without sex and stay faithful to that one person in a monogamous relationship, knowing full well they can't and/or they are not even thinking about the long-term.

I do not think it is fair that some heterosexuals pretend they are asexual when they are not; this is cruel, misleading and dishonest.

I don't think it's fair for any sexual person to want a casual relationship or serious relationship with an asexual, while having sex with others. This is not love and can be very hurtful and painful emotionally, not to mention how can you be fully committed in the relationship and working hard to make it work and to make your asexual partner happy, when you have this flippant attitude, 'oh well, today I want sex and as my asexual partner won't give it to me, I am just going to pick someone who is willing to' – why don't you just stay single and sleep with whoever?

I do not think it is fair for a sexual person to have sex with an asexual person, knowing full well the asexual person is only having sex to please them. How is this real or true love?

I don't think it is fair for a sexual to say to an asexual who has feelings for them of more than friendship, 'yeah, I can be with you now (to get this, that, and the other out of the relationship), but I cannot stay with you or be in a permanent relationship with you'. While I think this is actually being more honest and realistic with the truth, isn't that like using the asexual? A bit like using someone for sex, but in other ways? Oh, yeah, no emotion involved, just get what you want and go! This could be kissing; a meal, to be there to talk to when they are lonely and their other friends are all busy! I think you can get my point.

Equally it is not fair if an asexual ever hides their asexuality from a potential sexual partner, or a partner they are already with, unless their life is in jeopardy. I am always upfront with people, I usually mention I am asexual within the first five minutes of talking to guys, or at least the first conversation I have with most guys – maybe one day an Indian guy will turn around and say "Guess what? So am I" and want the same things as me. Nothing is impossible. It states I'm possible.

It is also not fair if the asexual says to the sexual they can be in a relationship with them and have sex, without first discussing how much and how often, and if they know full well they can't do that, just because they so badly want to be in a relationship with that person.

I think for an asexual and sexual to be truly happy in a relationship, unless the asexual likes or enjoys sex, as some asexuals do, then it is not going to be a fair relationship and there will always be problems. The only time I can see it might work is if the asexual was with a sexual who is celibate, or impotent, or had a really low sex drive and genuinely did not have a mental drive for sex and a need for it in their life. However, I would always personally be worried that the celibate person may decide to change – especially after kissing me passionately and the impotent person may be cured with the way I like to passionately kiss and then they would want sex – especially as I believe that a major cause of impotency is stress and anxiety – if there is no pressure to sexually perform from my end and they had their body intertwined with me with clothes on passionately kissing me, they may all of a sudden be cured and no that isn't an advert for heterosexuals to contact me to cure their impotency incase you are reading this and are not asexual. And also, it is not meant to be insulting in any way to impotent people. From the point of view of an impotent guy not being able to 'perform', that is great for me as I don't want sex ever, but not good for them as they don't feel like a 'real man' a lot of the time, due to what society perceives a real man to be. To me, a 'real man' is a guy who is not afraid to show his emotions and is sensitive and if he wants to write me love poems, all the better, I love those. In the case of having a low sex drive, a low sex drive is not the same as not having one, and that person may still want sex, and *their* not often, may not match your asexual ideal of not often. The reason I go on about kissing so much, is because all sexual guys who I have kissed, usually want

510

to have sex with me within the first five minutes of kissing me. It is because it is very arousing for them, and even it is for me, just we have different thinking.

Asexuality is the lack of sexual attraction, as an asexual, what does this mean to you?

As a female heteroromantic asexual who is only ever attracted to guys, I don't ever look at a guy and think I want sex with him.

Do you believe sexual attraction and sexual desire are the same thing or different?

I think sexual attraction and sexual desire can be the same thing or different. For me, I could not sexually desire someone without being sexually attracted to them first and as sexual attraction is a 'desire' to have sex with someone or something, they are the same thing (and some dictionaries define them as one and the same thing). I can still find a guy 'sexy' with the way he looks, without being sexually attracted to him, because I think he is stunningly gorgeous and I want to snog his face off. However, I think for some sexual people they can experience sexual desire separately if they want sex with just anyone, so for example when you overhear a guy at a nightclub saying, "I am going to get laid tonight", he doesn't care who with, he just wants; desires; the sex, and women go 'on the pull' for the same reason. I have known of two asexuals who say they desire sex, but it isn't aimed at anyone and I guess this would also be sexual desire without the sexual attraction. I also think asexuals confuse sexual desire, with a desire to have sex for the sake of having kids or pleasing their partner. They believe these are the same because of the word 'desire', but they aren't. Sexual desire means a desire for the sex itself with someone or something. A desire to have sex to get an end result of kids or gratification for their partner – does not mean they desire the sex itself, but rather the outcome of what having sex will bring. Aven Wiki I think confuses this issue because of their definition of Primary vs Secondary sexual attraction, which defines both of these instances as 'sexual desire'.

Do you think sexual arousal and sexual attraction are the same or different.

They are different. Sexual attraction means being attracted to someone or something with a desire to have sex with it or them. Whereas arousal is a response to stimuli, this can be physical or mental. So for me, I can get aroused by nothing and no one; just by thinking of the word aroused in my mind and feeling aroused in my body. I can also get aroused involuntarily by talking about kissing or thinking about it; at the mention of the word sex, even though I do not want it; or if I happen to see nudity for example on Twitter, even when I hate nudity and am repulsed by it because it gets me thinking about my own bits and arousing myself not thinking of other people being involved with it.

What's your view on living with someone?

I have lived on my own in a beautiful self-contained flat, in the middle of a house for 12 years and I absolutely love living on my own and specifically the flat I live in, and I do not want to live with someone. To reiterate what I said before, I do not want to share household bills or responsibilities such as housework and cleaning, been there, done that, and never again thanks. This is where a lot of the arguments stem from in a relationship; different lifestyle and home environment preferences, I just want to have fun and love in a relationship, not all that rubbish. Even though I desire a romantic relationship with an asexual foreign guy, I still want a Living Apart Together relationship. Ideally he would live next door to me, but as that would currently be impossible where I live given that the homeowners either side of me are not going to move anytime soon, if ever, then it would ideally be around the corner from me; a five minute walk. My preferred time to sleep is 4am as I love to work throughout the night in my bedroom on my business stuff and play music until this hour, but most guys are not going to want to live with a person who does not go to sleep at normal times or play music the amount I do, and I use music to constantly energize myself and keep myself happy so it is essential for me.

Would you like kids and if so how many? And how do you hope to conceive these? If you already have kids, did you know before you had them that you are asexual and how did that impact your life?

I categorically do not want kids, ever. I would rather be single forever than ever have this in my life. I am personally pregnancy repulsed and have known since 15 that I never want kids in my life. Unlike most women, I look forward to when I can no longer physically have kids. In my day job, I work opposite the Nursery department in a large retail store and it took me about two and a half years to not feel sick every time I saw a pregnant woman, to me it is personally gross. I actually get on really well with kids, because I am like a quirky teenage kid in my lifestyle and I think of kids as little beings in their own right that I can have conversations with and we can relate to each other. So for example, if I see them in my work and their parents are nearby trying a bed and the kids look bored, I will talk to them about films such as superhero movies or Disney or Pixar movies, it's great because I am on their level. Besides writing non-fiction books, I actually like writing children's picture books for 3-5 years and I love reading them too, but so far the two I have written have not been published.

What's your view on marriage? And if you were to get married, would it need to be with another asexual?

Despite the fact my parents have been married for 48 years, I personally don't like marriage for myself. I think it is a way of getting a woman to be contracted to be a housewife slave to a guy – I am not that woman. I hate housework, cooking and cleaning, so why would I want to chain myself down to a life of that for years? Living on my own, if I want to store my washing up to do in one go by hand I will, as I prefer to write and get on with my business stuff and see it as a pointless waste of time other than being necessary, and dusting – what's that? It's only going to get covered in dust again, most likely the next day, so what is the point in wasting one's life on this? I only iron clothes now, as and when I need them, and I never iron bed linen as it's a pointless waste of time, I am only going to ruffle it up again when I sleep. I am a business girl and an entrepreneur and not a housewifey type of person at all. I do the minimal I have to do to get by. My guinea pigs are usually cleaned out every day though – they are a top priority. The only thing I don't mind being married to is my writing and I don't need a piece of paper to prove my love for that! Oh, the irony of what I just said! Let's face it, if you end up marrying someone who changes or who tries to change you, and you are no longer compatible, it is much better to be able to break-up without a messy divorce. I am not saying every relationship will or does end up like this, as my parents are happily married but I have never liked to be tied down by permanently wearing a piece of jewellery so what does that say about my view of marriage? I was engaged years ago and I hated my life back then, I love my life now. Marriage is not for me.

What's your view on nudity? On porn? On masturbation? On BDSM and kinks?

I am nudity repulsed and always have been. I hate nudity, in movies, on TV, in sculptures, paintings, and anywhere and every-where. I do not think it's natural to see other people's bits and I particularly do not feel comfortable seeing naked women at all, ever. I was once at Centre Parcs when I was 24 in birth certificate age, and there was a woman stood in front of me in the women's changing rooms, completely stark naked, I felt so uncomfortable and sick, I really tried hard not to look at anything but her face and could not wait for her to stop talking to me and for me to get away. My earliest recollection of being naked was on my potty in the kitchen in front of my mum. This is when I became con-sciously aware that my mum was seeing me naked and it did not feel right. Because I am never attracted to women I would rather see a guy naked if I had to, but I don't like the male anatomy – it looks like a sausage with a sack of two potatoes tied to it, often wizened potatoes, where is the appeal in that?? (Sorry if I of-fended you x.) I would rather not look at that unless I really had to or needed to. I think it's pretty gross. I get attracted to a guy's face and frame, not his penis! I also prefer a guy without chest hair as I love baby soft skin and shave my own legs and arms ev-ery day in the shower – but I may have to put up with that as I know it's natural for most guy's bodies to produce this hair and I would not expect him to wax.

I never go to look at porn ever I my life; I think it is disgusting and totally unnecessary. I do not wish to get aroused by anyone who I am not in a relationship with and I can get aroused by myself without thinking of anyone if I want to.

Yes, I have tried masturbation; ironically this was after I discov-ered I am asexual. I never felt I needed to try it prior to that and had always thought it was a gross thing to do because I don't like touching myself; I preferred a boyfriend to do that for me but don't like touching a guy below the waist even though I have done so in the past. And even though I don't like it much, and it often makes me feel sick and I think 'yuk!' I've found it can be quite addictive – like playing a squirting game with myself and seeing how many times I can complete the round. But after completing 5 times in a row once, I was still left thinking, "Is this it?" It doesn't do much for me other than release the arousal feelings if I want to and wake me up if I feel sleepy (but I usually use dance music to do that). And in this respect I do not understand why people go crazy for sex? Why does squirting some fluid feel that 'orgasmic?' Why do they need it or want it so badly? Why go to all that bother with intercourse? They can obviously feel something that I can't. And maybe that is the sexual attraction and/or the desire part that I don't experience but they do? The only time it feels good to release fluids is naturally through passionate kissing – then it can be soothing and exciting at the same time and if I had been with my partner for a while and I trusted him (if I had one), and he was to gently touch me in a certain way, then that can be quite nice and I can like it, but sometimes that can become overwhelming for me beyond a certain point and I prefer the kissing. (This is an instance of why some behaviour that is seen as sexual, does not automatically equate to that person being sexual in orientation because I still don't feel sexual attraction and think I want sex with anyone.) But I would seriously rather not masturbate, even though I have become good at it. I prefer to feel non-aroused with myself and just focus on my business stuff, writing and other pursuits.

BDSM and kinks; I have no experience of either. They do not enter my vocabulary or life! Kinks sound yuk to me! Dirty somehow! Not going there! And BDSM, well the only knowledge I have of this is pleasure through pain and I cannot for the life of me understand why anyone would want to inflict pain on someone they loved? Why would you want to hurt someone? Why would that be a nice and loving thing to do? That does not compute in my head; there is enough pain in the world, without purposefully adding more!!

This is my personal opinion, I know not every asexual will share it and it's up to you what you think and how you live your life.

How difficult is it for you to be asexual, in a sexualized world?

The hardest thing is finding a suitable asexual life partner; that is really tough. If more people knew about asexuality and it was globally accepted then we would have more chance of finding someone as there are probably more asexuals than is statistically recorded. Also, there would be far less fear of people admitting they are asexual and maybe more asexuals on traditional dating sites, at 'singles' events and posting singles ads. There would be more choice and diversity of choice.

I hate nudity and sex but can choose to not look at TV shows, movies, and books with nudity and sex in them, so that is more within my control. It is horrid when my Twitter stream fills up with porn, even though I am not following these people, I just have to keep blocking and reporting them.

It is difficult being an admin of an asexuals only dating group because it is so time consuming to check each prospective member's profile to ascertain if they are really ace and only they themselves know for sure.

It is also hard when you discover that some people on asexual dating sites and in asexual Facebook groups, are not really asexual and that can be very disappointing if you have a lot in common with them and want to date them.

It's difficult to keep having to explain what asexuality is to people who really do not care what you say, they are not believing it anyway, but it is great to educate people who genuinely want to know more.

It is difficult refusing to date very attractive sexuals, whom you have lots in common with and who you would no doubt be in a relationship with, if they were ace or you were sexual.

But it does not bother me than I am asexual as it is a better life for me; it's who I really am. And I am proudly out to the world, and from that point of view, it's easy to be the real me and not difficult at all.

Can you tell me about a time when you have had to deal with intrusive questions or a difficult situation due to your asexuality, and what happened?

In the first year I found out I was asexual, there was a sexual Indian guy who was interested in a relationship with me, we seemed to have a special connection online and he was due to move to the states but said he may change his plans to come to the UK to have a relationship with me, but things did not go well and he turned out to not be so nice. Not only did he start lying to me and at a time when one of my guinea pigs was dying, he originally said he accepted my asexuality and that I wanted a relationship without sex, and changed and said there was no way he wanted to stay a virgin all his life and therefore he meant he would be with me and other women too – which was totally unacceptable and horrid. He was the first Indian guy to break my heart and after that I decided I would not date sexuals again as there was no point, we both need different things. At the beginning of the following year, 2015, I had my heart broken by an Asexual Indian guy because I seemed to like him a lot more than he liked me and when I found out he was 'lazy'; his words not mine, and he did not like to work and he seemed to think he would come over here and not work and I would do the work and get the money, I sent him a long voice message pouring my feelings out to him but saying I would not like to be with a person who wanted to be lazy and I did not want a lazy guy. It took me months to stop feeling anything for him.

There was another Indian guy I liked who turned out to not be asexual, despite being on asexual sites, but impotent according to the third girl who he was after. He implied to me that he was going to come to the UK and kept saying things like "when I come to the UK we can go to …" and I thought he started talking to another girl because he suddenly stopped talking to me and in the end I found out he was, and then again with another girl. It was a painful experience for us all.

I was in a nightclub and a guy who claimed to be an off-duty security guard there started chatting to me and inviting me to his home. I said, "no I am asexual" and he added, "as friends", and then asked me a series of intimate questions about if I have had sex before? If I have had oral sex? "What is a guy supposed to do then if he is aroused and wants sex?" I told him he can pleasure himself with his hand, it's not my problem. The look on his face was a picture and that was quite amusing.

As I like to spread awareness at every opportunity, I tell a lot of taxi drivers, especially if they are foreign, and especially if they seem remotely interested in me in a non-business way, that I am asexual. One particular time this happened, I explained what asexuality meant and he said, "You are in a trance?" I replied, "So you are in a trance because you are sexual then?" He didn't like that very much. It was a bit nerve-wracking, as he seemed to be getting more frustrated and agitated by the fact I am asexual and as he was driving my life was in his hands. Some taxi drivers have been awesome about my asexuality though and one even started talking about his wife and said if his wife did not want sex then he would not do it and still love her. I thought that was very sweet and understanding.

What are the positives about being asexual?

Everything, apart from the difficulty in finding a suitable life partner.

- I don't ever have to have sex again in my life – hooray!

- No pain through intercourse.

- No chance of ever getting pregnant.

- No chance of STIs or STDs.

- As I refuse to date heterosexuals, I can date again without feeling anxious that the ace guy is going to want sex with me at some point and I can focus more on getting to know if he would be a good match for me, rather than the sexual tension getting in the way and my hyper-romanticism and high arousal levels being mistaken for heterosexual attraction.

- I can find love without sex.

- I can make more friends and I have a lot more friends, because I now know that many guys are only suitable to be my friend and not a potential sexual partner. Also, I have made a lot of wonderful asexual friends since helping asexuals online, some of whom I see in person and would never have met or thought about talking to, had I not found out I am asexual.

- I can meet others who are asexual and understand me, both online and through meeting up with them offline, either one-to-one or through the asexual meet-ups that I organise locally.

- I have a deeper understanding of myself and even more self-love now.

- I am more fearless because I have to talk about intimate personal details online, in order to help other asexuals.

- I know my body better and my physical needs and limits in a relationship more now, and what I do and don't like.

- I am more self-assured and confident with who I am, my relationship goals and my life purposes.

- I feel honoured and blessed to help other asexuals as much as possible and that gives me great satisfaction and a sense of achievement in my life.

- I can link other asexuals to each other and spread awareness of asexuality on a more global scale.

- I can be part of a world-changing mission to get asexuality recognised as a sexual orientation in its own right throughout the globe, so that no asexual has to live in fear of ridicule, ever again.

- I feel I can bridge the gap between asexual and sexual understanding, as I have lived a heterosexual life in the past, despite being asexual. Even though I have not had as much sex as some would have had, I am still very experienced in this and knowledgeable.

- I can write more asexual books as I have the experience of being asexual, and I am well connected to a lot of asexuals around the globe and I adore writing; it's my life purpose.

- I live and breathe asexuality every day of my life, I am constantly seeking to understand asexuality better despite whatever personal view I hold.

- I have become much more open-minded to increase my understanding, awareness, knowledge of asexuality and to help others.

- I can design more asexualise T-Shirts and enjoy that creative pursuit at the same time raising more awareness of asexuality.

- I always love to be not normal and stand out, so being asexual really suits me and my already quirkiness.

- I believe I really can make a difference to the lives of asexuals and that is empowering.

If you could have one wish about being asexual, what would it be and why?

I wish asexuality was recognised as a sexual orientation in its own right throughout the globe, so that no asexual has to live in fear of ridicule ever again and every asexual could be open about it to have a greater chance of finding a suitable life partner or friends. On a personal note, I wish to find my asexual Indian soulmate life partner and be happy together, forever.

If you were to look back at your life, what advice would you have given a younger version of yourself in regard to asexuality?

This is a really difficult one for me to answer because part of me likes the fact that I discovered through my heterosexual relationships that I did not like sex and despite not having a good heterosexual relationship and some of my sexual experience being awful, I am not sure I would change anything in that regard because otherwise I feel personally for me, I would always have been wondering what it is like to have had sex, and would I like it and I would probably have not got the kissing experience that I love so much, because it is usually used in foreplay leading up to sex, even though I never actually want the sex. Because I have had sex with 5 different guys, 3 British and 2 foreign, with different sized penises and in different sexual positions and frequencies of sex, and sex was the best thing in the end about my long term ex; I feel I have had enough of sex to last me a lifetime and to know it is not for me and that I am definitely asexual. There is no confusion with me and no misunderstanding about myself, and no thinking 'what if' and no trying to date sexuals anymore on conventional dating sites – so I have far less heartache in my life now, than I may have done had I thought when I was younger that we are only 1% of the population and there was no internet stuff around back then.

If I were to give myself some advice when younger, it would have been that there are definitely others who want a relationship without sex and you can actually find love without sex. Maybe then I would have been more inclined to have a traditional and conventional asexual relationship that so many other asexuals seem to want. Years ago I wanted to get married and live more of a normal relationship life and live together, but I have always been different, got bored easily and enjoyed being quirky – looking back I would never have been happy or fulfilled being that person because I am the happiest I have ever been living on my own and living a teenager lifestyle and being young and unconventional and fulfilling lots of life missions, and had I stayed living with someone then I could not have been myself in this way. I have always known since 10 that I have a soulmate and since 15 that I will be famous and in the media somehow – I used to want to be a professional Radio Presenter and was a Hospital Radio Presenter for 17 years, but then my love for writing took over. I also intuitively knew that I was not normal and was born for a very special purpose, although I did not know when younger what that was and it was this that kept me going when being depressed in the past. In truth, writing is my life's purpose but I also have many other life purposes, such as getting asexuality recognised as a sexual orientation in its own right throughout the globe, this is a huge challenge and one which I gladly accept and feel blessed to be part of. So I guess things have worked out the way they should even though the path in my past has not always been a good one. Now I believe I am on the right path and maybe changing my past by giving advice to myself about asexuality would have been too soon as I was not ready to accept it, but now I am in a great position of strength to help others to unleash their inner ace.

What advice would you give to others who are just discovering about asexuality and considering whether they are or not?

To think about if you have ever looked at anyone and thought 'I want sex with you', if you haven't, then it's highly probable that you are asexual and if you have thought that but only on rare occasion, or under specific circumstances, it is likely you may be on the Grey Asexual or Demi-sexual end of the asexual spectrum, but it's up to you to read about asexuality and chat to other asexuals to discover if you believe you are asexual or not. Visit the 'Aven Wiki' page and look at the explanations of the different variations of identities across the asexual spectrum to see if any fit you. Don't be worried if you think you may be a combination of variations of the spectrum, some people are. It's a minefield sometimes and lots to learn, but it is awesome to find other asexuals who can understand you and you can relate to.

To find other asexuals online go to www.asexuality.org that is a free to join online community of asexuals – the largest in the world. On there, you will find a ton of information and forum discussions about all matters concerning asexuals and asexuality. Be proactive, rather than reactive, ask questions to learn more, and be prepared in the future to travel to asexual meet-ups if it is safe to do so, because you will be lucky to find a few asexuals in your own city and never give up on finding that special ace someone for a relationship, if that is what you want. Also, join www.ace-book.net for asexual dating and to socialise online with other aces for free and check out www.asexualitic.com that currently costs $15 a year for full membership at the time of printing this book. There are other asexual dating sites too that usually cost money per month – just Google 'asexual dating sites'. There are lots of asexual Facebook groups you can join too – just search for 'asexual groups' in the Facebook search field and click 'join' to request to join them. You can find some of the asexual Facebook groups I am in, some of the asexual YouTubers I follow and some of the asexual Tweeters I am connected to by going to my www.asexualise.com website and click on the 'Resources' tab. On my site you can also watch some of my educational, informative and empowering videos for asexuals and subscribe to my channel "Asexualise My Asexual Life" (www.youtube.com/c/asexualisemyasexuallife) to learn more about asexuality and matters affecting us. I also have a newsletter that is free to join and provides useful how-to advice about matters relating to asexuality, asexual news, asexual videos and offers on Asexualise merchandise, you can join for free and unsubscribe at any time.

Do you have a story you would like to share or anything else you would like to say?

Being asexual is beautiful and although asexuality is not a choice, if I had the choice to be a heteroromantic asexual or heterosexual, I would choose to be asexual every time and without hesitation. I am happy to not like sex for me personally and would much rather kiss than ever have sex again in my life and now I know that is possible, it is acesome.

If my asexual soulmate is reading this – just message me via my 'Contact' page on www.asexualise.com and put in the subject line 'I'm Your Soulmate'. If you are not my soulmate but want to get in touch, please connect with me and stay ace.

Remember, you are beautiful just as you are, asexuality exits and so do you, there is nothing wrong with you being asexual, you are a member of the elite 'Ace Team' now and that is something to be proud of. Never let your voice be drowned out or your true identity be crushed, always be your true authentic self, and embrace your quirky no matter what.

Extra Info

What name would you like to go under for this book?

I am the Author Sandra Bellamy. Otherwise known online as 'Asexualise' or 'Quirky Books'.

What country do you live in?

I live in the UK and hate flying on a plane, so likely to live here forever and I love the UK too – if you are asexual you should come and visit one day and attend an Exeter asexual meet-up.

What age are you specifically? Or what decade age range are you – 20, 30. 40s?

I believe age is a state of mind.

My lifestyle mindset age is currently 23.

I live like a 15 year old and love it.

I predominantly get attracted to 21-27 year old foreign asexual guys.

My birth certificate age is older and is really not who I am, that is why I usually only tell an asexual guy who wishes to date me the exact age; for the purposes of this book I am in my 30s and if you recently saw me in the national press then you will already know my birth certificate age.

What nationality and ethnicity are you?

I was born British and I am British and white.

Links to your website/social media.

Website: www.asexualise.com

Free newsletter for asexuals sign up here for free: http://eepurl.com/cpYIWv

YouTube: www.youtube.com/c/asexualisemyasexuallife

Twitter: @asexualise

Facebook: www.facebook.com/acexualise

www.facebook.com/acexualisedating

www.facebook.com/groups/acexualisedating

www.facebook.com/groups/acebusiness

www.facebook.com/groups/acefriendsrus

53. Surprising Conclusions

It was interesting for me to read interviewee answers to the question, "Do you believe if a sexual person had a relationship with an asexual, it can work? And what do you think about it being fair or not?" And discover that some automatically thought I was implying if it was fair for an asexual to be with a sexual and deny them sex. Which just goes to show how much society conditions us to think this way and how often sexuals must ask this question to imply this. This is not at all what I thought when I wrote the question. In fact, I thought the opposite, because I wrote about the 'sexual' first, having a relationship with an asexual and I was thinking just how unfair it is that some sexuals pretend to be asexual when they aren't. Some sexuals expect an asexual person to give them sex regardless of how the asexual person feels about it and that is not fair if the asexual doesn't like sex. It's not right that a sexual should 'seek' a relationship out with an asexual if the asexual cannot have sex and that is what they want. I have had sexual guys in the past say they don't need much sex and are not that bothered by it, as a way of charming me to be so comfortable with them and that they are the 'one' for me and then get sexual with me and want intercourse, which I don't want. By then I have an emotional connection with them and it hurts emotionally that they could do this. This is not fair!

I was somewhat shocked at how many interviewees said they

would facilitate a polyamorous relationship whereby the sexual person could get their sexual needs met outside of the relationship, I can understand this if they themselves are poly but if they are not, to me this is like letting the sexual have their cake and eat it, if you pardon the cake expression. I mean surely this is the dream situation for many highly sexual people, to have sex when they want with whom they want, yet still get their emotional needs met with the person they are with? Isn't that the reason so many have affairs because they want the best of both worlds? If this is the case then I am surprised more sexuals don't be with asexuals, I mean, what have they got to lose?? The asexual gives and the sexual takes – lovely for the sexual – This is just my personal experience and opinion and if you are in this type of relationship then I am sure you can see and list the benefits of it and will say that the sexual does not just take and I would hope they don't, you are a gorgeous individual – never forget that! I am a monogamous person and there is no way I would want to facilitate this type of relationship; they either want to be in a relationship with just me, or they can take a hike!! I am worth more than that and may as well remain single and happy. Unless a guy can add value to my life in some way and keep me as happy as I make myself or make me happier – there really is no point to the relationship. I love my life so much and love living.

While it would seem that most people who identify as asexual, are born asexual, but many did not realise it until later in their life when their circumstances lead them to find this out; there are people who identify as asexual even though previously they did not, because they did experience sexual attraction and have led a fairly heteronormative life for years, then all of a sudden things changed like in Jo's Story. This does not invalidate their asexuality because they still fit into the definition of asexuality according to Wikipedia. So what is the full definition of asexuality?

According to Wikipedia at the time of publishing this book:

"Asexuality is the lack of sexual attraction to anyone or low or absent interest in or desire for sexual activity".

And it is this latter part of the definition, "or low or absent interest in or desire for sexual activity" that often gets overlooked. So in theory, a person who *was* very sexually active and whom has previously experienced sexual attraction could quite comfortably say they are asexual if all of a sudden they lose interest in having sex and that interest does not return. That in turn will mean these asexuals will have different learned sexual behaviour and thinking, to the 'born this way but didn't realise it and/or never had sex or been in a relationship in my life asexual'. And this could cause conflict in a potential relationship between the two types. We could almost do with a separate classification directly under the 'asexual spectrum umbrella' at the top of it, before the sub-identities: NBA (Not Born Asexual), and BA (Born Asexual). Even though I have had sex in the past, I am still a born asexual as I don't experience sexual attraction, although I did not realise it until later in my life, I guess this may then need another classification of BABDR (Born Asexual But Didn't Realise) under BA. But as it can be hard enough to understand asexuality as it is, do we really need another set of classifications? Some will argue no. Some hate labels and classifications but I think it is good for finding like-minded people, for finding those who are different and we want to know their story to help us understand our own and in particular for asexual dating and finding a suitable partner/s.

It is interesting to read different perspectives about what sexual attraction, sexual desire and arousal means – because as we tend to judge others on our own interpretation of the meaning of something, if we interpret those differently, we could think an asexual person is sexual according to our interpretations. So hypothetically, if for example I had a partner and I liked him to touch me, but I am not sexually attracted to him because I don't want sex with him and don't think this way, if another asexual believes this is sexual behaviour and that a person can't be asexual because of such behaviour, they will then view me as not being asexual, but I know I am because I don't experience the attraction. I know asexuals who will strip and pretty much do most things, just not have the intercourse. I don't even like being nude, so I could interpret them as being grey sexual, grey asexual or borderline sexual, when they define themselves as a heteroromantic. This is how we can end up telling someone what they are and are not and how people can be denied the right to be themselves and their own identity. But I hope this book has showed you just how beautifully diverse the asexual spectrum is and that we all have a place in it and are valid to be here in our own right.

However, if sexual behaviour is not the same as sexual attraction, but may or may not be a result of it, what does the 'sexual activity' part of the asexuality definition mean? I personally understand it to mean sexual intercourse, because although I don't experience sexual attraction and I don't desire the intercourse, if I was in a relationship and enjoyed my partner touching me, it still does not make me any less asexual in my mind and the asexuality definition is "Asexuality is the lack of sexual attraction to anyone *or* low *or* absent interest in or desire for sexual activity". Some asexuals still like masturbation, which is a solo sexual activity; and other asexuals like to touch each other through mutual masturbation when in a relationship. As it is a Grey Area – that is why I define myself as a Heteroromantic Grey A; I am still asexual as I have no desire to have sex with anyone and especially not with women but I am attracted to guys in many other ways.

In my experience of being a born asexual but didn't realise it, looking back on my life since my potty days, I can understand that I always thought differently to others when it came to nudity and sexual exploration. I didn't like being nude on my potty and after an 'exploring incident' with a boy the same age as me at the time – 6 years old, I felt invaded, even though I said okay to it, I felt pressured into it. I have loved passionate kissing from that age and desired to be loved at that age by a guy but did not want sexual activity. I saw a counsellor years later at college and she could not understand why I was so upset by that 'doctors and nurses' incident. I felt horrid and devastated that I let him do that because in my mind it was so very, very wrong and all I wanted was love. I did not take his offer up of exploring him. Back then I didn't have the immense self-love I have now and even though I have yet to experience that 'good love' from a guy, I still desire it, but I only look to find that with an asexual guy. If I don't get the right guy for me, then I will remain happily single forever. I love being asexual. The thought of me being a full-blown heterosexual is repulsive to me and even though I have some highly sexual friends and would never be without them and am happy for others to like and enjoy sex, I would never want to be a heterosexual in my life. I don't want, need or like sex and it is not necessary to have that again in my life. No one needs sex, unless they believe they do and they can't satisfy their sexual urges through other means, which it would seem most sexuals feel they can't. I will always prefer kissing hands down over sex, any day. It's the best feeling in the world if you have a good and compatible kisser who you are in a stable and secure relationship with.

If you have read through this entire book, then maybe you have also reached the surprising conclusion that many interviewees believe sexuality is fluid and their advice is if one day you think and feel like you are asexual and fit somewhere on the spectrum, then you do. If another day you decide actually 'this' fits me more accurately, that is okay too. And this is the beauty of diversity and individuality, it is all about exploring what we do and do not like as an individual and not about meeting society's expectations or that of other's within our own community, but discovering what really works for us and makes us feel great. It is about embracing our own quirkiness, just as we should embrace other's quirkiness too.

It is strange because I always feel like I know what sexual attraction feels like, despite not experiencing it, which I can only conclude from the fact that everything works as it should, my arousal levels are sky high (which I only consciously became aware of since discovering I am asexual), and I can feel the whole sex thing, but my mind does not want or desire it, even if my body pulls me that way at times. Because I am a born asexual I just think and feel differently to the usual heterosexual and in this way I feel rigid in my sexuality and sexual orientation. The great thing about the people in this book who believe sexuality is fluid; I know if one day I changed my mind and became a demi, that they would not dismiss me out of the asexual community, they would not ridicule me or make me feel like I don't belong, but I have no *intention* to be a demi-sexual and quite happy to lead a sex-free existence forever. In fact as a hyper-romantic I can easily make strong emotional connections fast and fall in love quickly, which is the opposite to a demisexual or demiromantic, who usually take time to form a strong and deep emotional connection with someone and fall in love.

As you can see from reading this book, although we share asexuality in common, the asexual spectrum is vast and wide and we all have different views and opinions on what asexuality means to us and to the world at large. There will have been stories that you resonated with in this book and maybe others that made you want to scream, 'I don't agree with that, it's wrong!' Maybe some of what I said resonated with you and at other times you thought, 'no way!' Take time to read this book again and discover the hidden treasure of opinions and experiences within it. Go out into the world with renewed hope and confidence that there are people just like you, people that are ace!

About The Author

Sandra Bellamy is a Heteroromantic, Hyper-romantic, Grey A, Asexual (younger) Cougar, who does not like sex, just kissing. She has had sex in the past because she felt she had to, but upon discovering she is asexual in 2014, she realised it was possible to have love without sex and that there were others, just like her, who desired a relationship forever, without sex.

On December 14th 2016, Sandra was featured in the online national newspaper The Mirror (mirror.co.uk) and Newslocker.com news site, in which she was interviewed about the UK asexual dating scene and asked to share her personal asexual story. The story was even displayed on the Nigerian www.onigeria.com site. She was also featured in the Daily Star and although they included that Sandra was sex and nudity repulsed they omitted the 'asexual' and 'asexual dating sites' part, which was the focus of the original interview and beefed up the story with a sexual "minx" connotation slant. Despite this, Sandra is determined to keep moving forward and promoting awareness of asexuality at every opportunity.

"I would rather have the media on my side. I understand they have a job to do to reach their target market and they are going to whatever they can to please that market, unfortunately for asexuals, most of that market is heterosexual, but I will not give up! The Mirror stayed truer to my original interview and featured the fact I am asexual and my story was based on that and this is a great leap forward for national press! When you are trying to make a difference in the world you need to break into the national and international press and don't let fear hold you back. Not everything is going to be true about you, for example, in regard to the Daily Star article that made it sound like I actively date younger guys in Exeter and go to the cinema with them and kiss them and hold hands, the last time I had a date with a sexual guy was in 2014 and that wasn't at the cinema!! And the last time I actually did this was with the Bangladesh guy in 2013!! But the people who matter know the real me and that's what counts."

Sandra lives in the South West region of the UK with her two furry kid daughter guinea pigs Chestnut and Angel, who are all the children she will ever need. A self-confessed insomniac and "night owl", she prides herself on being quirky, unconventional and different. She overcame depression in 2012, without the need for meds, using her "Embrace Your Quirky" philosophy, that is all about being your true authentic self, regardless of what anyone else says, thinks or does. This is the philosophy she lives by throughout her life and businesses.

Sandra believes age is a state of mind and says her current lifestyle mindset age is purposefully 23, meaning she can do anything a 23 year old can do if she wants to. She loves living like a teenager with cuddly toys around her bedroom, a fiber optic lamp, an Iron Man alarm clock, coloured boxes and sparkly things and is the happiest she has ever been, living her life, her way!

Currently single, Sandra has lived on her own for 12 years in a beautiful self-contained flat and has no desire to live with anyone, but would like a romantic, quirky and unconventional Living Apart Together teenage style relationship near to her home, with a younger foreign guy, ideally in his 20s and Indian. At the time of writing this book, she believes she has an Indian soulmate somewhere in this world and will not give up on discovering him but still loves her single life so much.

Sandra founded International Celebrate Being Single Day #ICBSD on February 14th 2015, not to be confused with 'Singles Day'; so that no single person has to feel alone, ever, on Valentine's Day; instead they can celebrate this as their special day and that being single is awesome. They can go out on a self-date like she does, celebrate it at home, or with other singles, or any way they choose. The focus is on, 'it's great to be single and being happy to be single'.

Sandra currently works in a full-time retail specialist "day job", while pursuing her entrepreneurial passions and maintaining her own businesses. Her work includes social media training, and mentoring/quirky coaching. But her huge passion is writing. Sandra is a published Author of two e-books on Amazon: "BREAK THROUGH THE BARRIERS OF REDUNDANCY TO GET BACK INTO WORK – AN A-Z 'HOW TO' GUIDE" and "How To GET STARTED WITH TWITTER For Absolute Beginners GET GOING AND GET GROWING A Step-By-Step Guide".

In 2015, Sandra became so involved with the asexual community, that she felt it was taking over her life and either she became less involved with it or she made it part of her business portfolio and went all out promoting it. That was when she turned her attention from helping redundant workers and made a conscious decision to get asexuality recognised as a sexual orientation in its own right throughout the globe, so that no asexual has to live in fear of ridicule ever again. She created a YouTube channel called "Asexualise My Asexual Life", to "Empower and Enhance the lives of Asexuals and Educate others." And took the bold decision to incorporate asexuality into her World Of Quirky organisation, under the brand name of Asexualise. She created www.asexualise.com with products, resources and services for asexuals. On Aven there were many people asking for asexual merchandise and in October 2015 she started selling T Shirts on Amazon.com under the brand name of "Asexualise", that was revolutionary for asexual merchandise because although others sell asexual merchandise on Amazon, they don't usually go under a brand name with the word Asexual in it. Sandra has purposefully done this to raise awareness of asexuality and get it to be taken more seriously. You can also find Asexualise merch on Redbubble.

As if that wasn't enough, Sandra runs the "Asexual Business, Gurus and Entrepreneurs" group on Facebook and the "Asexualise

Dating" for Asexuals only group, that is for asexuals who are looking to have a serious relationship with another asexual without sex ever being involved. Her latest addition is the "Asexual Friends" group.

You can also find her on Twitter (@Asexualise) and Facebook (www.facebook.com/acexualise).

If you would like to hear from Sandra on a regular basis with advice; help; support; inspiration and information about Asexualise merchandise and special offers, please sign up to her free newsletter. Your details will remain confidential and never passed on to third parties.

If you enjoyed reading this book then please leave an honest review on Amazon to spread awareness of asexuality and so that others may benefit from it.

Stay Ace and Acesome.

Connect With The Author

For **free** advice, help, inspiration and information, please sign up to the free *Asexualise - What's Happening?* Newsletter at

www.asexualise.com

You can also find Asexualise at:

www.youtube.com/c/asexualisemyasexuallife
www.twitter.com/asexualise
www.facebook.com/acexualise
www.facebook.com/acexualisedating
www.facebook.com/groups/acexualisedating
www.facebook.com/groups/acebusiness
www.facebook.com/groups/acefriendsrus

Remember, if you have enjoyed reading this book then please leave an honest review on Amazon to spread awareness of asexuality and so that others may benefit from.

Made in the USA
Lexington, KY
16 September 2017